C016636764

ABOUT THE AUTHOR

Photograph © Jeannette Breward

Dr Stuart Shanker is a distinguished research Professor of Psychology and Philosophy Emeritus at York University in Toronto, Canada. He is a former president of the Council of Early Child Development. Dr Shanker attended the University of Toronto, where he received his bachelor's and master's degrees. He obtained a first in PPE and BPhil and DPhil with a distinction in Philosophy at Oxford University. He is the founder and CEO of The MEHRIT Centre and science director of the Self Regulation Research Institute.

His expertise has been sought internationally, and he has been an adviser on early child development to government organisations across Canada and the United States in addition to a host of other nations, including the UK, Ireland, Western and Eastern Europe, Latin America, Australia and New Zealand.

The book was written with Teresa Barker who is a journalist and has co-written many books, including the *New York Times* bestseller *Raising Cain: Protecting the Emotional Life of Boys.*

DR STUART SHANKER

HELP YOUR CHILD DEAL with STRESS – and THRIVE

The transformative power of Self-Reg

yellow
kite

First published in Great Britain in hardback as *Self-Reg*
in 2016 by Yellow Kite
An imprint of Hodder & Stoughton
An Hachette UK company

First published in Great Britain in paperback in 2018

First published in the United States of America by Penguin Press, New York
an imprint of Penguin Random House

1

Illustrations by Stuart Shanker, Amanda Davey and Meighan Cavanaugh

Some families are struggling with extreme or atypical problems. The
strategies in this book will be helpful, but they may not be enough to
adequately address all the complex issues. This book is for self-help
purposes only. It is not intended as a substitute for medical, psychiatric
or psychological diagnosis, advice or treatment, for specialist teaching
methods or for consultation with a qualified legal professional.

A CIP catalogue record for this title is available from the British Library

Paperback ISBN 978 1 444 78870 9

Printed and bound by CPI Group (UK) Ltd, Croydon, CR0 4YY

Hodder & Stoughton policy is to use papers that are natural, renewable
and recyclable products and made from wood grown in sustainable
forests. The logging and manufacturing processes are expected to
conform to the environmental regulations of the country of origin.

Yellow Kite
Hodder & Stoughton Ltd
Carmelite House
50 Victoria Embankment
London EC4Y 0DZ

www.yellowkitebooks.co.uk
www.hodder.co.uk

To my wife and children

Contents

PART III

Teens, Temptations, and Parents Under Pressure

HELP YOUR CHILD DEAL with STRESS – and THRIVE

Introduction

I've lost track of how many children I've seen in my work across Canada, the United States, and the world. Not just thousands but easily tens of thousands. And among all those children I have never seen a bad kid.

Kids can be selfish, insensitive, and even spiteful; refuse to pay attention; be quick to shout or push; or be disobedient or downright hostile. The list goes on and on. I know—I'm a father myself. But a *bad* kid? Never.

We all have moments when we immediately label children "bad." We might say "unmanageable" or "impossible" or "the problem kid" or use a clinical label like "ADHD/ADD" or "oppositional defiant," but no matter what words we use, our conclusions can be harshly judgmental.

One day I bumped into a neighbor walking down the street with his four-year-old son and the family dog. When I leaned down to pat the dog, it snapped at me, and the father smiled ruefully and said apologetically, "Alfonse is just a puppy," but the little boy stopped to scold the dog and slapped it on the nose. The father exploded. It was okay for the dog to act up but not his four-year-old son. We've all been that dad at one time or another, reacting to our kids in the pressure of a moment in ways we wouldn't if we were thinking more calmly and clearly.

These behaviors are expressions of a child's inability *in the moment* to respond to everything going on in and around him—sounds, noise, distractions, discomforts, emotions. Yet we react as if these were problems with a child's character or temperament. Worse yet, children come to believe it.

There isn't a single child who, with understanding and patience, can't be guided along a trajectory that leads to a rich and meaningful life. But stereotypes of the "difficult child" color our views, as do our own hopes, dreams, frustrations, and fears as parents. Don't get me wrong: Some children can be a lot more challenging than others. But often our negative judgments of a child are just a defense mechanism, a way of shifting the blame for the trouble we're having onto the child's "nature." This can make a child more reactive, defensive, defiant, anxious, or withdrawn. But it doesn't have to be that way. It never has to be that way.

I once shared this thought with a conference audience of two thousand kindergarten teachers, and a voice piped up from the back: "Well, I've got a bad kid. And his dad was a bad guy. And his grandfather before him was bad to the core." Everyone laughed, but I was intrigued. I thought, "Well, there's always an exception to the rule. I really want to meet this child." So the teacher arranged for me to come to the school and meet the little boy in question. And the second he shuffled into the room it was instantly clear that what she saw as *misbehavior* was really *stress behavior*.

He was sensitive to noise; twice, before he'd even sat down, he had been startled by sounds in the hall outside the room. What's more, he was squinting, which suggested that he was sensitive to the fluorescent lights in the room or perhaps had a visual-processing problem. The way he squirmed in his chair made me wonder if it was difficult for him to sit upright or feel at ease on the hard plastic chair. The real problem was something biological. Under these circumstances, raised voices or hardened facial expressions would only make him more distressed and distracted. Over time, this kind of habitual interaction can make a child disobedient or defiant.

This is especially true with issues that run in families, as it seemed was the case here. Did his father and his grandfather before him have the same biological sensitivities? Had they met with the sort of punitive responses from the adults in their lives that can so easily set a child on a troubled path that eventually seems only to confirm the thinking "You see, I told you he was a bad kid"?

My immediate concern was for the child in front of me, and to help the weary teacher see and understand the significance of his behavioral cues. I gently closed the classroom door, turned off the overhead lights (which not only have a harsh glare but also make a constant buzzing noise), and lowered my voice. She saw him suddenly relax, her expression softened, and she whispered, "Oh my God."

It's a response I've seen and heard from every adult who has discovered that a child's problem wasn't irreparable. It had been so easy to see this boy as having a genetically flawed character. That changed the instant she saw his sensitivity to sound and light. This wasn't his choice.

In a flash the teacher's entire behavior toward him changed. Before she had been grim; now she smiled to the corners of her eyes. Her tone of voice changed from clipped to melodic, her gestures from choppy to slow and rhythmic. She was looking directly at him, not at me. The two of them had connected, and everything about his body posture, facial expression, and tone of voice mirrored the changes in her own.

This sort of transformation isn't just a case of seeing the child differently or, for that matter, seeing a different child, but of changing the whole teacher-child dynamic. She had put aside her need for *compliance*, even her ego, if you will, and had seen the child—truly seen the child—for the first time. She now could begin to teach him; for his part, he hadn't the first clue that he was so sensitive to noise and light, let alone that this made him difficult to handle. This was his reality, what was "normal" for him. Now she could help him learn when and why he was becoming hyper and distracted and what he could do about it to stay calmly focused, alert, and engaged in his own learning.

Looking from the Right Spot

There isn't a parent reading this book who hasn't, at some time in their child's life, been in exactly the same place. Probably more than once! We try so hard to help our children, to provide them not just with material comforts but with the life skills they will need to be successful. Yet all too often we find ourselves failing to connect and understandably frustrated or angry. We know that what they are doing isn't working well for them or isn't good for them, and we wonder why we can't get them to see it. Just like this teacher, we have the best of intentions, but that's not enough. Self-Reg, or self-regulation, starts by *reframing* a child's behavior and, for that matter, our own. It means *seeing the meaning* of the child's behavior, maybe for the first time.

When I was in graduate school, my supervisor, Peter Hacker, an amateur Rembrandt scholar, once offered to show me around a Rembrandt exhibition. Arriving early at the gallery, I spent twenty minutes alone studying a self-portrait, and for the life of me I couldn't see what all the fuss was about. When Peter arrived, he asked me what I thought, and I said it just looked blurry to me. Peter smiled and walked away from the painting, staring intently at the floor. He pointed to a small dot on the floor and then asked me to stand on that spot and look at the picture again. What I saw was astonishing. The painting had suddenly sprung into perfect focus. Instantly I saw and felt the full force of Rembrandt's genius.

I had wanted so badly to be able to understand why this painting was considered a stunning artistic achievement. I had read the notes about its history. I knew when and where Rembrandt had painted it. Yet I could have come to the museum every day for years to study that painting and never have discovered its secret. I would always have been standing in the wrong spot.

Self-Reg will show you where to stand: how to bring your child's behavior into focus, respond to your child's needs, and help your child help himself. It will strengthen your relationships. This is not about getting your child to "behave"—to stop doing or saying things that irritate you or others or create problems for himself. Self-Reg is about making a dramatic difference in mood, concentration, and the ability to make friends, feel empathy, and develop the higher values and virtues that are vital to your child's long-term well-being.

This technique is the result of the scientific revolution in our understanding of *self-regulation*. The term "self-regulation" is used in so many different ways—hundreds, in fact—but the original psycho-physiological sense refers to how we manage the stresses that we are under. And "stress," in its original sense, refers to all those stimuli that require us to expend energy to maintain some sort of balance: not just the kinds of psychosocial stresses that we are all familiar with, like the demands of work or what others think of us, but, as was the case for that little boy I discussed above, things in the environment, like auditory or visual stimulation; our emotions, positive as well as negative; patterns that we find it difficult to recognize; the demands of coping with the stress of others; and for too many children today, the things they do or don't do in their free time. If a child's stress load is consistently too high, his recovery may become compromised and reactivity to stressors, even relatively minor ones, becomes heightened.

Self-Reg is a five-step method for (1) recognizing when a child is overstressed; (2) identifying and then (3) reducing his stressors; (4) helping him become aware of when he needs to do this for himself; and (5) helping him to develop self-regulating strategies.

It's not easy to know when a child is overstressed or what counts as a stressor for a child, especially because children have to cope with so many *hidden stressors* these days. Too often we think that we just need to *tell* a child to calm down, even though that never works. There's no simple recipe for what helps a child to self-regulate; children are all different and their needs are constantly changing, to the point where what worked last week may not work today. But by mastering the first four steps you'll be able to experiment and discover what works for your child and what doesn't. Most important, your child will too.

Since Plato's time self-control has been celebrated as a measure of character. This assumption has profoundly shaped how we think about children and how they develop into adults of sound mind, body, and character. For adults too the assumption has been that willpower is essential to resist temptation and to persevere through challenge and adversity. What the classical philosophers and the generations that followed them didn't know is that something much more basic is at work.

Self-control is about *inhibiting impulses*; self-regulation is about identifying the causes and reducing the intensity of impulses and, when necessary, having the energy to resist. This distinction has not been clearly understood; indeed, the two are often conflated. Self-regulation is not only fundamentally different from self-control: It is what makes acts of self-control possible—or, as often happens, unnecessary. Unless we understand this fundamental distinction, we run the risk of adding to the factors contributing to a child's poor self-control, rather than helping him develop the self-regulation foundation needed to succeed in school and in life.

Self-Reg sees "problematic" behaviors as invaluable signs of when a child is overstressed. Think of the child who is highly impulsive or explosive, has trouble regulating his emotions, has frequent meltdowns or is highly volatile or irritable, can't tolerate frustration, gives up at the slightest obstacle, finds it difficult to pay attention or ignore distractions, has trouble managing relationships or experiencing empathy. Behaviors that trigger our automatic thought that the child is "bad" or "lazy" or "slow" are often a sign that his stress level is way too high and there's no gas left in his tank—no energy left to manage anything else. So Self-Reg teaches us how to figure out what the stressors are for that particular child and how we can reduce them. Then we need to help the child learn how to manage all this on his own.

Self-Reg starts with how well *we* can identify and reduce our own stressors and how well we can stay calm and attentive when we're interacting with a child. Just like the teacher who raised the question at my talk, when we're angry, worried, or at wit's end with a child, we need to be able to say, "What is this really about? What am I missing?" Sometimes we'll need to be able to say, "I was wrong." That's big. Nobody likes to do that.

stayed in touch with that kindergarten teacher. She once told me that a lot more had changed that day than just how she interacted with that young boy and the other children in her class. Her whole life had changed. The way she treated her own family, her friends, and most of all herself had transformed. All of this, she insisted, had happened in that one split second.

Why? Had she been callous before, burned out on teaching or weary of working with this boy, ready to give up on him? Nothing could be further from the truth. In fact, she was deeply compassionate and a devoted teacher. But despite this, she had come to the determination that there was "something wrong" with him. Such a determination is never right. Something is going on, certainly, but it is not "something wrong." It is something *else*. This book is about figuring out what that thing is for your child.

There's a method for doing that, for tackling these problems at their roots. It's called Self-Reg. We created The MEHRIT Centre to teach parents and teachers Self-Reg and the results have been nothing less than extraordinary. This book will show you how to use this approach and teach your child how to do the same. But it's not just a method for helping kids who have problems; it's a method for all kids. This is something that we all need to do. Now more than ever.

PART I

Self-Reg: Essential for Living and Learning

ONE

The Power of
Self-Reg

ry harder!

You hear it all the time. You say it yourself. Have more willpower, more self-control over what you eat, or drink, or say to your boss, or do in your free time. You need to exercise. Control your spending. Resist the endless temptations out there, and if you fail—when you fail!—try harder.

That's the message we get constantly, and so much of the conversation about helping our kids succeed focuses on the same thing. But for them as for so many of us, it seems that the harder we try, the harder it is to impose self-control and the more distant the goal becomes. We berate ourselves for being weak. Children do the same thing, and the self-blame and shame work against every good thing we hope for them in school and life.

New advances in neuroscience are unlocking the secrets of why we behave the way we do and, more to the point, why it is so hard at times to behave the way we want. These same advances are also telling us how to change our behavior and that self-control has little to do with the solution. In fact, research now shows that the more we focus on self-control and the harder we push for it, the harder self-control and positive behavioral change can become.

Don't get me wrong: Self-control is important. We're all aware of individuals who have risen to the top of their field who are models of self-control. But much more fundamental is the stress load that we're under and how well we deal with this: how well we *self-regulate*. In fact, the closer you look at these "success stories," the more you'll see that what really sets them apart is their remarkable ability to self-regulate.

The more aware we are of when we're becoming overstressed, and know how to break this cycle, the better we self-regulate: in other words, manage the myriad stresses in our lives. The autonomic nervous system (ANS) reacts to stress with metabolic processes that consume energy and then sets in motion compensating processes that promote recovery and growth. The greater our stress load, the more constrained this recovery process, and as a result, the fewer our resources to exercise self-control and the more intense our impulses become. Once you understand the brain's natural response to stress and practice Self-Reg, the very need to impose self-control often disappears.

Advances in Neuroscience Upend Stubborn Myths About the Roots of Behavior

The association between poor self-control and weakness is the most punishing aspect of a remarkably ancient outlook that viewed self-control as a matter of strength and character. That idea has held sway for thousands of years. Being judged as having poor self-control has been the source of untold guilt and personal recrimination. Modern science tells us that this outlook isn't just archaic; it is fundamentally flawed.

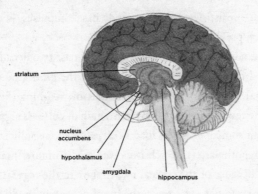

striatum

nucleus
accumbens

hypothalamus

amygdala

hippocampus

The Limbic System

One of the big modern breakthroughs in the science of self-regulation was the discovery of the operation of the limbic system, what Joseph LeDoux called the "emotional brain." This subcortical complex lies below the *prefrontal cortex* (PFC), and its main structures are the *amygdala, hippocampus, hypothalamus,* and *striatum.* The limbic system, and in particular the amygdala and nucleus accumbens (in the ventral striatum), is the source of our strong emotions and urges. It plays a critical role in the formation of memories and the emotional associations that get attached to those memories—positive as well as negative. Love, desire, fear, shame, anger, and trauma share a neurological home base here.

In times past it was initially tempting to see the brain's functioning as a kind of hierarchy in which "higher" executive systems in the PFC rule over and control the urges coming from the "lower" limbic system. The idea was that when we give in to desires, it is because our PFC is too weak to inhibit the strong impulses emanating from the limbic system. The ancient and unchallenged idea of willpower and self-control as a kind of mental muscle fit right into this view. Just as in Socrates' day, the remedy, it was thought, was to strengthen the executive systems for self-control much as you'd strengthen a muscle, through rigorous practice and discipline. In that paradigm the exercise of self-denial—resisting temptation and "base" impulses—becomes a kind of bench press for self-control.

However, advances in brain science in the past two decades reveal a strikingly different picture. The capacity of the prefrontal cortex to play a rational, inhibitory role—for example, by weighing the value of an immediate reward against a long-term gain or cost—is significantly reduced when someone's stress load is excessive. Especially important here is the hypothalamus, which is viewed as the brain's "master control system" because of the critical role it plays in the regulation of an extraordinary number of systems: the immune system, body temperature, hunger, thirst, fatigue, circadian rhythms, heart rate and breathing, digestion, metabolism, cellular repair, and even important aspects of hearing, speaking, "mindreading" other people's social and emotional cues, parenting, and attachment behaviors. All of these different functions are tied to the brain's most primitive response to anything from relatively minor stressors to full-on threats—or at least what our limbic system "decides" is a threat. When we can calm that response, we begin to bring all the other self-regulation processes into sync.

Self-control is important but not the central organizing feature of a strong, healthy mind and life success. Self-regulation is.

Three-Part Harmony: The Triune Brain

In the 1960s Paul MacLean, a neuroscientist at Yale, developed a theoretical model of the brain that remains highly instructive. According to his "triune" model, we actually have three distinct brains, each of which evolved at a different time in our evolutionary past and which are layered on top of one another. On top and at the front is, as its name suggests, the "newest" brain, the *neocortex*. It supports higher-order functions like language, thinking, mindreading emotional cues, and self-control. Underneath this is a much older, paleomammalian brain, which houses the limbic system and strong emotional associations and urges. And at the very bottom is the oldest and most primitive, so-called reptilian brain, which works closely with the limbic system to regulate our arousal and alertness.

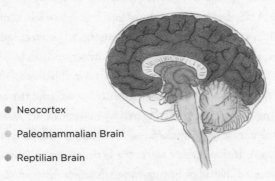

● Neocortex

● Paleomammalian Brain

● Reptilian Brain

The Triune Brain

MacLean's model is now seen as an oversimplification, yet it is helpful in understanding the neurophysiological difference between self-control and self-regulation. For self-control is very much a neocortical phenomenon, supported by a small number of systems in the PFC, while self-regulation operates on systems deep in the mammalian and reptilian brains: systems that are not only activated independent of, and even prior to, prefrontal functions but can also seriously constrain the operation of those prefrontal systems.

The Vigilant Brain: Wired to Protect and Defend Around the Clock

The hypothalamus oversees our internal milieu, making sure, for example, that our body temperature is close to 98.6 degrees, that we have the right amount of sodium and glucose in the bloodstream, that during sleep some systems rest and recover while others make repairs and promote healing. If the temperature outside suddenly drops, the hypothalamus triggers a metabolic response to generate body heat: Our breathing and heart rate go up, we shiver, our teeth chatter. All of these processes consume a considerable amount of energy.

The cold outside is a classic example of an environmental stressor that the ANS monitors and reacts to. If there are too many of these external "costs," on top of the usual emotional, social, and cognitive stressors, the limbic system can become hypersensitive to the slightest hint of danger. It registers something as a threat before the PFC has a chance to decide whether or not it really is one, tripping an alarm— something like a car alarm triggered by movement or vibration—that causes the release of neurochemicals for dealing with danger: fight-or-flight mode. If that doesn't work, the brain resorts to freeze—akin to the "play dead" behavior of some animals when threatened. The most ancient part of the triune brain, the so-called reptilian brain, responds to the danger by releasing *adrenaline* and setting in play a complex neurochemical chain that results in the release of *cortisol*.

These neurochemicals raise heart rate, blood pressure, and the rate of breathing to deliver glucose and oxygen to the major muscles (the lungs, throat, and nose all open). Energy surges. Fat is metabolized from fatty cells and glucose from the liver. Alertness and reactivity increase: Pupils dilate, hair stands on end (which allowed our hominin ancestors to appear larger and more formidable), sweat glands open as part of a cooling mechanism, and endorphins are released, increasing pain tolerance. This is just what you need in a dire situation that demands a quick response: fight or flee.

This alarm system is very primitive, at least in terms of contemporary life. As far as it's concerned, there's no difference between a real enemy and the pretend enemy of, say, an online role-playing game: Both trigger the release of adrenaline. These systems were designed for reptiles and mammals in the wild and cannot judge the severity of a threat or how long that threat might persist. The alarm stays on and the system remains in a state of fight or flight, pumping out stress hormones, which, in excess, can disrupt normal functioning of organs and organ systems and even cause cellular damage in parts of the developing brain.

In order to have enough energy for this continual heightened stress response, our hypothalamus shuts down whatever functions consume energy but are not necessary for survival in this perilous moment: nature's way to channel maximum energy to systems needed to deal with the threat at hand. The list of these nonessential functions that get slowed or shut down is quite extraordinary and the fundamental key to why it is so hard to exercise self-control when we most need to.

Fight or Flight Diverts Energy, Drains Reserves

In a fight-or-flight response energy is diverted from systems considered nonessential in emergency mode, such as digestion. The sluggishness you feel after a big meal is a reflection of how much energy digestion requires—roughly 15 percent to 20 percent of the body's total energy, the same amount the brain requires for the day-to-day job of keeping everything running. Digestion takes anywhere from four hours to a couple of days and is "energy expensive" because it takes a lot to produce the right chemical balance in the stomach to digest food and to produce the enzymes that will break down and distribute the nutrients throughout the body. Some of the other metabolic functions that are slowed down or suspended under stress include the immune system, cellular repair and growth, blood flow to the capillaries (so you're less likely to bleed to death if you get wounded), and reproduction.

You might wonder what any of this could possibly have to do with your losing your temper or eating that extra slice of cake you intended to leave on the plate, or with your child's tantrums, meltdowns, or math anxiety. The answer lies in the effect of fight or flight on our rational, inhibitory functions supported by the PFC.

Think of a time you've been absolutely furious with your eight-year-old for doing the thing you've told her a thousand times not to do. How well were you able to speak, let alone think? We tend to splutter when we're in a rage because when the mammalian and reptilian brains are running the show, the left side of our PFC has been side-lined. We lose all of those wonderful higher-order functions served by the PFC: language, reflective thinking, mindreading, empathy, and, of course, self-control!

Fascinating discoveries are being made by molecular biologists about the functions that get turned off in fight or flight. For example, sudden, pitched stress affects the muscles in the middle ear, reducing the child's ability to process speech and amping up his hearing at-tuned to low-frequency sounds. That makes eminent sense for the mammalian and reptilian brains: Those low-frequency sounds might be signs of a predator lurking in the bushes. But for us it explains why our distressed or distracted child appears to be ignoring us unless we stand right over him. And if we're standing right over him, chances are our tone of voice and body language are perceived as all the more threatening.

In fight or flight our modern, language-based social brain is put on hold and we instantly regress to what is in essence an ancient, pre-social, prelinguistic state in which the primitive survival mechanisms of a cornered animal are called into play.

Self-Regulation: How the Brain Balances Arousal and Arousal Regulation

The autonomic nervous system (ANS) regulates transitions between arousal states, from being sound asleep, our lowest state of arousal, to the highest, full-out flooded state, which you see in a child having a temper tantrum.

Arousal regulation is a function of the complementary forces of sympathetic nervous system (SNS) *activation*, which makes us more aroused, and parasympathetic nervous system (PNS) *inhibition*, which slows everything down: in effect, the brain's way of putting its foot on the gas pedal or the brakes. How much activation or recovery is necessary for any particular task varies from situation to situation and, of course, depends on our reserves. All day every day we are shifting up and down this arousal scale. As arousal goes up, energy consumption naturally does as well; as arousal goes down, we restore our reserves.

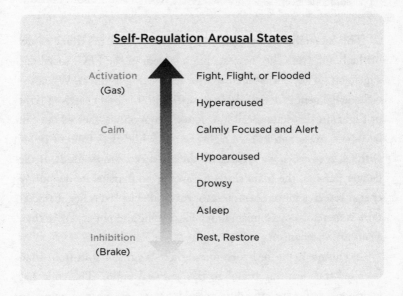

Self-Regulation Arousal States

Activation (Gas)	Fight, Flight, or Flooded
	Hyperaroused
Calm	Calmly Focused and Alert
	Hypoaroused
	Drowsy
	Asleep
Inhibition (Brake)	Rest, Restore

The more stress a child is under, the harder his brain finds it to manage these transitions. The recovery function begins to lose its resilience and the child can become "stuck" in hypo- or hyperarousal. Think, for example, of the child who finds it hard to get going or is always on the go and finds it hard to sit still.

Maybe most serious of all is when the fight-or-flight response becomes "kindled," or sensitized, making the child much more easily and repeatedly startled. When this happens, the child pulls away from us. Parents tend to experience this behavior as a sort of rejection, but, in fact, it is the function of a different kind of brain hierarchy—a series of natural biological responses to threat:

1. Social engagement
2. Fight or flight (sympathetic arousal)
3. Freeze (parasympathetic arousal)
4. Dissociation (the "out-of-body" state in which subjects report looking at what is happening to them as if it were happening to someone else)

This hierarchy of stress responses reflects MacLean's triune model of the brain, from the "newest" brain system in the PFC, social engagement, to ancient mechanisms for responding to threat. When social engagement is not available or sufficient, the brain shifts to fight or flight. In this state social interaction is not only eschewed but can become a stressor in its own right, i.e., the child flees from or fights with us, even when we are exactly the resource he most needs. If the danger persists, the brain shifts to "freeze" to marshal its dwindling energy reserves for one last push for survival. The last stage, dissociation, is more of a mechanism to reduce psychic and physical pain than a survival mechanism.

In chronic hypo- or hyperarousal there is a major shift from what is called the "learning brain" to the "survival brain." The child has enormous difficulty attending to and processing what is going on around or indeed inside him. He is now highly susceptible to "shutting down," impulsivity, and/or aggression (against himself as well as others). Children who are chronically zoned out or hyperactive are not somehow "weak" or simply *not trying hard enough*; they are experiencing too much stress.

Children cannot be forced to "calm down," and threatening to punish them if they don't can add considerably to the stress they're already under. They aren't *choosing* to be hypo- or hyperaroused any more than they can choose to calm down when they don't know how. Self-Reg gives them the tools and skills to do that.

At War with Ourselves: The High Cost of the Battle Within

A chronic state of heightened arousal makes the limbic alarm so sensitive to stress that it takes very little to set it off. Perception itself changes as the system becomes primed to look for threats, even where they are nonexistent. In experiments it is remarkable to see how when children are chronically hypo- or hyperaroused, they are much more likely to label neutral pictures of actors' faces as hostile.

This makes perfect evolutionary sense in a dangerous environment. The problem is that the more the alarm goes off, the more it is primed, or kindled, to go off again. Unfortunately, alarms are triggered way too often and way too easily, to the point where we no longer even notice when this is happening.

Consider your typical workday: Your alarm clock goes off (there's a reason why this common household device goes by that name), jerking you into a sudden state of hyperarousal, especially if you haven't been getting enough sleep or slept poorly the night before. You have to rush your children through their morning routines, drive them to school, and then commute to work, dealing with crowds, traffic, noise, and delays. Your stress load is high even before your workday has begun.

Maybe a midmorning coffee and doughnut calms you. There are physiological reasons why such a treat is soothing, including positive emotional associations. But maybe your need for treats is getting out of control and you're feeling guilty when you indulge, so you start to resist. Just fighting these urges can put you into a state of fight or flight, and being angry with yourself afterward—once your PFC has come back online—for your lack of self-control makes you that much more vulnerable to tripping into the fight-or-flight cycle you know and dread.

The 2,500-year-old idea that we experience a sort of "war" between our executive functions and our impulses turns out to be the perfect metaphor for the state we're in when we berate ourselves for our lack of self-control. The idea behind self-control is that if you can develop the "muscle" (grit, determination, self-discipline) to win this war, this carries over to things like suppressing the impulse to give up when the going gets tough—with your child, your partner, your work. You are basically learning how to deal with a feeling of discomfort without "giving in" to it. But, then, the cost of war is always high and in this case takes a heavy toll on our energy reserves.

This toll *will* eventually be felt, if not in the moment, then later, in an even more uncontrolled bout of negative emotions or self-gratification, or some deeper problem in our physical or mental health or emotional well-being. In fact, scientists have shown that increasing the stress on subjects *increases* the potency of their impulses and *reduces* their self-control. Rather than ignore these feelings, Self-Reg teaches us to recognize them as signs that our stress is far too high—our alarm system is stuck in the "on" mode—and what we really need to learn is how to turn it off.

The Stress Cycle: When Colliding Stressors Kick the System into Overdrive

The point of Self-Reg isn't to label a response or a behavior as something you must resist or control. The question we always need to ask ourselves isn't "Why can't I control this urge?" It's "Why am I having this urge—*why now*?" That's where Self-Reg becomes a powerful tool for positive and lasting change.

It's not just cravings we are talking about here. It might be a constant worry or, for that matter, something unspecific: a general sense of dread or simmering anger, an intrusive thought, or a dark outlook. The list goes on and on: strong associations that trigger arousal—a sudden fight-or-flight or freeze response, sudden impulses, powerful emotions, strong needs.

But arousal isn't the enemy. We depend on it when we need to transition from asleep to awake, from daydreaming to attentive, from play to work. A child needs it to learn. It is normal and healthy to *up-regulate*, to cycle through those transitions that require an uptick in energy. We normally move through a number of such cycles in an ordinary day. Up-regulating and the cyclical nature of it reflect purely biological states, having nothing to do with "bad" or "good" behavior.

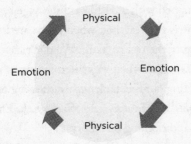

The Physical/Emotion Nexus

It's when the cycle gets *stuck in overdrive* and we can't "downshift" that we need to intercede, need to break a "stress cycle" that is spinning out of control:

I'll add more elements to the stress cycle, but we'll start with this simple version, which shows us how the physical and emotional elements of a cycle are interlocked and mutually reinforcing.

For example, the tingling or painful feelings associated with adrenaline can trigger an emotional association, a sudden sense of fear or worry. But equally, feeling a sudden fear or worry can trigger an uncomfortable physical sensation. When stress is chronic, the adrenaline response continues too. The effort of trying to forcibly stop the cycle through an act of self-control can leave us even more out of control as both the physical and emotional arousal responses intensify one another and further deplete our already depleted resources for responding. Bursts of impulsivity are so often seen as moments of weakness when they are actually signs of this physiological chain of events: the different regulating processes that are activated or deactivated.

Rather than insisting that we must exert greater self-control to restrain ourselves from acting on our impulses, Self-Reg teaches us how to recognize the source of the impulse and interrupt the cycle. Often just recognizing the powerful link between the emotional and the physical is enough to make a serious start on this.

Cars come equipped with a dashboard message system that alerts us when our engine is running hot, when fluids are low, or when the fuel supply is down to the reserve tank. We don't have such a system. There's no gauge to tell us when we've become stuck in a stress cycle that is rapidly draining our fuel tank *and* overheating our engine. *Negative feelings, thoughts, and behaviors are those signals.* They tell us when we're overstressed and running on empty.

This is especially important for regulating our children. The problem is that children and even teens find it very hard to articulate what they're feeling. It is through their actions—or lack of action—that they show us. Once we learn how to read their signals, there are effective steps we can take to help them manage their arousal. But often the very first step for parents is to recognize the significance of their own signals, which, in the heat of caring for their child, they ignore or even deny.

Parents Are Nature's Appointed Partners in the Self-Reg Process

Bernice and Autumn:
At the Self-Reg/Self-Control Crossroads

Bernice came to see us for help with her twelve-year-old daughter, Autumn, who was struggling with serious anxiety. But Bernice herself was incredibly anxious. She fidgeted nonstop and the stains on her fingers showed she was a chain-smoker. All this was perfectly understandable: She was consumed with worry about her daughter.

Bernice was the sort of mom who wouldn't put her own needs above her daughter's, but the problem was that she was in the firm grip of a stress cycle herself and in full-blown, relentless hyperdrive. She was having a great deal of trouble sleeping, which contributed to her worries about money, her other child, her marriage, and her job. When she woke up in the middle of the night, her mind would race from one worry to another. She was, as she admitted, "a nervous wreck," and this state of chronic tension only made her more vulnerable to the waves of worry that struck when Autumn was having a bad day. The repeating loop of worry, tension, vulnerability, and more worry only increased her tension and reduced her energy still further.

Bernice presented us with a fascinating pattern that I've seen so often that it deserves a title of its own: the "Self-Reg/Self-Control Parental Dichotomy." She immediately saw the importance of doing Self-Reg for her daughter; but for herself she was absolutely convinced that what was needed was more self-control: for her daughter's sake! She instantly saw how her daughter was overstressed because of a number of biological, emotional, and social stressors;

but she felt responsible for and in fact guilty about her daughter's anxiety and was certain that she needed to try much harder to control all her own worries.

It took time, but eventually she recognized that she needed to do Self-Reg for herself as much as for her daughter. Bernice decided to start attending a yoga class with Autumn. She had done yoga when she was younger—before she became a mother—and had found it calming and enjoyable. Before long, Bernice and Autumn were showing up at their weekly sessions with their yoga mats strapped to their backpacks.

Of course, there was much more behind this result than just doing Pranayama breathing exercises. For one thing, Bernice had a strong drive to do whatever it took for them both to feel better. For another, the fact that Autumn was benefiting from her own Self-Reg exercises did wonders to undo Bernice's feelings of helplessness. But the biggest driver was Bernice recognizing that she needed to do Self-Reg every bit as much as Autumn did.

It was fascinating to see the two of them improve very quickly, not so much *with* as *through* each other.

Self-Reg: The Five Core Steps to Transforming Behavior

The self-control paradigm represents a one-size-fits-all response to all challenges. In contrast, self-regulation creates an open, expansive system designed to channel our energy to help us function at our best under any circumstance. The better we understand self-regulation, the better we can turn challenging behaviors into active opportunities for engagement.

Children of all ages can learn Self-Reg skills, and my primary goal is for you to learn how to help your child self-regulate. Like Bernice, you'll learn to read your child's signs and understand the significance of your child's behaviors, to identify stressors and reduce them, and to engage your child in this process of self-awareness rather than trying to suppress or control what he is thinking, feeling, or doing. You'll help your child experience what "calm" feels like and learn how to access or create that state when he feels the need. These five Self-Reg steps will become second nature to you:

1. Read the signs and reframe the behavior.
2. Identify the stressors.
3. Reduce the stress.
4. Reflect. Become aware of when you're overstressed.
5. Respond. Figure out what helps you calm, rest, and recover.

Each of the five steps is something you can learn to do routinely for yourself in the moment.

Read the signs and reframe the behavior. A lot of the work we're going to do will involve learning how to understand the meaning of behaviors that you would otherwise find only troubling or irritating. This starts close to home with learning how to read your own signs and recognize them for what they are, something every bit as significant as a fever or a rash.

Identify the stressors. Ask, "Why now?" Stress usually means work, money problems, social worries, having too much to do and not enough time. These are certainly all stressors, but the concept of *stress* is much broader and subtler, especially when we turn to *hidden stressors*. For some people noise or certain kinds of sound can be significant stressors. For others light or visual stimulation (too much or too little) is stressful. Other common stressors include smells, textures, sitting or standing, and waiting. Remarkably, our environment may be highly stressful and yet we block this out as conscious information. But those monitoring systems deep in the brain, the mammalian and reptilian brains, aren't blocking it out, and they are in a constant dialogue with our internal receptors about how to deal with all this stress.

Reduce the stress. If you are very sensitive to light, replacing your on/off light switch with a dimmer switch gives you a way to adjust the lighting so you can be comfortable. In Self-Reg the dimmer is a useful all-purpose metaphor. We have physical, emotional, cognitive, and social stressors, and it's helpful to have a dimmer switch for all of them. In some cases you may be able to eliminate your exposure to a stressor altogether.

Reflect. Become aware of when you're becoming overstressed and why. We can get so used to feeling excessive stress that this state becomes "normal," so much so that sitting still and focusing on our breathing—something typically considered calming—can be a thousand times more distressing than being manic. Self-Reg develops this awareness of your inner state, sometimes very slowly, so that the shift isn't just tolerable but inherently enjoyable. The ultimate goal is to become aware of the causes of being overstressed and not just the symptoms.

Respond. Figure out what brings you back to being calm. Finally, we need strategies to reduce our tension and replenish our energy. This is what makes Self-Reg a completely personal journey. No one size fits all here. What one person finds calming might have the opposite effect on the next. What you find calming one day may not have that effect the next. This is why the first four steps are necessary to empower the fifth. For with the ability to read the signs you'll be able to distinguish between adaptive and maladaptive coping strategies. The reason why maladaptive coping strategies are so called is that they provide only short-term relief and then leave us even more drained, tense, and vulnerable to hypo- or hyperarousal. Self-Reg strategies are by nature adaptive—of lasting impact and value—because they focus on bringing your natural systems for self-regulation into balance and help you keep them that way.

The big appeal of popularized mindfulness practices is that these represent an important—nonpharmaceutical—way of dealing with troubling symptoms. But it's important that we don't overlook the fact that troubling symptoms like "monkey mind" are signs of excessive stress. What's more, we always need to take individual variability into account: how there are those—especially among children—who find focused breathing or meditation exercises stressful in their own way. As we'll see, a number of mindfulness practices are generally helpful, but because they can trigger greater anxiety—one more thing to control—they can at times in some cases be counterproductive to self-regulation. There are many options for relaxation practices, and what's most important is that you help your child find the right fit.

It's Not Strength We Need but Safety

It's natural to assume that when, say, you wake up in the middle of the night worried, the reason you can't get back to sleep is all these urgent problems. But it's not. This kind of anxious rumination is a sign that your internal alarm went off while you were asleep. You were likely in a high state of tension when you went to bed and stayed that way. Whatever triggered the alarm woke you with your heart rate, blood pressure, and breathing all elevated. It's the surge of adrenaline that's keeping you up and fueling the anxiety. And those systems in your PFC that you need to reappraise the worries? Forget it. They're on hold.

One way to interrupt this looping stress response is deep belly breathing and mindfulness practices that you find calming. Simple mindfulness exercises that have been shown to calm the brain include following your breath as you slowly inhale and exhale, visualizing something or someone reliably calming for you, or meditation of one kind or another. The point is to go for the so-called multiplier effect: rather than a "magic bullet"—a single activity to promote self-regulation—your child should explore all sorts of self-regulating activities, including exercise, music, art, or other mindfulness activities. You might draw or listen to a particular piece of music that you find calming. With Self-Reg you don't do this to distract yourself or suppress what's bothering you; you do it to break the stress cycle. The very act of reframing an intrusive thought or worry can instantly release tension, which then sets in play your recovery functions and brings the PFC back online.

Humans aren't very good at noticing when we're in a state of low energy and high tension. I suspect there's a strong evolutionary reason for this: No doubt it was better to stay focused on the threat and not on how we feel. The problem today is that stressors are ubiquitous and we can frequently be overstressed without even knowing it.

The real power of Self-Reg is recognizing and knowing what arousal state we're in and how to release our tension. The result is not that we finally have the strength to vanquish our internal demons but that as the intensity lessens they simply fade away.

TWO

More Than Marshmallows

Self-Regulation Versus Self-Control

It was gymnastics night. I was really looking forward to watching my daughter's class from the parents' viewing gallery upstairs, something I didn't get to do often. It was a chance for me to be "off the clock" and see my eight-year-old do things I could never have dreamed of doing.

On the bench right beside me were a young mom and dad with a three-year-old child who, to use a clinical term, was "full of beans." He was such an energetic little guy, chirping away with endless questions, running around the room, knocking on the glass to get his sister's attention, trying desperately to get other children to play with him. His parents found his behavior extremely annoying. Pretty soon I had completely forgotten about my daughter and found myself counting how many times they said "no" in a five-minute period. (Fourteen.)

The intensity of their reprimands grew. Mom and Dad had started off gently, but soon they were irritated and in short order genuinely angry. They wanted him to sit quietly on the bench, but he was finding that next to impossible. They tried healthy snacks from home, bought him a bag of popcorn, gave him a handheld video game, even a bribe, but nothing worked for longer than a minute.

At one point his mother gave him a smack on the bottom and sat him down on the bench fairly forcefully. The little guy sniffled a bit and did the best he could to sit perfectly still. He managed this for a couple of minutes. Then, ever so surreptitiously, he got up off the bench, warily watching his parents. Sensing that they were fully engaged, he took off running—but just briefly! The same scenario played out all over again. And so it went for the rest of the two-hour session, a sort of waxing and waning of family strife.

I felt deeply sympathetic watching this. I'd been there myself with my own kids. I suspect everyone has had times when they couldn't help but be irritated by their child. "Why can't you come to dinner the first time I call you?" "Why is it so hard to get you to wash up?" "What could possibly prompt you to say that to your mother?" Here's the thing: What if we treat these not as laments but as *genuine questions*?

The night that family drama played out in front of my eyes at gymnastics, there were quite a few children the same age sitting quietly in the viewing room. So what was making this little guy so restless? Why were his parents' efforts ineffective? *Why now?* That's *the* question.

Maybe he found it hard to be in a small and crowded room and needed to move around a lot in order to feel secure. Maybe he found the hard wooden bench uncomfortable or found the gymnastics painfully boring—or so exciting to watch that he had to jump around too. Lots of "maybes" could be added to that list. But that's the point. His behavior was saying more eloquently than he ever could have done that he was overstressed. His mom and dad were admonishing him to control himself, but the more they tried, the more he resisted and the more desperate they became.

In fact, neither the boy's behavior nor his parents' frustrated and eventually angry response reflected some innate lack of willpower or self-control. Each of them was worn out and desperate. We all know the feeling. In our own trying moments with our kids, is there a way to change the behavioral tug-of-war and, most important, the outcome? The answer is yes, but for that to happen we need to make the dramatic change in our thinking that makes self-regulation—not self-control—the focus of our efforts.

The distinction between the two can be confusing at times, even to experts, as we'll see in a moment. As parents it's natural to assume that when our child's behavior or our reactions feel "out of control," then control is what's missing. But to focus on control is also to shut down opportunity: end of conversation, end of a potentially constructive interaction, end of a teachable moment of lasting value. Self-Reg instantly opens the moment to opportunity. That begins with the simple act of asking, "Why now?"

It is critical that we make this conscious distinction between self-control and self-regulation. Otherwise the default explanation is that children are either "good" or "bad." With that come flawed assumptions about a child's genes, character, learning, and life potential.

The Marshmallow Study Meets the Myth of Self-Control

In 1963 American psychologist Walter Mischel, a Stanford University professor, performed a simple experiment that came to be an iconic reference for the importance of self-control to children's life success. The study involved six hundred children four to six years old. Mischel showed that children who can resist the lure of a marshmallow for the promise of more marshmallows later, if they wait, perform better in school over time. Follow-up studies indicated that the young kids who had been able to delay gratification that day did better in all sorts of ways when they grew older: They were more likely to complete high school and go on to college; had fewer health problems, mental as well as physical; were less likely to engage in mindless risky behaviors; were less likely to get in trouble with the law or succumb to an addiction, and scored higher on "life satisfaction" scores.

It's easy to think this was all about self-control. It's also a bit scary that a measure as crude as whether or not a young child can resist a temptation can be used as a predictor of his life trajectory. The "marsh-mallow study" seemed to confirm the age-old belief that self-control is the key to future success. What's more, the age of the children in the study was taken as evidence that we can detect poor self-control at a remarkably young age. These two assumptions taken together fueled the hope that if we intervene early we can strengthen a child's self-control and ensure life success. That, in turn, led to classic behavior modification becoming the mainstay in parenting, education, and far too much of professional counseling.

This "delay of gratification" task has even become the theme of a *Sesame Street* song circulating on the Internet. But what is not well known is that you can manipulate how a child will perform on the task—or, for that matter, a teenager, a college student, even an adult. If you tire out the child before the task or make the child anxious, the chances rise dramatically that he won't be able to wait: even if he previously had no trouble. In fact, if you have the child do the task in a noisy or crowded or strong-smelling environment, or just prime him with some sort of negative thought or emotion, he'll have a hard time waiting.

The marshmallow task may seem like a harmless bit of fun, but it was carefully designed to see how well a young child deals with stress; and for a lot of children the test is incredibly stressful. The child is left alone in a sterile room with nothing to do but sit at a table on an uncomfortable chair and stare at a marshmallow that's been placed directly in his line of vision. On top of that there's the stress of waiting for a strange adult to return in order to get a reward, with no way of knowing how long you've waited. Watch children suffering through the test and you can see that to them it *feels* like an eternity.

This is a stress test pure and simple: a version of the isolation chamber that astronauts have to undergo, tailored for four-year-olds.

Science now tells us that a child's response to this demanding situation depends most of all on his arousal state. How calm the child was before the plate of marshmallows appeared and the instructions were given is relevant information. The fact that a particular child chose to take the single marshmallow instead of waiting longer for the reward of more marshmallows doesn't really tell us much. *Why* the child did so takes us into the realm of self-regulation. That's where the power lies for behavioral change and for lifetime strategies for resilience and thriving in a stressful world.

We saw how the brain responds to a stressor by triggering metabolic processes that consume energy and then another set of metabolic processes that counteract the first and promote recovery. These counterbalancing mechanisms are in constant use maintaining a stable internal environment. They keep your core body temperature—which varies by close to a degree over the course of a day, typically with lower temperatures in the morning and higher temperatures in the late afternoon or evening—close to a set point of 98.6 degrees. If you get too hot, your body restores balance by radiating heat and sweating. If you get too cold, you shiver or your teeth chatter.

These processes all require energy, and most expensive of all in energy terms is when our limbic system—the "emotional brain" that governs strong emotions and drives—sounds the alarm: We respond to the threat and then recover. I liken this to the gas pedal and brakes on a car: When the amygdala registers something as a danger, the hypothalamus floors the gas pedal; when the amygdala turns off the alarm, the hypothalamus presses on the brakes. The problem is that if the amygdala sounds the alarm too often, the hypothalamus is constantly pressing on the gas pedal, then the brakes, and the brake pads wear out: The recovery system loses its resilience. When that happens, you start to see problems: behavioral problems, learning problems, physical, social, and emotional problems. Self-regulation calms the emotional brain and quiets the alarm and the systemwide arousal so that the dual response and recovery systems can work together smoothly.

Here's the important point: If a child is in a depleted state, he is going to find it much harder to resist an impulse, whether that is to snatch a tempting marshmallow or to run around when orders are to sit still. Jump to the conclusion that the marshmallow study is about self-control, however, and you miss this crucial point about the energy it takes to be still and quiet, the biological fact that remaining still and quiet under stress consumes energy. The more stress, the greater the energy drain. Further, if you focus on self-control as the goal, you're more likely to respond in ways that increase the stress on the child and make things much worse.

The young, restless boy at gymnastics class is a case in point. When his parents' initial efforts to quiet him failed, they upped the ante. They reprimanded him repeatedly for squirming, then smacked him on the bottom, all of which only added to the boy's overstressed state and agitated him all the more. The worst outcome of all is that the parents' harsh behavior pushes the child past fight or flight into freeze, which is all too easily misconstrued as compliance. The parent might think, "Well, now he's listening. Now he knows I mean business!" But unfortunately a child in a state of freeze is processing very little of what you're saying. And the more a child's fight-flight-or-freeze response is triggered, the more sensitive his reactivity to stress becomes. The nervous system becomes quicker to alarm and harder to calm.

The distinction between self-regulation and self-control is much more than a simple quibble over semantics. Words and ideas have lasting power, especially as we see them play out in the way we view children. In this case the lasting power of this long-misunderstood idea of willpower or self-control distorts our understanding of children and limits the potential we see, or even allow, for them. It leads us to assume, for example, that the reason a young child can't resist the lure of a marshmallow is that he is innately weak-willed.

It's a basic misunderstanding that we teach a child self-control through punishment and rewards. The behaviorist view, as it is called, found its voice a century ago in American psychologist John Watson's argument that by judiciously using a scientifically based system of punishment and rewards, you could mold any child's character in any way you wanted. The view held that you needed to start with how you responded to your baby's cries when you put him to sleep. The notion was that to comfort your crying infant only rewarded him for behavior you wanted to change; that he must learn to control his upset by himself and that withholding your comfort was the more effective way to teach him.

Following this line of thinking, the marshmallow study would indicate that if a four-year-old is weak-willed, it's because his parents have failed to teach him how to inhibit or control his natural desire for instant gratification. These misguided theories have become entrenched in widespread attitudes about child rearing. It is only in the past few years that we have come to realize how harmful this outlook can be.

We are witnessing an explosion in the number of children who struggle with the very sorts of psychological, behavioral, and social problems that historically were blamed on poor self-control but that we now understand more accurately as problems with self-regulation. The epidemic levels of childhood obesity and diabetes, for instance, reflect more than a lack of willpower to resist junk food.

Something more basic is out of balance for our kids, and hammering harder on the need for self-control isn't the answer. It doesn't build or restore the self-regulating skills needed for them to be at their best each day and make meaningful changes in behavior and health. Unless we understand this, we risk adding to the factors contributing to a young child's poor self-regulation.

From Marshmallows to Meltdowns: Stress Drives Behavior

Countless variations on the marshmallow study have been done over the years. By far the most interesting finding is that individuals' performance can be manipulated by increasing the stress they're under. All sorts of stressors have been studied. For example, subjects might be asked to think about or look at something distressing. They might be exposed to a loud noise or a strong smell while doing the task. The testing room might purposefully be made too hot, too cold, or too crowded. Or the test might be timed so that the subjects perform the task when they're hungry or haven't slept enough.

Studies show that the greater the emotional, physical, or psychological stress, the harder it is for us to delay gratification. That tells us that a child's ability to resist an impulse is first and foremost a matter of arousal: the result of too much stress and the effect this has on energy reserves. How hard is it to think clearly when you're stressed out or exhausted? Notice how much easier it is to resist a temptation when you're feeling calm. In this context a child's behavior is an expression of physiological and emotional factors, and the role of self-regulation stands out in sharp contrast to self-control.

Running on Empty

Stressors come in all shapes and sizes, including environmental, physical, cognitive, emotional, and social. Every one of them affects the self-regulation processes. Put a child in a cramped chair in a noisy classroom, with an assignment that requires concentration, add a distracting classmate nearby, and that can be a tall order. Send him to school without a decent breakfast or a good night's sleep, and the resulting stress and energy consumption are that much greater. Just think of the last time your child had a blowup or a meltdown, even in the privacy of your own home. Look for the stress factors and you'll find them.

To make matters even more complicated, these different kinds of stress are all intricately bound together. It's a common playground scenario. Something happens that makes the child anxious. The anxiety makes him tense and the tension depletes his energy. It becomes even harder for him to pick up the subtle social cues going on around him, leaving him even more anxious and less able to connect with friends who would otherwise be a calming influence. If tension continues to escalate as energy runs low, the child is headed for a meltdown. These cycles occur throughout a child's day, and much more powerfully for some children than for others, depending on their individual sensitivities, temperament, and resilience under stress of various kinds.

When children are under too much stress from these many varied sources, they generally can't tell us in words, but they show it in their behavior, their mood, their inability to listen or to get along with other children. A child who is overstressed by environmental factors— sounds, smells, visual distractions, the feel of a chair or a sock, for instance—may have a hard time paying attention or may have a short fuse around someone who annoys him. Another child, generally unfazed by environmental factors and at ease socially, may nonetheless be devastated by his parents' divorce or some other sudden change in the emotional status quo. Yet another child may be depleted from lack of sleep, exercise, and sound nutrition—a common trifecta of deficits in kids' lives today. The underlying cause is the same: These children are under more stress than they have the energy to manage. Excess stress drains their energy for the long, steep climb of the day.

The problem goes still deeper than that. As stress drains their fuel tank, they rely on adrenaline and cortisol to keep themselves going. That's why they become hyper or manic, and this is as hard on them as it is on us. This is definitely not the sort of behavior that a child can control "if only he chooses to do so." Because he's not *choosing* the way he's acting. The part of his brain that serves intentional behavior is precisely the part that shuts down when he becomes hyper or manic. I'm not even sure that the little guy at the gym heard, let alone understood, what his mom and dad were demanding, because the listening part of the brain shuts down as well.

"Reframing" a Child's Behavior for the Answer to "Why Now?"

The instant you recognize when a child's troubling behaviors are caused by too much stress, your whole relationship is transformed. In Self-Reg it's called *reframing your perception of a child's behavior*. Once you can distinguish between misbehavior and stress behavior, you find yourself better able to pause and reflect when he does something you find disturbing, rather than reacting automatically. Instead of being irritated you become inquisitive. Instead of disciplining or instructing, you listen—with all of your senses. Instead of reacting in a way that only adds to the stress and causes the child to burn even more energy, you can help the child to calm, restore equilibrium, and recover. That's Self-Reg.

Self-Reg is based on five developmental domains: physical, cognitive, social, emotional, and prosocial. All of these domains interact with and influence one another; all five of them hold answers to the question "Why now?" Except in the case of very young children, for whom social and prosocial stressors are not significant factors, all five always have to be addressed.

Some of the simplest signs that a child's stress is too high are behaviors that are often mistaken for misbehavior or a bad attitude:

The child . . .

. . . has a lot of trouble falling asleep or staying asleep
. . . is very crabby in the morning

. . . gets upset easily—even over little things—and has trouble calming down when this happens

. . . has a volatile mood, happy one moment and distressed the next

. . . has trouble paying attention or even hearing your voice

. . . gets too angry too often or seems to be overly sad, fearful, or anxious

Blaming, shaming, or otherwise punishing a child for these sorts of behaviors can make things worse. The punishment becomes a stressor in its own right. Make the punishment severe enough and, as I mentioned, the child will likely freeze. Freezing is a worrying step in the brain's hierarchy of strategies for responding to stress. It may look like self-control but it is the very opposite of self-control: Overwhelmed, the response system is disabled.

A dramatic change results when we start to think in terms of behavior as a reflection of self-regulation in response to stress, arousal, and energy levels, rather than in terms of self-control and compliance. Sometimes the fixes are surprisingly simple—lowering your voice, tidying up visual clutter in your child's room, or changing the lighting in a room. For some children the struggles are deep and more complex, often as confusing to them as they are to us. We see them trying and failing. We see them not trying and are at a loss to understand why, or what to do about it. Or we see them give up and we do understand why but are still at a loss about what to do. Whatever the circumstances, reframing your child's behavior instantly changes the dynamic and opens the way for greater understanding and lasting change.

Steven

Steven's parents knew from the start that their baby boy needed an extra measure of patience and TLC. Steven had a difficult birth, with low scores on the Apgar test of critical measures of newborn health: jaundice and high measures of heart rate, breathing, and irritability meant he spent the first four days of his life in the neonatal intensive care unit under the bilirubin lights. One of the biggest challenges in the beginning was that he was unusually sensitive (what we call *hypersensitive*) to light, taste, and odors, but he was undersensitive (*hyposensitive*) to touch and voices; although his hearing was good, he had trouble distinguishing some word sounds. Further, the more tired or stressed he was, the more pronounced these hyper- and hyposensitivities became.

Not surprisingly, Steven's first year was difficult. He had a great deal of trouble eating and sleeping. He cried a lot and was very difficult to settle. Their pediatrician recommended that they come see us and, together, we began to figure out what Steven's stressors were and to develop calming strategies. His parents learned that when they softened their voices and slowed down their speech, gestures, and movements, he grew calmer. When he was agitated, they learned to soothe him by rocking and swinging, and they avoided taking him into environments like the supermarket, where they knew he quickly became overwhelmed by the sensory overload.

By the time he was two years old, Steven was still highly irritable but he was starting to fall asleep at the same hour every night and sleep through. He was beginning to eat well and, most important of all, he was starting to take enormous delight in his parents. Just the sound of Mommy's voice could cause him to smile, and a gentle caress or being held on Dad's shoulder could usually soothe him.

Over the next couple of years, as Steven began to interact with other children in nursery and preschool programs, new obstacles arose. Activities that some children might find energizing were draining for Steven. His low sensitivity to voices meant that he didn't pick up on routine auditory cues such as someone's tone of voice when they spoke to him. His lack of response was confusing or sometimes irritating to others. At home his parents understood and had developed warm, supportive ways of engaging him in conversation. But in social settings it made for tense moments when communication went awry with teachers or other children, and tempers flared.

Steven also had trouble with his fine motor skills. Simple activities like coloring or playing with building blocks or manipulative toys easily frustrated him. His frustration made ordinary social and learning activities especially challenging—and stressful—for him and everyone around him.

On the plus side for Steven were fairly strong gross motor skills involved in movement. By his first birthday he was already starting to run. His parents regularly took him on long walks, and with each walk he would go a little farther before asking to be picked up and carried back to the car. He absolutely loved rough-and-tumble play. He was already doing somersaults by his third birthday, and when he turned four he wanted nothing more than to learn to skate and play hockey. Steven was what we call sensory craving, a child who needs a lot of movement and contact to feel in touch with his body. The more he skated, the calmer he became, the better he ate, and the earlier he went to sleep and stayed asleep.

By age five Steven was an active kid but had trouble staying out of trouble in social situations. He could be sweet and easygoing when he was relaxed at home, but he had a short fuse when he got frustrated and had a hard time making friends. He didn't know how to behave with playmates. In school he'd get grabby over toys or pushy when things didn't go his way. His mother thought one-on-one playdates at home might work out better, but they didn't. At school or at home, a minor quarrel over a toy could quickly escalate and Steven was prone to shove or hit. His reputation grew as the kid nobody invited to playdates or birthday parties.

It was difficult for Steven to sit still and join group activities like circle time or to follow instructions. The fact that he didn't easily pick up on social cues in those settings only made miscues and misunderstandings more likely. By age five Steven had been kicked out of a gym club for kids, an art club for kids, a summer camp for pre-schoolers, and a progressive nursery. He would either simply refuse to engage in the group activity or, when he was involved, become so disruptive that he was soon asked to leave.

He was consistently singled out as a "difficult" child, even though when he was calm he was sweet and engaging. Instead of experiencing the sort of consistently warm and encouraging response that his parents gave him through ups and downs, at school and after-school activities he was constantly being scolded and placed on time-outs. His engaging moments went unappreciated and became fewer and fewer. Not surprisingly, by age seven he was showing all the signs of low self-esteem and, connected to this, a reluctance to own up to his transgressions, which often only infuriated the adults in charge of him even more.

Despite their devotion, there were times when his parents feared that Steven's outlook was poor, and their anxiety mounted with every new challenge or setback. But they continued to focus on ways to reduce his overall stress at home, for example, by limiting TV and holding fast to early bedtime. They were patient instead of harsh when Steven had a meltdown, and they noticed that when the melt-downs did occur he was starting to be able to regroup more quickly.

I mentioned how at four he had begged to learn to skate and play hockey, but it was soon clear that, as passionate as he was about wanting to play, he was also extremely anxious about actually playing—enduring the stressful social aspects of a team sport, listening to the coach. But with his parents' help he persevered. He routinely needed help tying his skates and he was extremely fussy about the fit, but his parents, instead of getting angry when they had to undo his skates for the umpteenth time because they were too tight and then too loose, just tied the laces again and asked him if the skates were all right now. Somehow they recognized intuitively that this was as much about the anxiety he was feeling as about the real or imagined discomfort of his skates.

They also discovered some teachers, coaches, and others along the way who were eager to work with Steven to minimize stressful aspects of his school day and help him use strategies to lessen his anxiety and help him focus for learning. There was the Tykes hockey coach who used humor and pylons to keep Steven on the ice and practicing when he was new at the game and barely able to move in his skates. There were the teammates cheering him on and celebrating his small triumphs with him. And there was Steven's own desperate desire to skate, which, with the other support, gave him an extra boost of energy to keep trying.

There was the kindergarten teacher, one of those naturally gifted educators who knew just how to ease this fraught young boy into his first experience of leaving the security of Mommy to brave the school day. She recognized that Steven was easily overwhelmed by the noise of the classroom, so she arranged for a quiet spot at the back where he could go whenever he needed to regroup.

In second grade a supportive teacher took additional steps to reduce classroom distractions so Steven was able to focus his energy more effectively on learning to read, which was a struggle for him. Once again the important step was to reduce the stressors and thus reduce the effort required to focus so he could master a skill that he himself was eager to acquire.

Over and over, by reducing his physical and emotional stressors supportive adults helped Steven to engage more calmly and master important skills and content that he needed and wanted to learn. He became able to pay attention and listen closely to instructions from a teacher or a coach; to organize his thoughts and actions effectively for schoolwork and hockey; to pick up on what other kids were thinking and feeling; and the effect of his own actions or utterances on others. The key to all these achievements, including the last, was not sheer willpower: It was self-regulation that enabled him to marshal his energy for challenge and change.

Over time Steven learned to recognize his stressors, to adjust for his emotions, to understand how his physical state affected his moods and ability to cope with stress, and to shift from agitation and anger to more useful ways of dealing with stress. In other words, Steven himself was learning how to do Self-Reg. There were lots of ups and downs, but eventually Steven went on to academic and athletic success. As a teen he became captain of his high school hockey team and a natural leader at his school. He became the sort of teenager we all hope for, with strong friendships, strong values, and grit and resilience. Nothing in the marshmallow study or behavioral modification models would have predicted that this was likely or even possible for the Steven everyone knew at a young age, or for so many kids who are written off because of early behavioral challenges.

Steven is no anomaly. Whatever challenges your child may have, self-regulation is the single most critical component for positive change and growth. Self-Reg is a process. In some ways it transforms your relationship and your child's behavior immediately, but other significant changes emerge over time. Most important, Self-Reg deepens and expands your child's inner resources. Yours too.

To Bully or Nurture a Child: The Buck Stops Here

The foundation of Self-Reg is that *it is only by being regulated that a child develops the ability to self-regulate*. This does not mean "the only way a child will acquire self-control is if we first control him."

Self-Reg is about becoming aware of and enhancing the internal processes of arousal regulation, not behavior management, about the critical role that an adult plays as an "external regulator" of a child's arousal states until such time as the child is able to manage this on his or her own. All sorts of things can trigger a state of hyperarousal or a drop to low energy, low interest (which we call *hypoarousal*) in a child. When this happens, it's critical that we help him get back to being calm and that, whatever else happens, we don't add to the problem.

Steven is a perfect case in point. Becoming a skilled hockey player required endless hours of discipline and focus on the ice; but this is not a story about grit. The reason Steven spent so much time on the ice, at least initially, is that he found it so regulating, a point that applies to most children who spend a great deal of time engaged in some particular activity by choice. The reason they become so good at baking or art or playing the piano is not that they want to "be the best" but that engaging in the activity makes them feel good.

Steven's turnaround wasn't instant when he started working on Self-Reg himself. He went through many ups and downs. Generally the setbacks were precipitated by something physical—for example, getting sick or not getting enough sleep. He found it difficult to cope with some challenging emotions: Shame and guilt were hard for him, as they are for every child. When he got sick, overly tired, or acutely embarrassed, Steven could regress to the level of a young child. He would become highly irritable and aggressive, responding to the most innocuous of remarks with a string of colorful expletives that only complicated matters. Or he would become belligerent, even threatening, and utterly irrational. In an athletic boy, and a pretty strong one at that, this could all be a bit intimidating, even scary. But the serious setbacks were *always* the result of how someone had responded to him during one of these episodes. It was seeing this happen to so many children that made me want to write this book.

Trading Carrots and Sticks for the Self-Reg Tool Kit

Steven's story is essentially about the paradigm shift his parents made when they chose to put Self-Reg at the heart of their parenting philosophy and everyday interactions with their child. His parents learned to respond to his outbursts in exactly the same way they had when he was a young child: by soothing rather than reacting angrily themselves. I once asked Steven's mother how she managed to stay so calm during these storms, and her response continues to guide me in my work with other parents and teachers. She told me: "He doesn't actually know what he's saying or doing: It's just his way of letting me know that he's in distress." That is the key to *reframing*.

We tend to take so seriously what a child says when he's in these states. We have become so used to language as our primary mode of communication that we listen only to the child's words and not to his tone of voice. But if we can tune out *what* he is saying and listen only to *how* he says it, what we hear are the sounds of a young child who is lashing out because he's in distress. Our child—even our older teen—needs us to return to the role of external regulator in these moments.

Steven's parents worked with him on developing self-control as needed but discovered that when he got enough sleep, ate well, exercised, and practiced Self-Reg, self-control wasn't often an issue. As Steven grew more attuned to his inner state and how particular stressors affected him, he was better able to sense when he was growing tired or tense and knew what to do about it. As a teen he was even known to pass up a sleepover or party the night before a big game or a test: He knew that he needed a good night's sleep to be at his best the next day.

Our days as parents are filled with all manner of stress. Our babies are needy and they cry at inopportune times; there isn't a parent of an infant who isn't routinely sleep deprived and running on empty. Throughout their childhood and adolescence we continue to struggle with their moods and continually shifting preferences. Or, at the extremes, total screaming meltdowns, fits that fill entire public places, shred the nerves, and drain all available energy (yours and your child's) to simply cope. Like kindling ready for the match, the small stuff adds up until a spark of anger or frustration—theirs or ours—ignites the emotional bonfire.

It's only in the past few years that science and clinical practice have provided a clear understanding of the biology of mood and behavior, the essential role of self-regulation, and the Self-Reg toolbox of skills and habits to support it. It's never too late to learn Self-Reg, and it's never too early either. In fact, nature has designed us to do just that. Self-Reg naturally starts at birth.

THREE

No Small Matter

Arousal Regulation and the Interbrain

The great American biologist Stephen Jay Gould wrote in *Ever Since Darwin* that human babies are all born prematurely. Literally they are "fetuses outside the womb" for the first stages of life. "Human babies are born as embryos, and embryos they remain for about the first nine months of life," he wrote. This idea is a game changer. Whenever I begin one of my lectures to parents with this, it is greeted by a sort of audible gasp. But compared with the rest of the animal kingdom, the human brain at birth is remarkably immature for a remarkably long time.

We're born helpless. We enter the world unable to feed ourselves, and we can't walk for nearly a year or perform the simplest tasks required to fend for ourselves. The capacity for self-regulation is barely in start-up mode, as your baby's frequent and frantic cries tell you. Yet this is a defining characteristic of our species. Why would nature leave this critical bit of unfinished business for the newborn brain? And what does it have to do with contemporary parenting?

The explanation is rooted in two equally desirable traits, each of which gave early humans a distinct evolutionary advantage over all other species. One is walking on two legs (bipedalism), and the other, having a big brain. Being upright had many benefits in terms of energy efficiency. One of the biggest advantages was that this freed up the hands, eventually enabling our ancestors to fashion labor-saving tools for hunting and homemaking. Bipedalism also triggered a variety of anatomical changes, the most important of which was the growth of the brain and all the technological and social developments this made possible.

There was just one problem. Females could give birth to only so big a brain and still be able to walk upright. Nature's ingenious solution: to grow more and more of the brain after birth. Forty weeks' gestation resulted in the maximum head size that could pass through the birth canal without a major overhaul of the female anatomy. (Once when I was explaining this idea to a very large audience, a lone voice called out from the back, "Nature went too far!")

As the adult brain evolved to be larger, each evolving species of humans gave birth to babies with a smaller percentage of that adult-sized brain developed. Today a newborn's brain at birth is about one quarter the size of an adult brain. Birth triggers a burst of neural growth so rapid and extensive that it is unique in the life span. Axons and dendrites—the roots and branches of the neural networking system—begin sprouting and forming connections between different parts of the brain. The connections between these roots and branches are called synapses, and hundreds of new ones form every second in the first year of life. The scientific name for this process—*exuberant synaptogenesis*—says it all. How the connections are formed between these synapses depends vitally on a child's interactions with her caregivers.

Around the eighth month the brain begins to prune away the excess synapses and strengthen the important connections. There is less flailing, more strategic movements as she explores her world, crawling, reaching, holding, pulling. This period of robust synaptic growth and pruning continues at a remarkable pace until around the child's fourth birthday, and by the time she is six and a half years old, approximately 95 percent of her brain will have developed. This process of growth and pruning in the brain's early development underpins all other aspects of development. Its impairment can lead to a range of physical and mental health complications.

A child's *stress reactivity* throughout life is literally being wired in the first years of life. The neural systems and connections that underpin language, emotional and social development, thinking, and behavior are all being wired in the crucible of early parent-child interactions. As parents we understandably tend to focus on the pressing physical, practical needs of a newborn, but that early caregiving is an essential part of the even deeper and more complex neurological process under way. From birth the unfinished business of the baby brain defines our role as parents. This understanding of the premature baby brain and continuing advances in brain science offer striking evidence of the dramatic brain growth and sculpting stimulated by the close and continuing interaction between baby and parent or caregiver. Nature not only intends for human parents to play a close, nurturing role with their offspring but depends on us to do it.

Birth: A Startling Start-up (or Storm of Stimuli) for All

Talk about a shock to the system. After nine months of relative quiet and calm in a cozy uterus, the fetus is suddenly forced from its sheltered environment through a cramped passageway in which it is squashed and bruised and finally delivered, only to find itself assaulted by all sorts of sensations it has never experienced before: light, noise, air, cold, the touch of hands, and a dry towel or blanket on its skin. Then comes the poking and prodding, the weighing and measuring and testing of heart rate, muscle tone, and reflexes, the sting of eye drops, injections of vitamin K and a vaccine, and a prick on the heel as someone draws blood.

The newborn also has to deal with all sorts of new, unfamiliar, and sometimes uncomfortable internal sensations. Breathing alone is an entirely new experience. In the womb the fetus had oxygen and nutrients delivered straight to its bloodstream through the umbilical cord. The umbilical cord also removed the waste products and carbon dioxide that built up around the fetus in this compact space.

Nature saw to it that the newborn has reflexes to drive these processes, but that doesn't mean the effort is any less physiologically demanding. All this is draining enough, but then add to that the first dominant behavior of the newborn: crying. Some evidence suggests that fetuses cry silently in the third trimester, but even so, this new kind of crying is loud, shrill, and utterly exhausting.

Despite all these sudden changes in her internal and external environment, the newborn's basic needs haven't altered from when she was inside the womb. She still needs to feel warm, safe, and secure, and she still needs sustenance. She now must figure out how to communicate her needs to another human being—all this while her ability to regulate and recover from her exertions is limited. Just as was the case with the fetus in the womb, during the first year of life outside it the parent (or attentive caregiver) has to carefully monitor and manage the baby's needs.

Soothing a baby is a crucial part of early care because babies startle so easily, and every time a baby startles her nervous system uses a great deal of energy. The startle response is an infant's fight-or-flight reaction, causing muscles to tense from head to toe. She may flail her arms and legs or arch her back, and her heart rate, blood pressure, and breathing all intensify. To compensate for this energy expenditure, the brain releases restorative neurohormones, but if the stress level is too great, this means energy use has to be cut, inhibiting a number of processes, including the immune and growth systems. This shutdown becomes a further stressor in its own right. For instance, in an environment that is constantly stressful, the digestive system can slow and the infant may be deprived of the very nutrients needed to thrive.

In adults thoughts, memories, and emotions, as well as external events, can all trigger the stress response. In babies we are primarily concerned with internal and external stimuli, which include the primitive emotion circuits, such as fear or anger. These reactions are the brain's most primitive responses to danger, real or perceived, and are governed by systems in the mammalian and reptilian brain that are activated in the last trimester and never go "offline." They monitor the environment for threats even in the womb and even while the baby sleeps.

Because startle reactions consume such an enormous amount of energy, it's imperative that a baby not be startled too often and that she have a chance to recover when this does happen. *Arousal* in the physiological context refers to how alert and reactive the baby is—physically and emotionally—to internal and external sensations. When an infant is startled and doesn't have a chance to recover, she quickly becomes *hyperaroused*, a state of heightened physiological and psychological tension that makes her even more likely to startle again. Some babies grow listless when hyperaroused, instinctively withdrawing to protect themselves—the infant's version of *flight*. Others become irritable, the infant's version of *fight*.

Melanie: The Baby in the Bistro

Rachel and Simon had asked to see me because they couldn't get Melanie, their three-month-old daughter, to sleep more than six to eight hours a day. Ordinarily an infant this age needs to sleep about fifteen hours a day. At their suggestion we agreed to meet at a popular bistro near their house. I thought it would be just us three, with

Melanie at home with her sitter. To my surprise, they showed up at the bistro with Melanie in tow in a baby carrier. When I remarked on this, they laughingly told me this was the only place they could get her to cooperate, that they brought her to the bistro every day and that shortly after she crossed the threshold she'd fall asleep and stay asleep the entire time she was there. And that's exactly what happened when we met.

This peaceful picture and predictable bistro sleep routine might not seem problematic at a glance, except that Melanie's parents had called because she was having so much trouble sleeping at home.

I certainly understood why taking her to the restaurant might have seemed so alluring. It was a chance to have a break from all the crying and fussing that was going on at home. And it seemed like such a simple way to get her down for a nap, just like taking her for a drive, only without the traffic to contend with. Plus, there was the nice bonus of the chance to eat in peace, with the only interruption the admiring comments of people who remarked on how angelic she looked, asleep amid all the hubbub.

Rachel and Simon told me they had tried cutting back the amount of time that she napped during the day in the hope that this would help her get to sleep earlier and stay asleep. They had tried playing soothing melodies at bedtime and, when this didn't help, tried a sound machine. They had even moved her bassinet next to their own bed in case she just needed to be near them. Nothing they had tried so far had worked.

Recognizing the immaturity of the newborn brain opens up a new way to view the situation and understand what might have been going on. Perhaps the noise and hubbub of the bistro were overwhelming Melanie, and falling asleep was a primitive defense mechanism for protecting herself from stimulus overload. That is, maybe she wasn't being lulled but rather found the experience overly tax-ing. That meant that her bistro naps were part of the problem. It meant that she wasn't getting the quality of restorative sleep that the rapidly developing young brain and body need. Her sympathetic nervous system was in overdrive.

Melanie not only found it hard to go to sleep but also seemed not to *want* to. This is quite common in young children but often misunderstood. Her parents knew she surely must be tired, but it seemed as if she were trying to keep herself in a state of upset—a heightened state of arousal. It's easy to imagine that a child who clearly resists going to sleep doesn't really need to sleep and there's no point in trying to force the matter.

This phenomenon of fighting sleep when it is most needed is common in children and teens (adults too). But here we were seeing the seeds of this behavior in a three-month-old baby. Why would an infant routinely fight sleep? We needed to understand why this had become a pattern, but much more important was the question of how to break it. Here is where Gould's idea of the embryonic baby brain, coupled with Self-Reg, suggests that the solution to this struggle is the opposite of what we might assume.

Melanie's parents had mentioned that they had tried reducing and even eliminating her naps at home. Like so many parents, they were concerned that the afternoon nap was the culprit in her night-time resistance to sleep. In fact, this idea that a child has to sleep through the night has almost become an obsession. The result is that desperate parents wind up keeping their baby up late or giving him heavy feedings at bedtime so that he won't awaken during the night. Melanie actually needed to nap more so she could sleep bet-ter. But how?

If this is viewed strictly as a "sleep problem," the conventional solution might be to focus narrowly on sleep itself and nap and bedtime routines. Self-Reg shifts the focus to the child's hyperarousal and how to interrupt that exhausting cycle that burns through the child's energy reserves. The process needed to begin with a kind of energy audit—and then implement steps to help her burn less and store more *throughout the day*. Melanie not only needed more sleep for more energy but also needed more energy to be able to settle down at bedtime for more and better sleep.

Sleep was the issue that prompted Melanie's parents' concerns, but the real lesson concerns the importance of learning how to recognize the signs of excessive stress in your child. The first step in Self-Reg is reading your child's behavior for signs of excessive stress, bearing in mind that your child will be unique. The same underlying issue of the energy needed for self-regulation comes wrapped in very different behaviors. In Melanie's case it was a baby who didn't sleep enough; but we've had other cases where it was a baby who slept *too* much. There was the baby who cried too much and another baby who never cried at all. In one instance a baby was extremely tense when her parents tried to hold her; another would grow limp in her parents' arms. The variations are endless and not necessarily signs that a baby doesn't feel safe and secure. But this is always a possibility that we need to take seriously.

The Arousal Cycle: Energy Ups and Downs

Over the course of the day a baby moves through a number of different arousal states. This is the role of the sympathetic and parasympathetic nervous systems, which meet the demands for energy expenditure and then for recovery and replenishing energy. Sleep is the lowest arousal state (see next page), burning only the energy required to main-

Sympathetic/Parasympathetic Nervous System

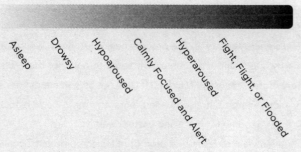

Asleep   Drowsy   Hypoaroused   Calmly Focused and Alert   Hyperaroused   Fight, Flight, or Flooded

Sympathetic nervous system releases adrenaline and cortisol, and activates energy to up-regulate

Parasympathetic system releases acetylcholine and serotonin to down-regulate

tain basic functions for health and healing. Flooded, or overwhelmed, is the highest and most energy-demanding state. A tantrum is one familiar sign of overwhelm; but a child whose nervous system is flooded may also withdraw—shut out the stimulus and dull her own responses—as a defense. That's what we saw with Melanie. At either end of the scale, the nervous system kicks in to up-regulate or down-regulate arousal, with the aim being to achieve that calm midpoint.

The Birth of the Interbrain: Relationship Completes the Baby Brain

If the infant is, neurologically, an "embryo outside the womb," then what takes the place of the umbilical cord and its role in the regulating process? Think of it as a sort of Bluetooth or wireless connection, which tethers the caregiver's brain to the baby's brain for purposes of arousal regulation. This shared intuitive channel of communication, called the *interbrain*, is established and maintained by touch,

The Interbrain

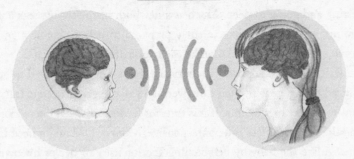

Parent and child are in constant communication
via the interbrain connection

shared gaze, voice, and, most of all, shared emotion. The interbrain lays the deep neurological, psychological, and sensory circuitry for co-regulation that evolves as your child grows.

The interbrain provides the conduit for the neural and neurobiological connections for arousal regulation that are not yet developed in the newborn brain. This is a direct brain-to-brain linkup that connects the infant brain to a higher-order parental brain that possesses this capacity for arousal regulation.

A baby has a limited number of self-soothing reflexes. Sucking is an important one, as are self-distraction, gaze aversion (looking away), and shutting down. Depending on her stress load, an infant may persistently shut down, just lie in the crib staring at nothing, or be highly reactive, crying for long periods of time and hard to settle. Not surprisingly, given their primitive brains, they shift erratically among arousal states, unable to move smoothly up and down through these states on their own. If left to themselves, they easily get stuck. They need us to smooth the transitions for them, "up-regulating" them when it is time to play or feed and "down-regulating" them when it is time to rest.

The higher-order brain—let's just call it Mommy or Daddy—reads the baby's cues: facial expressions, posture, movements, sounds—and adjusts its own behaviors accordingly to up-regulate or down-regulate the baby as necessary for feeding, playing, learning about the world, or resting and going to sleep. Much as a newborn instinctively seeks out the nipple, he also arrives innately prepared to help us connect and provide the internal regulation he can't yet manage for himself.

Babies come equipped with curiosity, but all newborns need to be enticed to engage with their caregivers, and all caregivers need to learn how to entice their infants. If it is time for feeding or social interaction and the baby is listless and nonresponsive, Mom or Dad might need to up-regulate the baby by heightening the intensity of her or his own smiles, vocalizations, gestures, and so on. If it is bedtime and the child is hyperaroused, with jerky movements or a wide-eyed expression, Dad or Mom might need to down-regulate the baby through such time-honored routines as bath time, singing a lullaby, reading a story, or gently rocking. The challenge here is that every baby is different in terms of what kind of sensations he or she finds energizing or soothing and what kinds of sensations feel unpleasant or draining.

Typically a baby is drawn into engagement by the emotional rhythm of your voice and gentle touch, your big smile and sparkling eyes. These cues from you or her caregiver enhance her arousal, helping her summon sufficient energy to engage in those critical social interactions through which she will develop her emotions and learn the meaning of facial expressions, vocalizations, gestures, and words. By the same token, your soothing sounds or caresses serve to down-regulate your child when it is clear she is becoming overloaded and needs time to recover.

As a parent you respond to your baby's needs in the same way that you respond to your own. In fact, in responding to your baby's needs you *are* responding to your own, for the interbrain works both ways. The caregiver's responses are physiological and not just cognitive. You're not just *aware* of but actually *feel* what your baby is feeling. You feel distressed when your baby is distressed, feel angry or frightened when your baby is angry or frightened, and in calming your baby you are also quite literally calming yourself.

"Left brain/right brain" theory maintains that the two hemispheres of the brain are responsible for different modes of thinking. The left brain is associated with logical, rational, objective thinking and, most of all, speech; the right brain with intuitive, subjective thinking based on the cues that we pick up, often unconsciously, from someone's body language, facial expressions, tone of voice, posture, and movements. While the two are much more highly integrated than once thought, the left-brain/right-brain model is useful as a kind of shorthand to refer to the different modes of communication that Self-Reg taps into.

The interbrain begins as a "right brain–to–right brain" communication channel between parent and baby, delivered through touch, sounds, looks, even smells. By the end of the first year of life the baby's left brain is starting to join the party: Language is emerging. Within just a couple of years speech will become the child's dominant mode of communication, although the earlier right-brain modes of communication will always continue to function "below the surface," as it were, shaping how we feel about and react to others.

This intimate exchange helps set what is to become the child's baseline state of arousal, her brain's "idle speed." In an engine the idle speed is set to generate just enough power to keep a number of core and accessory systems running smoothly. The idle speed varies for different engines; there is no single standard idle speed, and often a setting has to be adjusted for variable environmental factors—seasonal changes in temperature, for instance—or for internal mechanical stresses unique to that engine.

Your baby's "idle speed" must generate enough power to drive the metabolic and cellular processes needed for the immune system and for growth and restoration. However, that baseline adjusts upward in response to prolonged stress. This would include physiological stress, such as hunger, lack of sleep, or biological sensitivities, and emotional stress, such as fear, anger, or negative experiences. The more stress a child is under, the higher her baseline level of arousal, the more energy she's burning while "at rest," and the more reactive she is to stress.

Babies can respond very differently to a heightened baseline. Under prolonged stress they might become withdrawn or irritable or shift between these responses, sometimes in the blink of an eye.

A baby's baseline arousal level develops in the crucible of the interbrain as a result of the interaction between biology and experience, powerfully shaped by your responses and the climate of your relationship with the baby. But some babies have a biology that makes them much more susceptible to heightened arousal, much harder to calm. This is what was happening with Melanie.

Simple Changes Make Sweet Dreams on the Home Front

Bistro Baby Rebounds

Melanie's parents took a fresh look at their home environment and their patterns of activity and downtime with Melanie. It was reasonable to assume that a combination of inborn sensitivities and her pattern of chronic low sleep and high stress had elevated her baseline arousal, making her more prone to startle and trigger the fight-or-flight response. This would mean that even while she was sleeping, both her breathing and her heart rate would be elevated and that her heart was always working harder than normal for an infant. Furthermore, when there was a stressor, her heart would beat even faster and when the stress was over, her heart rate would stay elevated, which, in turn, would continually signal the primitive brain to stay on high alert. All the signs indicated that this elevated level had become her natural idle space.

Not only did Melanie find it hard to down-regulate, but she actually seemed to dislike what we would call being relaxed and calm. This can be a function of becoming habituated to the higher arousal state, or it may be the mammalian brain's way of saying, "I don't want to let my guard down" or "This feels unfamiliar and scary." Unfortunately, a nervous system poised to pick up danger senses it everywhere, even if there is none. The chronic stress constantly depleted Melanie's energy. She was burning way too much and finding it increasingly difficult to recover.

Calming the "Hyperarousable" Baby

Melanie's pattern of sleeplessness and startling easily throughout the day is an example of what is called "heightened arousability." Self-Reg strategies for reducing stress for a hyperarousable baby start as they do for any baby, with steps to make the home environment calm and comforting, as close as possible to the idyllic womb. Rachel and Simon committed wholeheartedly to the makeover challenge, including my suggestion (met with groans by both) that they set about turning their living room into a "livingwomb."

For starters, they turned off the TV. This was a family where it was always on. All too often the morning news was peppered with the sounds of explosions from war fronts, fraught voices in other reports, and newscasters speaking in urgent tones. Rachel, who is a graphic artist, told me how she liked the background sound of the TV while she worked. But now she noticed how Melanie would respond to the sudden volume increase when a commercial came on or the sound of a siren or angry voices on the TV. The sound of ordinary appliances such as the vacuum, blender, or doorbell could startle Melanie as well. Even smells had to be toned down. The pine scent that reminded Rachel and Simon of the time they spent hiking seemed to bother Melanie.

Step by step, Rachel and Simon identified and removed the things that upset Melanie, and within a few weeks she was starting to sleep sixteen hours a day, including nice long morning and afternoon naps! This does not mean that we all have to go out and turn our living room into a "livingwomb." Every single baby is different in terms of what she finds soothing and what agitates her. The key for Rachel and Simon, as for every parent, was to recognize when Melanie was startled or overstressed and to read the signs that she was becoming hyperaroused. Instead of trying to suppress her sleep problems, they reduced the stressors for Melanie and continued with their calming interactions with her, and they soon found that she became less sensitive to startling and more responsive to calming influences. Melanie's sleeplessness proved to be the wake-up call that helped her parents learn to recognize when she was overaroused and needed their help to calm herself.

The intimate interconnectedness of the interbrain can, in one sense, be considered the master tool in the parenting tool kit for Self-Reg. We can use it with intention, with the aim of helping our child ride the ups and downs of the day and learn, over time, to self-regulate. The shared experience and emotional intimacy not only enrich the parent-child relationship but also enhance the child's capacity for healthy relationships and the regulating benefits of social engagement.

The Connection That Calms, Comforts, and Completes Us

My introduction to the power of the interbrain happened during training under Stanley Greenspan. He showed me a video he had shot of himself with a mother and father and their four-year-old daughter with autism. At the beginning of the video the little girl wanders aimlessly, oblivious to her parents and surroundings. She mindlessly picks up a toy, plays with it for a bit, and then discards it for another. After several minutes of this, Greenspan remarks on the tape that he'd like to get a bit of an interaction going, and the mother responds with what primatologists call a "fear grin," an expression of anxiety rather than pleasure.

At this point Greenspan turned the video off and asked me to speculate about the child's developmental level and what her prospects in life might be. I had found it very hard to watch the video, to see this mother longing to connect with her child and unable to, while Dad sat physically and emotionally apart from all this on a couch, clearly finding the whole process unbearably hard. The situation looked bleak. I couldn't help but respond pessimistically to Greenspan's questions. I've repeated the same exercise with my own students over the years and they have all responded in the same gloomy manner.

Greenspan then restarted the tape and I watched, utterly mesmerized, as he was able almost instantly to change the entire dynamic of the interaction by helping the parents adjust their behaviors. They needed to slow down and soften their speech and their gestures, to wait patiently for her to respond. In front of my eyes the child became first aware of and then absolutely entranced by both of her parents. She demonstrated the most exuberant pleasure in the game of hide-and-seek they were playing and even started to speak. The most moving part, something that still brings tears to my eyes when I watch this, occurs at the very end of the tape. Tired from their play session, both mother and child need a break, and the two of them come together in perfect harmony for a hug and kiss.

That image of the mother-daughter interaction showed the power of the interbrain. Two brains that had been disconnected suddenly came into sync, experienced deep pleasure in each other, then calmed each other, *all in that connection*. This was more than a mere connection; this was the dawning of attachment, of love. Suddenly I understood the deeper meaning of all the science that I had been studying for many years. Science is hard-pressed to fully explain the interbrain phenomenon, but Greenspan's research, our own at our institute, and that of others have documented various aspects of it that highlight its essential role in arousal regulation.

Using the sophisticated tools of video microanalysis, scientists have been able to show that when Mommy or Daddy smiles one of those broad, loving smiles, this stimulates pleasure in the infant and gives her a quick shot of energy. The baby's positive reaction is immediately communicated back to the parent via the infant's big smile, so that the two are said to be in a "symbiotic state of heightened arousal." The delight in each other is uplifting for both.

The opposite happens as well. In one of the most noted psychological experiments of our time, the eminent developmental psychologist Ed Tronick studied how a mother's facial expression affects her infant's emotional state. In the experiment mother and baby begin with a few minutes of play, which promotes an enjoyable state of arousal in the baby. Then Mom is instructed to turn her head away briefly and then turn back with a neutral and blank look on her face, which she maintains for several minutes.

The babies in the original experiments were eight months old, an age by which they have pretty good communicative skills but are not yet talking. In each mother-baby pair the babies initially respond to mother's "still face" in the same way: They try desperately to bring Mommy back, using all the cute smiles and gestures at their disposal, and become increasingly agitated when she remains distant.

These scientific discoveries tell us why the interbrain is such a powerful force in our lives. Why our need for one another is so strong and isn't simply emotional but neurobiological. Why the distress we experience when our child is distressed is so acute; why the pleasure that we experience in moments of attunement is a pleasure that we experience *only* in moments of attunement. Our brain responds to these moments, and so does our baby's, with a rush of "feel-good" neurohormones, and there's nothing else in life with quite the same effect. The joy when we connect with our child completes us. The interbrain serves not just the child's deepest needs but also our own.

Unlike the umbilical cord, the interbrain is never no longer needed. When the attachment between parent and infant is secure, the interbrain will always be an intimate and enduring tether between them that can deliver comfort, encouragement, and a calming influence that mitigates stress. The interbrain is forever a feature of the parent-child relationship and in many ways becomes the foundation for close relationships with others.

In Tronick's Still Face experiment the mother's initial lack of response to her baby's overtures represents a fundamental breakdown in the social-engagement system. Some babies become withdrawn and apathetic, while others become angry and aggressive. When Mom reengages, the babies return quickly to a regulated state. If they don't, this can be an important sign of a deeper problem.

Social engagement is not simply a learned coping strategy to add to our repertoire of self-soothing reflexes. *We are designed to draw energy from one another and restore energy through one another.* We are not just a social species that, like ungulates, feeds together. We are social beings who sustain and protect one another through looks, touch, conversation, and soothing vocalizations, as well as by sharing the spoils of our hunting and gathering.

A baby who does not experience this nurturing can have problems feeding and sleeping but also issues with slow physical and mental development, motor and communication delays, even cardiovascular or autoimmune disorders. Such a baby has an alarm that is on high alert, which means that she is constantly releasing adrenaline and cortisol. This continual push-pull pressure on her nervous system to respond, then recover, sets in motion subtle changes at the cellular level that can undermine a child's health and resilience early in life or take their toll over time.

Self-Reg can help infants, children, and teens alike become calm and stop burning through their energy reserves faster than they can restore them. When they're running on empty, the reptilian brain's response is to shut things down or dip still further into its reserves. That is why the interbrain is so absolutely vital for the child's or teen's well-being. Nature gave us, as adults, a higher-order brain to calm the reptilian brain until such time as the child or teen can do this on his own.

What Interferes with the Interbrain?

A number of factors can interfere with the smooth functioning of the interbrain. For example, severe illness might seriously interfere with a mother's or father's ability to cope with the intense demands made by this ongoing two-way psyche-to-psyche "conversation." Physical absence limits the opportunities to cultivate the connection, at least in the way that one-on-one engagement allows.

A parent's heightened stress also can disrupt the regulating influence of the interbrain. In my work with families and in our clinic, we have found consistently that a fixation on self-control turns into one of the biggest sources of parental stress. It is extraordinary how many parents come to our clinic genuinely concerned that, for instance, by "giving in" to their baby's cries they might be undermining their child's subsequent self-control, or who even worry that their infant is being deliberately manipulative when she cries. Just being unhappy with our child's behavior is stressful in and of itself.

Our focus on the power of interbrain is about helping a child to develop the ability to manage her stress load, not about "teaching self-control" or socializing a child. Self-control is very much a social construct, in terms of both the kinds of behaviors that different cultures deem desirable and when and where they expect a child to exercise self-control. Children need to have limits; indeed, the absence of limits is a stressor in its own right and leads to problems in self-regulation. Self-control is clearly a vital aspect of successful social functioning. But it is not the same thing as self-regulation.

Biology becomes central in Self-Reg and in understanding the interbrain because of the many biological challenges that make this close two-way interaction taxing for an infant or young child who has so few ways to communicate to us his distress. For the infant or child with hypersensitivities, for instance, the gleam in a parent's eyes or a hug or gentle touch, which normally would be a source of positive arousal, can be more than the baby can bear. Or a child who has no particular sensitivities but is short on sleep, or is hungry or spent from other activity, may be less receptive or less responsive to your efforts to engage.

Parents naturally tend to take these difficulties deeply to heart. A crucial part of Self-Reg is learning how to let go of personal recriminations or distress when this happens and instead become an objective observer, both of your baby's needs and of your own. The better we can understand what might be draining a child's energy reserves, the better we can tailor our interactions to reduce that strain. Self-Reg supports parents in this effort and in doing so strengthens the parent-child connection.

Relationship Creates the Conduit for Calming and Cultivating Self-Reg

Our relationship with our child is an environment in which we both change and grow. This is fundamental to the scientific study of child development today. Neuroimaging and sophisticated psychophysiological technologies, together with real-time studies of babies and their parents interacting, have dramatically advanced our understanding of the unique power of this relationship. Most important for self-regulation, we now know this to be a core truth: *It is by being regulated a child develops the ability to self-regulate. Regulating a child* is not at all the same thing as *controlling a child*. Rather, it is concerned with managing the child's arousal states until such time as the child can do this on her own. That's what you're doing when you gently rock your baby to calm her, sing to her to help her fall asleep, or playfully engage when it's time for her to be up and about.

I once gave a public lecture about this topic and a member of the audience, a car mechanic, came up to me afterward and said: "So it's kind of like seeing your child's behaviors as indicators of how his engine is running." I loved this metaphor and have used it ever since in my work with parents, teachers, and kids themselves. Everybody gets it. It helps us get to see our child's challenging behaviors as signs of an engine that, for one reason or another, is overheating. A chronically irritable infant, a child who can't calm down, a constantly anxious teen: All are indicators of an engine working too hard. Other indicators include issues with attention or poor study habits, overemotional reactions, anger, aggression, or weak social skills. But given the individual variability that is a defining feature of our species, we first need to learn how to recognize the indicators of how a particular child's engine is running in order to be able to assess what to do; whether *this* practice is effective for *this* child at *this* time.

So how does that engine run?

FOUR

Under the Boab Tree

The Five-Domain Model for Self-Regulation

Jonathan had just turned five and was only one month into kindergarten when his mother got the call. Jonathan was in the principal's office—again. It was the quintessential terrible, horrible, no good, very bad day. His mom arrived to find him sitting miserably in the school office, tearful and anxious.

His teacher explained that Jonathan had whined all through an assembly while the school band had performed, tripped a classmate in his rush to get back to the classroom afterward, and then, once there, refused to engage in any of the class activities. At snack time he wouldn't eat his own snack and had snatched food from other children as if it were a game. Then, when the teacher had asked everyone to put on their coats to play outside, he'd refused, grown belligerent, and howled in pain after bumping into a desk. When the teacher had tried to talk to him, he had looked away and wouldn't pay attention to a word she was saying. That's when she sent him to the principal's office. It wasn't the first time.

Soon after, I visited Jonathan at school. I had never seen a child who was quite so easily startled. Someone down the hall could sneeze and he would almost jump out of his skin. Alert to the slightest noise, he reminded me of one of my cats. Nan, his mother, told me that Jonathan had always seemed more sensitive to noise than other children. When he was invited to birthday parties, she practically had to drag him, and once there he would beg to leave. He was just a boy who preferred things quiet. She had hoped that the kindergarten experience would be a happier one for him, but Jonathan dreaded going to school in the morning, and Nan dreaded his going too, knowing that it made him so miserable.

There was more going on with Jonathan than just hypersensitive hearing. Physical sensations inside his body scared him—his heart beating, for instance. He found certain emotions hard to handle. When he got angry, or when he was sad, it was always full throttle; no modulation there. Social interactions and demands left him rattled. So the first step was to get a fix on the full range of his stressors.

It wouldn't have been possible to just make an itemized list of the things he found stressful and then address them one by one. With Jonathan, as with all children, his difficulty self-regulating involved a multiplier effect in which one kind of stress—the noisy assembly, for instance—made him more sensitive to other stressors. Put him in a crowded room and he became much more sensitive to noise and light; when he was frustrated, his pain threshold seemed to plummet and the slightest bump left him howling. Back in the classroom, one trigger after another brought him to meltdown in no time. The multiplier effect holds true for all of us but especially for children, who are still beginners in life experience and the highs and lows that come with it.

Our research team was surprised when we started doing Self-Reg on a large scale with school systems to see how many children were struggling with stress-related issues. I don't mean that we are seeing an explosion in the number of children presenting clinical problems—although health statistics do show that—but that we are seeing a generation of children with way too much stress in their lives. Kids at young ages are already showing signs of stress-related wear and tear on their physical and mental health, putting them at higher risk for more serious problems later on.

There is all the usual: the upcoming math test, the teacher whose angry voice rattles them, the tiff with their friend. Their limbic systems are on high alert, doing what they were designed to do—sound the alarm. In fact, multiple alarms on all fronts. The stressors and the stress alarm circuit get stuck in a repeating loop and the energy drain just keeps on and on.

School and sports have grown increasingly competitive, social media has created a more complicated arena for friendship and social interaction, and many of the opportunities for rest and restoration—playing outdoors and true downtime, for instance—have disappeared from children's lives. The sources of stress are so interwoven that instead of looking for a single stressor, like a splinter that needs to be removed, the task is to untangle the web of stress in which the child is caught.

The Five Domains of Stress and Self-Regulation

Stressors come in infinite variety, but most can be assigned to five basic categories, or domains. The domains give you a way to begin to identify the kind of stress triggering your child's behavior. With that you can dig deeper to identify the specific stressor and its source, and then specific ways to reduce that stress and help your child learn to do the same.

Because self-regulation involves these multiple dimensions, it is a "dynamic system," which means that anything that happens in one part of the system affects the other parts in ways that may stabilize or destabilize the whole. All five domains influence one another and create a complex yet seamless, integrated system. At the same time, each domain is a distinct energy-expending system in its own right, a system in which energy and tension are always in play.

The Biological Domain

This includes the nervous system and the physiological processes that burn energy and restore it. The balance of energy-in and energy-out varies widely from person to person and from situation to situation. Emotions have a biological component too, as they trigger biochemical responses that can energize or drain us, especially intense emotions, whether positive or negative.

Stressors in the biological domain include inadequate nutrition, sleep, or exercise; motor and sensorimotor challenges (a child finds it hard to run or to go down a flight of stairs without holding on to a rail); noise, sights, touch, smells, and other kinds of stimuli; pollution, allergens, and extreme heat and cold.

Signs of stress in the biological domain could include low energy or lethargy; hyperactivity; difficulty making transitions between active and less active activities; chronic stomachaches or headaches; sensitivity to noise or to sound, which may include both the volume and the tone of your voice or a teacher's voice; difficulty sitting on hard surfaces or sitting still at all for more than a few minutes; physical clumsiness or difficulty with fine motor skills such as holding a pencil; or a tendency to get overwhelmed by what most people would consider normal stimulation or stress.

Many kids don't even know what the physical sensation of "calm" feels like or what it feels like to be energetic without being hyper. It's up to us to help them learn to recognize their own physical states: how their body feels when they're calm, alert, and engaged or when they've gone into a low-energy/high-tension state, and what they can do to help themselves feel better.

The Emotion Domain

The headliner: the emotions that are so large in our everyday lives. Kids, especially, start from scratch when it comes to understanding and managing big emotions (positive or negative ones), learning what to do when emotions overwhelm them, and developing the language to express their feelings effectively. Not only that, but the neural connections are so strong that emotions can affect the intensity of physical sensations—pain, for instance—making a child more or less sensitive to any biological stressor. Temperament can affect whether a child might be disappointed by a rainy day or delighted at the prospect of puddles.

Stressors in this domain include intense emotions, new or confusing emotions, and emotional entanglements. Intense negative emotions drain considerable energy in children and parents alike. Positive emotions tend to be energizing, although at times they too can be overwhelming. A parent's task is to help a child tell when his emotions (or someone else's) are running high and learn how to take steps to feel less in the grip of emotions and more calm and collected.

The Cognitive Domain

This refers to thinking and learning and includes mental processes such as memory, attention, information processing, reasoning, problem solving, and self-awareness. Good thinking requires good attention. Optimal self-regulation in this domain means that your child can ignore distractions, sustain attention and shift it when necessary, sequence thoughts, keep several pieces of information in mind at one time, and plan and carry out steps to achieve a goal.

Cognitive stressors include limited awareness of internal and/or external stimuli; sensory information (such as visual, auditory, or tactile) that the child has trouble picking up; sensory experiences that a child has trouble understanding because he can't see any pattern; too much information or too many steps for him to handle; information presented too quickly or too slowly; information that's too abstract or presupposes more basic concepts that he hasn't mastered yet, and requiring a child to concentrate for longer than he's able.

Signs of excessive stress in the cognitive domain include attention problems, learning difficulties, poor self-awareness, problems transitioning between tasks or dealing with frustration, and poor motivation. Usually a child who is having trouble in the cognitive domain is also stressed in the biological and emotion domains, and attention to those helps relieve additional stress, making more energy available for cognitive tasks.

The Social Domain

This domain is about being able to adapt behavior and thinking appropriately in social situations. It includes social intelligence and relationship skills and the ability to develop and use socially acceptable behaviors. A child who is optimally self-regulated in this domain is able to pick up on social cues, including nonverbal cues such as facial expression or tone of voice, understand those cues, and respond appropriately; take turns in conversation; "repair" communication breakdowns; and understand how emotions affect other people's behavior.

Stressors in the social domain include confusing or demanding social situations, interpersonal conflicts, being the victim of or even just witnessing acts of aggression, and the social conflicts that result from not understanding the impact on others of one's own actions and utterances. Many parents are surprised to learn that their own expectations, opinions, or concerns about their child's social life and friends can add to their child's stress.

Signs of stress in the social domain include trouble making or sustaining friendships; difficulty in group activities or conversation; difficulty understanding social cues, whether from children or adults;

being excluded or withdrawing from a social involvement; social aggression or intimidation; and being bullied by or bullying others.

The Prosocial Domain

This includes qualities of empathy, selflessness, internal standards and values, collective engagement and behavior, and social responsibility, as well as the ability to put the needs of others or a higher purpose ahead of one's own. A child who is optimally self-regulated in this domain has the ability to shift smoothly from a me-centered moment to a we-centered one. He is able to connect with others, read their cues, recognize their needs, and, when needed, delay gratification of personal desires in order to consider and act on the needs of others. An awareness of a group dynamic and the ability to compromise and collaborate, contribute, learn, and benefit in a collective environment such as a class or club are also signs of success in the prosocial domain. The prosocial domain also includes aspects of spiritual, aesthetic, humanitarian, and intellectual development.

Stressors include having to deal with other people's strong emotions, being asked to put the needs of others ahead of one's own, tension between personal and peer values, moral ambiguity, and guilt. In the prosocial domain the stresses that the child needs to deal with grow exponentially. Now it is not just the stressors assaulting his own nervous system that are at issue but the stresses affecting those around him, even the stresses with which his entire group is struggling. He needs to help the group and not just himself stay calmly focused and engaged.

Signs of stress in the prosocial domain often overlap with those we associate with the social domain, starting with a lack of empathy, apparent in group-based social situations in which a child may feel anxious, excluded, or isolated, overwhelmed by dominant personalities in a group, or swept up by ideas that run contrary to the child's own moral or behavioral standards.

The Infinite Variability of Stress Emerges in Common Problem Behaviors

Each of the five domains represents a distinct area of potential stressors. The emphasis here is on *potential*. What makes something a stressor is how it affects us and how we respond, which can be a pattern for us or change, depending on other factors. Across domains, common behavioral signs of energy depletion and heightened tension include being crabby, inattentive, withdrawn, manic, restless, aggressive, or temperamental. Sometimes a child's behavior clearly points to one domain as a particular source of stress, and once you have that puzzle piece identified, the rest of the picture starts to come into view. That first piece is often hidden in plain view, as it was for Damien's family.

Damien and the Dinner Disaster

Thanksgiving dinner was the last straw for Damien's parents. His grandmother had come for the meal and everyone had just sat down when Damien, fifteen, suddenly fled to his room. He did this frequently: He'd come home from school, head straight to his room, and then refuse to join them for dinner. His parents had become resigned to bringing him his meal, which he'd eat while glued to his computer. They had long since given up lecturing him about manners, about their wish for family mealtime together, about anything.

Damien's parents arranged to come with him to the institute to see if our clinic team could help them. Our mental health clinician, Eunice Lee, started the session, chatting with them about what they'd done the evening before. They had gone to a restaurant for dinner, and when Eunice asked what they'd all eaten, Damien responded that he'd had a hamburger but wished he'd had the steak. Eunice asked him why he hadn't ordered the steak:

> "You know, because of this." Damien made the motion of using a knife and fork to cut a piece of meat.
>
> "You mean you didn't order the steak because you didn't want to have to cut it up?"
>
> "Yeah."
>
> "Why would having to cut up the steak have bothered you so much?"
>
> "You know, because of the sound it makes on the plate."

You could see the lightbulb come on in Eunice's brain.

> "Is that the reason why you bolted from the Thanksgiving dinner?"
>
> "Yeah, of course."
>
> "Is that the reason why you always leave the table?"
>
> "I don't always leave: I stay when Mom makes sandwiches or finger foods."

Damien was suffering from something called misophonia, a condition that makes ordinary sounds excruciating. Often it's the sound of cutlery, but it can also be muted sounds: someone chewing, sighing, drinking. We still don't fully understand the neurobiology of this condition, but what is clear is that a combination of auditory hypersensitivity, physical and emotional arousal, social stress, and past experiences can make ordinary sounds an extreme stressor. Reactions range from being agitated and highly anxious to full-on fight or flight.

But why hadn't Damien simply told his parents that the sound of the cutlery bothered him so much? When we asked him, he answered: "But I did, over and over." In his mind he had told them, even though he'd never said a word. Children often tell us when something is overstressing them through their body and their actions, and if we don't respond to the message, they take matters into their own hands as best they can.

Absolutely anything can be a stressor. What is especially problematic for children is when something is a stressor for them but not for the adult with whom they are interacting. Far too often a teacher or a coach responds to a child's stress behavior as if it were misbehavior, as if the child were "acting up" or "choosing" to be irritating.

This variability in kids' behaviors under stress often leads adults to assume a child is choosing to be troublesome. Adults with misophonia often get labeled as neurotic because the sound bothering them has no effect on those around them. But a child gets labeled "difficult." One of my biggest concerns is the number of children who get labeled "oppositional" for what are, in fact, defensive behaviors. One child digs his heels in, another becomes tearful, one bolts, another lashes out. Or the same child goes through all of the above. In an instance like this there is usually a stressor—and usually more than one—that has triggered these behaviors.

The postscript to the story about Damien is also illuminating. Shortly after this session, my wife and I took our children to the same chain restaurant. My kids have grown up in the rural countryside and found the noise of the restaurant more than they could bear; they both wanted to bolt. We all wanted to bolt. I found myself thinking about Damien. How, I wondered, had he managed to stay at the table the entire meal? For that matter, he didn't appear to have the same problem at breakfast; he didn't have this problem at all meals. What explained the fact that his sensitivity to sound was unbearable in some situations but manageable in others?

A child's capacity to manage a problem is determined by a host of factors from across the five domains. In Damien's case, perhaps he hadn't bolted from the restaurant the night before our meeting because going to the city was an adventure and the restaurant was fun, both of which boosted his emotional state. His physical state most likely played a role too. He had been allowed to miss school that day to travel to Toronto to see us; perhaps the trip gave him some welcome relief from the noisy school environment, which could be excessively draining.

The solution for a problem like Damien's wasn't to get the family to switch to finger food–only meals. It was to get a fix on the multiple stressors he was under from across the five domains and begin to look at how these all interacted. It's the whole system that we look at when we do Self-Reg, not just the most glaring stressor.

In Sync or Stressed Out: How Five Domains × Multiplier Effect = Stress Cycle

When Jonathan, the kindergartner, bolted from the band concert, his fight-or-flight alarm sounded across every other domain: He got pushy with his classmates, belligerent toward his teacher, more sensitive to the pain of bumping into the table, and finally overwhelmed and in a total meltdown, sobbing all the way down the hall to the principal's office. For Damien the sound of the cutlery was the catalyst for flight. Suddenly, stressors from all the different domains began to ricochet off one another, intensifying the effect of each one.

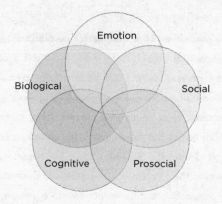

The Multiplier Effect: Five-Domain Stress Cycle

One of the most useful tools we have developed for our work with families is this concept of the stress cycle, illustrated on the next page. When a child starts to become overstressed in any one of these domains, depending on his energy and tension levels, the uptick in stress can trigger an escalating cycle of overarousal that, without the assistance of an external "braking" system, can quickly spiral out of control.

Any stressor in any domain can trigger a stress cycle, but a child is most vulnerable when in a low-energy/high-tension state. Once a stress cycle is tripped, the threshold drops for a stress response in any of the other domains, meaning the child becomes even more reactive, and the number of issues escalating the child's arousal response grows exponentially. The most important Self-Reg point is this:

The more a child is in a low-energy/high-tension state, the more difficult he is going to find any one domain or, in some cases, all of these domains. And the more challenging he finds one of these domains, the more this is going to deplete even further his overall energy reserves.

It can be very hard for parents to stay calm and composed and perform their designated role of the regulating "brake" when this is

Stress Cycles in the Shared
Interaction of the Interbrain

Parent-child communication can escalate hyperarousal for both

happening. In the heat of the moment your child's actions or comments can trigger hyperarousal for you too. At that point it's not just the stressors in the child's five domains that are ramping one another up but the parents' stressors and hyperarousal communicated through the interbrain. This is one reason why so often when a child is stressed, our attempts to help him end in conflict.

The Two-Way Stress Cycle

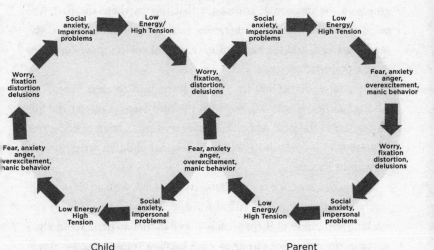

If parent and child become locked in a cycle of spiraling stress, the interbrain itself spins out of sync. Instead of serving as a regulating influence, reducing arousal, it amplifies arousal; pure exhaustion shuts things down in a hail of shouting, tears, threats, or recriminations. So much of the clinical work we do involves developing strategies to break a stress cycle. There are often multiple entry points for breaking a hyperarousal cycle, but the first step is always the same: We have to return our child, and ourselves, to energy/tension balance.

The question is this: How exactly do we do that?

A Trip to the Pilbara: Under the Boab Tree

The most powerful lesson I have learned about how to break a stress cycle was during a trip to Australia. I was in the Pilbara in Western Australia with Michelle Scott, the commissioner for children in Western Australia, to see the work her agency was doing with various children's organizations. The Pilbara is an enormous region ranging from vast beaches on the Indian Ocean to breathtaking rock formations and gorges in the interior. It is thought that this is where the first Aboriginals settled, sometime between forty thousand and fifty thousand years ago, and the extraordinary natural environment continues to be a powerful presence.

At a large dinner my first night, I arranged to meet "Stan," an Aboriginal healer who worked with troubled teens. We met the following day at the local school in Roeburne, a small town of under one thousand, in a community where Aboriginal children struggle with significant hardship.

Stan was a bear of a man, about sixty years old, with an air of quietness and compassion. He talked for a while about the kids he was working with, most of them because they had tried to harm themselves or someone else or because they were battling some addiction (typically drinking alcohol or sniffing gas). He asked me if I would like to see his clinic, and off we went for a twenty-minute walk along Harding River, through a natural area teeming with birds and wildlife.

The clinic wasn't a building at all. It was a small clearing dominated by an ancient Boab tree. The tree wasn't that tall, maybe twenty feet, but its girth was enormous: It would have taken at least ten adults holding hands to surround it. The scene felt not just remote but alien, as if we were the first humans ever to have set foot there. It wasn't quiet; on the contrary, it was filled with the clatter of kookaburras, herons, and other birds. Yet it was one of the most peaceful settings I have ever encountered.

Stan and I sat down side by side under the tree, which was in full bloom, and there we stayed, not talking, basking in the tranquility for I don't know how long. After a while I found myself thinking about new strategies that we had never tried in our work—I felt suddenly refreshed, alert, and eager to think through these emerging ideas, hardly typical for the end of a very long day. When I mentioned this to Stan, he replied that this is precisely what he did with teens who were shut down or agitated. He would just patiently wait until they felt like talking. Eventually they all opened up, although with some this might take a full day. Then the two of them would quietly talk about what was troubling the teen and explore ways to manage his life. That tree was probably more than 1,500 years old, and I couldn't help but wonder how many thousands of youths had come there and found this equanimity in the calm company of this and other sage elders.

What a clinic. What a lesson. When a child is in distress, we feel an almost reflexive need to try to reason it away. The problem is that the systems in the brain that he would need to process well-intentioned reason go off-line when he's hyperaroused. He truly doesn't register what you're saying. The very first thing to do is bring those systems back online. Every child needs this experience of sitting side by side with us under a figurative Boab tree. This is the first and the most important function of the interbrain: to instill that feeling of emotional safety and security that children need to replenish their energy. Jonathan needed to feel calm at school. Damien's mealtime exits were his effort to find a place he felt calm and safe. That's how to break the stress cycle. Only then can you begin to do Self-Reg—on yourself as much as with your child.

PART II

The Five Domains

FIVE

Eat, Play, Sleep

The Biological Domain

To enter the biological domain is to transform forever the way you look at your child's behavior—and your own! It's to shift from the "top-down" view of *behavior management*, which sees the parent as in charge and the child as having to submit, to the Self-Reg "side-by-side" view of *understanding behavior*. The whole point of the latter is that, rather than automatically trying to control or curtail "difficult" behaviors, we pause and consider whether they are signs of hypo- or hyperarousal and, when that is the case, set out to identify and mitigate the stressors that brought about this state. That is, the communication between parent and child has to be two-way, just as the arousal between parent and child is shared. Marie and Rosie present the perfect case in point.

Marie and Rosie

Marie fought back tears as she told me about her problems with her ten-year-old daughter. It was so hard to get Rosie to listen to reason: No matter what she said to Rosie, the two of them ended up "shrieking" at each other and Rosie would storm off and sulk for hours at a time. Sometimes it was over something that had seemed minor to start, sometimes over more important things, but regardless, the angry confrontations only made matters worse. Marie had even once tried writing Rosie a letter to explain why the tirades worried her but later found the note torn in shreds and left on the kitchen table.

The problems that pushed Rosie and her mother to the flash point amounted to a stock list of parent-child grievances, mostly lots of little things. "She won't come to dinner when I call her," Marie said. "Won't eat her dinner when she finally comes. Won't wear the clothes I put out for her. But the biggest fights always happen at bedtime, and usually they're over *nothing* at all." Just days before, Rosie had screamed at Marie for cleaning her room and moving all her stuff. Marie hadn't even been in Rosie's room that day.

I asked Marie how she had responded. "I told her that I wasn't going to stand for this. That if she didn't stop yelling at me, she'd lose her iPad for a week. Then it was a month! Then, when she still didn't stop, I told her that I was going to take her iPad back to the store!" When I asked Marie if she actually took away the iPad the next day, she looked at me sheepishly and replied, "Well, she was so much nicer that I let it go."

Was the problem that Marie didn't follow through? That Rosie pushed as far as she could, knowing that her mom was never going to follow through? The empty threats weren't changing Rosie's behavior. No amount of cajoling and pleading, no type of punishments or rewards seemed to work, and their relationship was suffering.

The first question Self-Reg prompts us to ask is whether this really is a discipline issue: whether we're dealing with *misbehavior* or *stress behavior.* This distinction is absolutely crucial.

Misbehavior Versus Stress Behavior

The concept of *misbehavior* is fundamentally tied to those of *volition, choice,* and *awareness.* It assumes that the child willingly chose to act the way he did. He *could* have acted differently, was even aware that he *should* have acted differently. But *stress behavior* is physiologically based. When this happens, the child is not deliberately choosing his actions or aware in a rational way of what he's doing. He's lashing out (with words if not physically) or bolting (emotionally if not physically) because his nervous system, triggered by a sense of threat, shifts to fight or flight.

There are some simple ways to gauge when we're dealing with misbehavior. Ask the child why he did such and such, and if he answers with any explanation—no matter what his rationale—there's a pretty good chance he knew what he was doing. Or ask him to tell you with a straight face that he didn't know that what he was doing was wrong. Stress behavior also reveals itself quickly. If you see confusion, fear, anger, or deep distress in that face, if your child averts his eyes or finds it hard to even just look at you, those are often signs of hyperarousal and of stress behavior.

The reason why the distinction between misbehavior and stress behavior is so important is that if you apply the carrot-and-stick techniques of behavior modification to stress behavior, you can make matters worse, adding to the child's stress load. And you've missed an important opportunity to help your child develop the type of self-awareness that's so important for self-regulation.

The Sweatshirt Incident: Containment Versus Control

It seemed clear that Marie was describing stress behavior. That Rosie was deaf to reasonable entreaties and, in fact, became irrational, that afterward she had difficulty remembering what she had said or done in those heated confrontations suggested fight or flight. So instead of trying to find some way to make Rosie be compliant in these episodes, Marie needed to reduce her daughter's arousal and then set out to discover the causes of the meltdowns.

I suggested that the next time Rosie started to spiral into the trouble zone Marie avoid making any disciplinary threats at all, and specifically not reason with Rosie. Don't try to explain anything, I told her. Instead, I said, drawing from Self-Reg basics, take a few deep breaths and relax your neck and shoulders. Turn out the light and go sit bedside or lie down beside her and gently stroke her hair or her hand or forearm or her back. If you do want to say something, just tell her how much you love her. The next day, when she's calmed down, you can go over whatever it was that you wanted to say the night before.

A couple of days later Marie got her chance to try this out. Rosie had asked for a new red sweatshirt like all the other girls in her class had, but when Marie went by the store to get one, they didn't have Rosie's size, so Marie bought a lovely gray one instead. She gave it to her when she got home from school, but Rosie didn't utter a word when she saw it. A few hours later, as she was getting ready for bed, she started yelling at Marie: "How could you buy me a gray sweatshirt! It's hideous. I'm never going to wear it. You never do what I ask. I hate you!"

Marie almost snapped. But this time she took some slow, deep belly breaths. This time, instead of trying to explain to Rosie why she had gotten the gray sweatshirt, or reason with her at all, Marie gently responded that they'd work it all out the next day. Having interrupted the escalating anger between them, she left the room and calmed herself before returning to tuck Rosie in. Calmer herself now, she lay down by Rosie and rubbed her back the way Rosie liked. Within minutes Rosie started to calm down. Just before she drifted off to sleep, she hugged Marie and murmured: "I love you, Mommy." The next morning, when Marie was all set to say that they could try another store after school that day, Rosie came downstairs wearing the new gray sweatshirt.

Counteracting the Effects of Limbic Resonance

Had we been able to hook up Marie and Rosie to a brain-scan machine during one of their bedtime battles, we would have seen something striking in a tiny little part of the brain that lies midway between the prefrontal cortex (PFC) and the limbic system. It's the *anterior cingulate cortex* (ACC), connected on one side (rostral) to the PFC and on the other (ventral) to the limbic system. In our neurolab when we scan the brains of hyperaroused children, the (ventral) limbic side is lit up like a Christmas tree and the (rostral) PFC side is quite subdued. This says the limbic system is dominant and the reasoning, rational PFC is going to have a very hard time having any say in the child's behavior.

That is what we would have seen in Rosie. *And we would have seen exactly the same thing in Marie's ACC.* The reason for this lies in a phenomenon called *limbic resonance*. Our limbic systems are hardwired to respond in kind when confronted with someone else's aroused limbic system, positive or negative. This is why laughter is contagious and if someone shouts angrily at us we instantly want to shout back—the reason we see road rage or see an argument escalate so quickly via texting.

The limbic system doesn't bother to make fine distinctions as to whether the source of the perceived threat is our beloved daughter or not; as far as it is concerned, a threat is a threat. For Marie, this limbic response triggered a flood of negative emotions. She felt rejected, unappreciated, and unloved, in addition to being just plain angry.

In the past Marie had felt compelled to respond to what Rosie was saying in the heat of the moment. Now she understood that in these moments Rosie's PFC was on standby and with it her capacity to think clearly, speak rationally, and have the presence of mind to manage her words and actions.

By first calming herself, Marie was able to counteract the effects of limbic resonance, bring her own PFC back online, and be in a better state to help Rosie. Marie had broken the stress cycle overpowering their interbrain. And as Rosie's limbic system calmed, she was able not just to fall asleep naturally but to experience and express her deep-felt love for her mother.

As the limbic system calms, the capacity for social engagement comes back online. Rosie was in desperate need of Marie's soothing presence and now she could be receptive to it. In this calmed state her limbic system switched from being in the thrall of primitive negative emotions to summoning up warm memories of Mommy's loving, protective presence when she was an infant. Her whole body relaxed and she drifted peacefully off to sleep.

Marie had sensed that something had to change about the way she and Rosie interacted, especially with adolescence only a couple of years away. She knew that what she had been doing was counterproductive. Learning how to get her daughter to calm down and fall asleep wasn't the *whole* answer, but it was the *beginning of the answer*.

Because the biological domain is so central to all the rest, and because understanding the inner workings of the nervous system can seem daunting or beyond our reach as parents, Self-Reg is designed to help you move step by step through the same discovery process that Marie underwent with Rosie. We rarely figure out what our child's stressors are on the spot; usually it takes what we call "hypothesis testing"—a version of the trial-and-error system you used with your newborn and the self-regulation detective work you're now doing as a parent.

Step 1: Read the Signs, Reframe the Behavior

When Marie and I spoke after the sweatshirt episode to review how it had played out, she confessed that she had found it excruciatingly hard not to shout back when Rosie turned on her.

Marie had thought what she needed was a new technique for controlling her child's behavior in trying situations, but what she needed was to be able to *read the signs and reframe the behavior.*

Rosie's behavior was a pure, unfiltered, right-brain expression of distress. Marie was able to calm Rosie down so quickly because she in turn responded with right-brain communication. By turning down the lights, softening her voice, stroking her daughter's hair, and gently rubbing Rosie's back, Marie was sending a message to the part of Rosie's brain open to communication: a part of the brain that is directly hooked up to neural systems involved in emotional arousal.

But Marie was reestablishing the lines of communication not only from her to Rosie but also from Rosie to her. This is very much the reason why Self-Reg is "side by side" or "bidirectional." Now Marie's right brain could fully receive the messages that Rosie's right brain was sending: "I'm scared. It hurts. I don't know how to stop this." And now the message Marie communicated back to her daughter was "I'm here. I'll protect you. I love you."

The change that Marie experienced when she started to do Self-Reg wasn't just a cognitive shift, a matter of sizing up the situation and concluding that she was dealing with stress behavior rather than misbehavior, then adjusting her parenting response accordingly. This was a matter of tapping in to right-brain messages that get blocked in the heat of limbic-to-limbic conflict. In the beginning you don't so much *infer* from your baby's behaviors as *feel* when she's in distress. And the long list of functions that are turned off in limbic hyper-arousal includes this form of nuanced experiential awareness. In fact, it is typically the first thing to go.

But there was definitely a cognitive shift as well: The behaviors Marie was seeing in her ten-year-old daughter harkened back to problems in arousal that had surfaced when Rosie was an infant. Marie explained that when Rosie was three weeks old she became intensely fussy every night at six o'clock and stayed that way for two hours or more. This was such a regular pattern, Marie observed, that you could set your watch by it. Rosie's bedtime battle behavior as a ten-year-old bore a striking resemblance to her fussy bedtime behavior as an infant.

The signs of Rosie's arousal-regulation issues had been there from infancy, but at ten the assumption was that she was being difficult or misbehaving. We know that an infant isn't choosing to be this way, and her behavior is certainly not manipulative. But as a child gets older we tend to become intolerant of these behaviors. A child can be "fussy" for so many reasons other than just being tired. This is why with infants we check to make sure they're dry, comfortable, not hungry or scared. In a case like baby Rosie's, we start to think about sensory issues. In my work with a broad range of children, I am seeing a significant increase in the number of children and adolescents with sensory issues that are easily and commonly overlooked. They aren't just "sensitive to" but are left drained by different kinds of stimuli, including light, sound, smell, and touch.

As an infant, Rosie had been very sensitive to noise, smells, and rough textures. Now, at ten, Rosie protested any time her parents wanted to take her to restaurants, complained about the noise and smells when they did, and still was notoriously picky about her clothes, especially sensitive to the feel of fabrics.

In the context of self-regulation Marie had a new way to read those cues about physical discomfort and sensitivities and a new way to understand Rosie's outbursts when stressed. A critical element in Marie's *reframing* of Rosie's behavior was the recognition that the problem had not, in fact, erupted "out of the blue."

I've known children hypersensitive to the feel of a shirt against their skin, the inside seam of their socks, the whir of an overhead fan, or the ticking of a clock. On the other end of the spectrum, some children are oblivious—hyposensitive—to sensory cues: not just in regard to what's going on around them but inside themselves as well. Young children typically don't pick up on internal cues that tell them they're running low on energy and they need a nap, a sweater, or a meal. But we've seen many older kids and teens who still don't know when they're cold, tired, or even hungry.

Marie's challenge was not at all unusual. Reading the biological cues in your child's behavior begins as early as birth, but those cues are easily misread when a child's behavior is labeled "difficult" rather than hyperaroused. For many parents it is only years later that, with hindsight, they recognize what were likely early signs of problems in arousal regulation in their infant or young child. The "aha" moment finally arrives when the parent discovers a new way to understand the behavior: reframe it. Self-Reg has been that opportunity for many parents of older children. However, if your child is young, then the sooner you can learn to read your child's signs, reframe the behavior, and use Self-Reg steps to guide your response, the sooner your child will begin to engage in the process and eventually learn to self-regulate—in many cases far sooner than you might have thought possible.

Step 2: Become a Stress Detective

Identify Stressors: Look for Patterns and Sources

A stressor, according to the classic scientific definition developed by Walter Bradford Cannon early in the twentieth century, is anything that disrupts homeostasis, the internal balance that an organism needs to deal with external challenges and to attend to its internal requirements, such as growth, reproduction, the immune system, and tissue repair. In the biological domain, being too hot or too cold is a stressor. Loud noises, bright lights, crowds, strong odors, new sights and sounds, surprising sights and sounds, certain kinds of movement, and not being able to execute certain movements can also be stressors. *Every child is different in terms of what constitutes a stressor.*

"Sensitive caregiving" means recognizing the signs that your baby is overly stressed and learning, mostly by trial and error, what has a calming effect and what has the opposite. When my son was born, my wife and I were eager to do everything we could to promote his robust early brain development. At a visit to the baby store, we spent an hour poring over all the different mobiles and chose one that, according to the package, had been "designed by neuroscientists to maximize the stimulation of your baby's brain." It had different sorts of geometric patterns and a battery-driven motor to make these slowly whirl around over the baby's crib.

The second we installed it, my son made it clear that he hated it. He turned over on his side and buried his head in his bumper! Determined to "stimulate his budding brain connections," we turned him over onto his back. His response this time was to clench his eyes shut. So back we went to the store, and this time we came home with an even more elaborate mobile. This one combined sounds with movement and light and had different speed settings so that you could find the one that "best suited your baby's brain."

This time we succeeded only in eliciting howls of protest from our poor baby son, who was clearly finding all this stimulation overwhelming. Thankfully, we gave up. We stuffed the mobiles in a closet and instead resorted to the time-honored—I suspect even prehistoric—technique of making funny faces to engage his interest. This worked like a charm.

The two mobiles lay buried at the back of the toy closet gathering dust when our daughter was born three years later. The scientist in me decided to see if she would respond in the same way as our son. She chortled with glee, loved the different colors and sounds, and would happily settle after watching for a bit. What was a stressor for one actually seemed to have a calming effect on the other.

When our child behaves in a way that we find troubling, or even irritating, we need to ask: What's the source of stress that's triggering this behavior? In the case of our mobiles, our son's reaction made that one easy to spot. In Marie and Rosie's case it might seem that Rosie was simply upset because she feared that all the other kids would tease her for wearing a gray sweatshirt. But if that was the sole cause, then why did she come downstairs happily wearing it the next morning?

Self-Reg takes us back to Marie's original observation that Rosie was getting upset just about every evening, and often for no good reason at all. This suggested she was becoming hyperaroused over the course of the day and in that state would find or fixate on some particular stressor. But the deeper issue was why she was becoming hyperaroused. This could well have been because of emotional and social stresses that she was experiencing at school, but when we do Self-Reg, we always consider all five domains, starting with the biological.

You don't have to be a neuroscientist to figure out this question, but you do have to become a bit of a stress detective. If you're in disciplinarian mode, you've already decided that your child is being self-indulgent or willfully disobedient and that you need to lay down the law. You're out to make it clear that this kind of misbehavior won't be tolerated and follow up on your reprimand. But when you suspect that you're dealing with a stress behavior, you need to be calm and reflective. You want to figure out what the stresses might be, and to do that you start by (1) not becoming a stressor yourself and (2) looking for patterns in your child's behavior.

Have you noticed that your child is typically agitated after doing something, like playing a video game or bingeing on sugary food? Does your child come home happy or agitated from a social outing or gymnastics or, to reverse this, does your child find a million excuses to avoid going to a social outing or gymnastics? Does spending time with a particular friend tend to leave her feeling happy or unhappy? Energized or down? Even talking: Does this seem to make your child less hyper or more agitated?

The fact that Rosie's worst meltdowns happened at bedtime was a sign that her stress load built up during the day; it could also have been a sign that she was a little deficient in the neurohormones that help the brain down-regulate from hyper to drowsy. Now Marie could start to think about whether there was anything different about the days when Rosie had one of these nighttime meltdowns and then reverse this to identify anything different about the days when she didn't have one. Marie also reflected on any possible patterns in her own reactivity. Were there days or times that she was less patient, easier to tick off, or more sensitive to Rosie's behaviors?

The biological domain is energy central for brain and body, so you want to check the most basic sources of energy and recovery. If they're low, that's a biological stressor. Your child's ability to self-regulate begins with having the energy she'll need to up-regulate and down-regulate to meet the demands of the day—all five domains humming with activity and expectations. The basic biological considerations are

- sleep
- nutrition and eating habits
- movement and exercise
- body awareness
- health status or special considerations

These biological factors are the core sources of energy, resilience, and potential stress reduction that help your child self-regulate, and as such they are also key areas of vulnerability, should your child be running low in any one of them.

The hypothalamus responds not just to something startling but also to fatigue, and when that happens a child can quickly become locked in a repeating loop of an escalating stress cycle that triggers reactions in all five domains—basically systemwide. From infancy it had been clear that sleep made a marked difference in Rosie's behavior. The less sleep she got, the fussier she was about every little thing throughout the day. The more sleep she got, the less fussy and more resilient she seemed. This was so at age ten too. Whatever might trigger her temper, on the nights that Rosie had the meltdowns she was then getting two to three fewer hours sleep. This sleep loss would leave her more tired and vulnerable the following day. A string of those nights in a row would easily put her in an exhausting cycle of underslept and hyperaroused that, once triggered, was hard to break.

There is also the matter of high-quality or restorative sleep. As was the case with Melanie, the "bistro baby," being in a low-tension state while asleep is every bit as important as the amount of sleep the child is getting. Exposure to light, especially blue-spectrum light, shortly before going to sleep can interfere with the release of the neurohormones that promote this relaxed state. Like so many parents today, Marie had always allowed Rosie to play on her iPad until it was time to turn out the lights, mistakenly assuming it was helping her unwind and relax for sleep.

Step 3: Reduce the Stress

"Reducing the stress" might seem rather straightforward. If your child is sensitive to noise, you "turn down the volume." You may be able to do this in your home or other environments where your wishes hold sway. But it's not that easy to control sound and other stress levels at school, for example. In terms of sensory stress, noise is a big problem in schools. Both decibel and reverberation levels are far too high in classrooms, cafeterias, gymnasiums, and hallways. For a child who is sensitive to noise this will drain the nervous system, affecting concentration, behavior, and mood. Crowded public environments, from playgrounds to shopping malls and restaurants, can present the same challenge. Avoiding noise isn't a realistic option for most of us.

In schools, techniques that help children manage sensory sensitivities include earplugs, noise-blocking headphones, and replacing loud bells and buzzers with chimes or ringtones. A different kind of seat or chair can make a pronounced difference if a child is sensitive to hard surfaces or needs a lot of movement to feel calm. A less visually "loud" or busy environment at school and home can effectively dial down visual sensory stimulation. To some extent you can also choose restaurants and other destinations with your child's sensory sensitivities in mind.

But there's another way to significantly reduce your child's stress load. A child's sensitivity to any single stressor is variable and strongly influenced by her overall stress level. Lowering this *core stress level* reduces your child's overall energy drain and boosts energy reserves for dealing with individual stressors. For example, when Rosie was well rested, she was quite able to deal with discomforts and frustrations that she found overwhelming when she was depleted. In fact, when a child is bothered by something that he happily put up with the week before, we have a tendency to think he's fickle and misbehaving, when what has really changed is his core stress level.

Step 4: Reflect to Develop Self-Awareness

The goal of Self-Reg is to help kids learn to recognize a state of low energy and high tension and then know what to do about it. For that to be possible they have to recognize when they are hypo- or hyper-aroused, but that is possible only if they're aware of what it feels like to be calm. The problem is that if "hyper" is all a child knows, then this is his "normal." Unfortunately, when children are habituated to being revved up, they resist doing any sort of mindfulness exercise that would help them learn how to be calm. So we have to make sure that they enjoy the experience. *Being calm* and *enjoying being calm* are two sides of the same coin. When Marie stepped out into the hall to do some deep breathing, she described it as feeling like "some sort of switch flipped" in her brain. Indeed, what she had experienced was the effect of a minute change triggering a sweeping shift in her brain activity. Neuroscientists refer to this as a "nonlinear transition," in this case triggering a shift in Marie's medial prefrontal cortex, from the top or "dorsal" side (dmPFC) to the bottom or "ventral" part (vmPFC). The former is involved when we ruminate or run through internal mono-logues, the latter when we become aware of what is going on inside or around us. Studies have shown that this simple deep-breathing ex-ercise can shift brain activity from the neural network for rumination to the network that creates more spacious awareness of internal and external environments.

The more we practice focusing being "fully present in the here and now," the easier it becomes to make the shift from dmPFC to vmPFC. It is as if the neurochemical pathway between the two systems be-comes more deeply etched, making it easier to consciously "flip the switch." That, of course, is precisely what we want when we tell our child to "calm down." But it takes practice before they're actually able to do so, and in the case of the child whose arousal baseline is set to hyper, parental admonishment has little if any positive effect.

We've developed a five-step method for helping children enjoy and master mindfulness techniques:

1. Explain how what you're doing promotes self-regulation.
2. Make sure the child is comfortable.
3. Help the child focus on what he's doing.
4. Help the child become aware of the connection between the activity and what's happening in his mind and body.
5. Start small and set up daily routines for practice.

Suppose you want to have your child do a breathing exercise. Ad-justing your storytelling style to suit your child's age and attention, start by telling her about the pathway from her nose to her lungs, how there's a big muscle underneath the lungs that draws the fresh air in and pushes the stale air out, and ribs around the lungs to protect them that expand and contract with each breath. Explain how when we breathe in this gives us a burst of energy that makes us more alert and how there is a calming effect when we exhale.

Make sure your child is comfortable. It's often necessary to support a child's back during breathing exercises in order for him to feel the sensations of his breathing. He may do best lying on his back on the floor or sitting up straight, though relaxed, in a chair.

Then help your child focus on his breathing: Ask him if he can feel the cool breath inside his nose as he inhales and the warm breath inside his mouth or on his hand as he exhales? Can he feel his lungs or belly filling up like a balloon?

Next help him become aware of the effect on his mind of concentrating on his breathing. Suppose he's been worrying about something. Lead him through the breathing exercise, helping him focus on his breath going in and out maybe ten times, and then ask whether the worry has faded or perhaps even stopped. Does the worry keep coming back? See whether bringing his attention back to the breathing interrupts the worry, eventually lessening or eliminating it.

Finally you might want to set a timer for, say, just a couple of minutes in the beginning and gradually make it longer.

Self-awareness is central to your child's ability to self-regulate. If a child isn't aware of what he's feeling, then he's helpless to do anything to improve it. The same goes for us, but the pressures of parenthood sometimes drive us to do the most self-sabotaging things.

When our kids were young, we used to regularly take them to a "child-themed" pizza restaurant in a small city a half hour's drive from our home; but these outings always ended in some sort of catastrophe. Sometimes the problems started the second they got into the car with the two of them squabbling over something inane. Sometimes the meltdown came at the end of the outing, when both kids would shift in a split second from being overly excited to being an absolute nightmare.

The distinction between "happy" and "hyperaroused" is every bit as important as the distinction between "difficult" and "hyperaroused." Our kids, who were so used to the quiet of our rural life, would instantly become as crazed as all the other children the second they stepped into the restaurant. What followed would be a struggle to get them to eat their slice and then a struggle to get them to leave the mayhem of the play area. The drive home was always harrowing. My wife finally decided to eliminate these outings altogether, but it was what she said to me afterward that made me conscious of one of the most easily overlooked aspects of step 4.

She told me how much she had hated these outings. When I asked her why, she immediately launched into a litany of woes. She hated everything about the place: the noise and hubbub, the uncomfortable tables and chairs, the harsh lighting and strong odors, but most of all she hated what it did to our kids. She wanted to leave the instant she got there, but she steeled herself and waited as patiently as she could. When I asked her why, if she found the whole experience such an ordeal, she put up with all this, she looked puzzled. Finally she answered: "Well, you know, because they were having so much fun." But why, if they were having so much fun, did these outings always end up in a family row?

It's important to keep in mind the benefits of family activities *for all of us*. There are all sorts of opportunities for calm and restorative outings where you live. A trip to the park with blankets and a Frisbee, or a walk through a forest collecting flowers and leaves, or perhaps to the beach armed with buckets and a shovel. In fact, there are all sorts of opportunities right in your home. In place of the trip to the pizza restaurant my wife instituted "Sunday pizza night." Every week the four of us would get involved in making pizzas from scratch. But what made it really fun was that we'd make four different pizzas, not one, so that each of us could design our own. This turned into a sort of competition as we'd all experiment each week and then taste one another's creations and have a family vote on that week's "winner." It was fun, it was tasty, and it left all four of us utterly calm—and satiated!

The real lesson here is that parents need to become just as aware of what sort of activity causes them to go into a state of diminished energy and heightened tension as of what causes this in their children. You need to become aware that, just like your child, you are much more likely when you're in a low-energy/high-tension state to explode over something that your child says or does than when you're calm and relaxed.

Step 5: Respond to Figure Out What Your Child Finds Calming

One of the most important distinctions that you learn in Self-Reg is the difference between "quiet" and "calm," and that's precisely what your child will learn too. Many parents ask us for advice about how to keep their child calm on a flight or a road trip, when what they are really after is something to keep their child *quiet*.

Video games clearly have a *quieting* effect: A child generally sits still and doesn't say much as he plays them. But no one would mistake these games as promoting a state of calm: Just look at the way your child reacts when you turn off the game. The same is true of medication that merely suppresses hyperactivity or impulsivity and does little to promote calmness (other than getting the adults interacting with the child to be less bothered by his actions).

Calmness is an entirely different state from being mesmerized by some movie or video game. When a child is calm, she is relaxed, aware of what's going on inside and around her, and enjoying the state she's in. These three components—physical, cognitive, and emotional—are the defining characteristics of "calmness." This is perhaps the most challenging but enjoyable aspect of the Self-Reg detective work for you and your child. For there is no one-size-fits-all answer to what a child will find calming. It's important to note that simply ordering a child to "calm down" rarely has this effect, although if you say it harshly enough your child might certainly become quiet. If you were able to peer inside your child's brain when this happens, using the imaging technologies applied in the brain lab, you'd see something quite remarkable. A child can be still and silent yet have an intense amount of activity going on in his limbic system, frontal and parietal lobes, thalamus, and other neural networks that are active when we have monkey mind. When a child is calm, these systems are subdued. What's more, there is a striking difference in brain waves between the two states: A child can be quiet and yet have surging beta waves, which are a sign of arousal; but when a child is calm, we see slow and rhythmic alpha, theta and gamma waves, which are signs of deep relaxation.

What takes you into a relaxed state may not work for your child. Once again, Rosie's Self-Reg journey with her mom offers helpful insight. Marie had long been a dedicated yoga practitioner. Her favorite moment of the week, she told me, was her Sunday-morning Iyengar class. So what could have been more obvious than to get Rosie to do yoga with her, especially in the early evening, when she was just starting to get wound up? Yoga is certainly something that we've found effective for children in a large number of cases. But Rosie hated it. She didn't like any of the poses that are supposed to reduce stress, and she got unbearably squirmy.

A few standard-issue stress-buster ideas were marginally useful—fidget toys, for instance—but it was Rosie, a serious stress detective herself now, who cracked the case. Rosie discovered that what worked for her was making bead boxes. She could become fully absorbed for hours and was always calm and ready for sleep afterward. But it's important to remember that this was the fifth of the five steps of Self-Reg. It was essential that Rosie first knew what calmness *felt like* and not just what the word meant in order to have settled on this as a self-regulating strategy.

One of the most interesting things we've found is that these five steps work for all children of all ages. Teens who have struggled with self-regulation issues for some time may need to experiment more than a younger child to find mindfulness techniques that click. They may want more detailed explanations of how self-regulation works and of the Self-Reg method. But whatever the age of the child, and whatever form the exercises take, you still need to move through the same five steps.

SIX

Monster in the Attic

The Emotion Domain

M any parents talk about their children's roller-coaster emotional lives using the same words: "perplexing," "exhilarating," "challenging," "frustrating," "mysterious," "weird," and, above all, "scary."

What is it that we find so scary about our kids' emotions? Again, parents offer up a familiar list: "My ten-year-old behaves like a two-year-old." "My child gets distraught for reasons she can't explain." "My child gets angrier or more frustrated than either of us can cope with." The comments turn to the son or daughter who "gets so excited that it's impossible to calm him down," "never seems to get enthusiastic about anything," "is always unhappy," "is like a pinball machine, pinging from one emotion to another," or "doesn't feel things that he should." As one weary parent put it: "My child's emotional outbursts just don't make any sense at all."

The confusion is understandable. Usually when your child is struggling emotionally, you know it—they show it—but sometimes you don't have the slightest suspicion. Even if you are aware of it, knowing what to do about it is something else.

The most common approach among parents is to talk with their child about it: get them to "open up," explain that getting angry only makes matters worse, or try to build up their feelings of self-worth and confidence. When children are upset, a parent's first impulse is to deal with the situation head-on with a rational, problem-solving approach. Unfortunately, reason doesn't seem to be much help for a child overwhelmed by strong emotion, and ordering her to get in control of her emotions only adds to her stress load. What's more, telling children to "use their words" isn't quite that straightforward when they are in the grip of the very subjective experience that they find frightening.

To be sure, it's important to help children voice their worries and other feelings. But this is always hard for kids and next to impossible when they're hyperaroused. When this happens, their emotions tend to get all jumbled together, so what they're feeling isn't simply, say, angry but angry/frightened/ashamed/excited. We need to help them disentangle all the different emotions (a process called emotional differentiation). Yes, we need to help them deepen and broaden the emotions they experience. We need to help them become aware of and articulate what they're feeling. There are excellent methods for working on these critical aspects of "emotional literacy" or "emotional intelligence." But we have to be careful that we don't approach our child's emotional development as purely a left-brain phenomenon: something that we can teach or explain or that we can promote just by having our child read inspiring books or watch inspirational films. Emotional growth has to be felt. And what children *feel* is much more complex than just a subjective feeling; it is a visceral experience that encompasses mind and body.

The rush of neurochemicals triggered by emotions—the tension, jitters, aches, and other physical sensations they create—and the resulting memories and associations: These are forces that shape your child's emotional experience and behavior. Every bit as important is how tension, jitters, aches, and other physical sensations trigger emotions, again as a result of these memories and associations. Physical and emotional experience are inextricably bound together: This is where we need to start, before we set to work on a child's "emotional literacy" or "emotional intelligence." Self-Reg takes hold where biological and emotional factors intersect: the *physical/emotion nexus*.

Emotions: What Are These Mysterious Elements of the Human Psyche?

Philosophers have talked about what emotions are for 2,500 years and they still can't agree on the basics. Even with scientists, psychologists, and psychiatrists joining the inquiry, there is no single explanation of emotion that simplifies your task much when it comes to dealing with your crying, sulking, fussing, fuming child. However we define them, emotions have a powerful effect on the body, and vice versa. In general, positive emotions enhance energy. Negative emotions drain energy. There are physical/emotional cycles in play. Children are more likely to experience positive emotions when they're well rested and more vulnerable to negative emotions when they're depleted. A child who is happy, interested, and optimistic will find it easier to tackle academic or social challenges. A child who is frightened, angry, or sad will find it difficult if not impossible to engage socially, academically, or even just physically through the day.

A "positive bias" leads to a greater capacity for emotional growth and a greater ability to

- modulate (up-regulate or down-regulate) strong emotions, positive as well as negative (excitement as well as fear or anger)
- recover from failure, disappointment, challenging situations, embarrassment, and other difficulties and move forward confidently and positively

- experiment and learn, on the child's own and in collaboration with others
- be proud of personal effort and achievement and appreciate the effort and achievement of others
- experience greater closeness with parents as a result of shared experience and emotional understanding

But more is involved here than just having the energy to deal with problems, emotional as well as cognitive and social. A child needs positive emotions in order to explore more challenging emotions and emotional situations. She starts off with a fairly constricted number of positive emotions (curiosity, interest, happiness) but this base makes it possible for her to acquire more complex emotions: to become ambitious and assertive, cheerful and decisive, honest and compassionate. Negative emotions have the opposite effect: They sap the energy needed to navigate new emotional territory. Negative emotions also "grow." What starts out as chronic fear or sadness can quickly lead to feeling alienated or awkward, bitter or cynical, demoralized or rejected.

A "negative bias" makes it hard for a child to recover from emotional swings, to deal with frustration or setbacks, to sustain warm interpersonal relationships. Where the child with a positive bias is drawn to character-building challenges and risks, the child with a negative bias is drawn to numbing activities or diversions. Where a positive bias enables the child to be in touch with the full range of his emotions, a negative bias leads him to repress his emotions—and not just the negative ones. Where a positive bias opens the child up to new emotional experiences, even "scary" ones, a negative bias closes the child to new emotional experiences—especially the scary ones. This can include scary emotional ventures like friendship, love, and any kind of emotional intimacy.

These differences between a positive and a negative bias add a significant element to what is going on in the marshmallow task. Negative emotions block those positive emotions that would enable the child to deal with the task: the confidence that he is capable of delaying gratification. All too often that "little voice inside his head" is his limbic system, telling him that he is not capable of resisting the marshmallow, so why even try.

Self-Reg can shift a child from negative to positive. There might well be strong biological factors that have tilted a child to a negative bias. But Self-Reg enables us to recognize and ameliorate the relevant stresses; to substitute energizing for draining strategies for dealing with negative states; and, most important of all, to help our child become the agent of such change.

The Duet of Emotion Regulation: Resonance and Dissonance

Emotion regulation begins at birth, even if science is not exactly clear about when "genuine" emotions begin to appear in babies. A lot of parents swear they can tell when their three-week-old is happy, but as far as scientific evidence is concerned, all we can really say for certain is that for the first few months of life a baby swings between two elemental states: distressed and contented.

Sometime between three and six months of age children start to have what are considered genuine emotions. Now they show us in all sorts of ways what they're feeling, with smiles that are a clear sign of happiness or other positive emotions and different kinds of crying to express different negative emotions. In the beginning they feel fear, happiness, anger, interest, curiosity, surprise, sadness. But they can't control any of this, leading psychologists to describe these first emotions as a kind of reflex, governed by genes inherited from some distant ancestor because of the function that they played in the survival of our species.

The "fear reflex" might have developed to trigger behaviors that served to bring a caregiver running. Joy would have cemented the infant-caregiver bond. Anger would tell parents they had better attend to their baby's needs—immediately. Curiosity would keep the baby glued to what her parents were saying or doing and motivate her to explore her environment, beginning with her parents' faces. Surprise was a great motivator to get parents to play peekaboo, which has all sorts of wonderful benefits in terms of integrating the different parts of the baby's brain.

This evolutionary perspective is useful. But sometimes it can lead us astray. For one of the complications that arise from treating "basic emotions" as reflexes is that this can lead back to the mistake of confusing *regulation* with *control*. If these emotions are just reflexes, then it follows that you're not going to be able to change them any more than you can change the reflex that makes you blink when something gets in your eye. The only way to not blink is by sheer will, and if emotions are reflexes, then the same must be true: If a child is having problems with "emotional control," it must be because he's not making a great enough effort. But children with emotional problems don't lack for effort; more often they are making too much effort trying to keep a lid on certain emotions.

Important here is how these reflexes get bound up with emotional experience that bears on the development of emotion regulation. Nature's design for emotion regulation shows clearly in infancy, and control has nothing to do with it. Mom and Dad don't calm an infant's upset by imposing control or *talking* to her about her feelings— the fear or anger triggered when she is startled, hungry, or overstressed. Rather they reduce her fear by soothing her, by showing on their faces and with their relaxed bodies that there's nothing to be frightened about. Other times they add to her joy or curiosity with sparkling eyes, animated facial expressions and vocalizations, and laughter. This is "right brain–to–right brain" communication, and it is critical for the baby's subsequent ability to modulate her own emotions.

Babies may not be consciously aware of any of this, but their intuitive right brain is highly sensitive to the emotional currents that play out on a parent's face and in the parent's posture and movements and are communicated via the two-way intuitive channel of the inter-brain. In your responses to your child's emotions you are helping to shape his physical/emotional nexus. Some parents find it difficult to stay calm when their child explodes with anger. They tense up and may hightail it from the interaction, becoming emotionally absent if not physically so. A young child—even an infant—may start to associate his parents' response, which can be frightening, with his angry behavior and for that reason become tense as he tries to repress anger when he feels it. A child whose parents delight in his exuberance and respond in kind, laughing and clapping their hands, develops a joyful, energizing association.

In all of these exchanges emotions become intimately wired to physical sensations. This is one reason why positive emotions can be so muted in some children, or negative emotions so powerful. For example, a child's exuberance can be unsettling for some parents, and if they tense up, seeking to restrain him, then the right brain begins to associate his joyful feeling with their tension. This physical/emotional association takes hold, and before you know it, the child shuts down when he feels himself starting to become high-spirited. Or take the child who is left all alone when he's frightened or lonely: When he gets older, these feelings are enough to trigger a surge of adrenaline and even pains in his stomach, chest, or head.

The associations are formed in the opposite direction as well: Physical sensations become associated with distinctive emotions. For example, if an infant is hungry and her cries go unheeded, her muscles tense up, which is associated with sensations of discomfort, and a distinct feeling of anger may begin to emerge. If the caregiver responds to these first signs of anger by scolding the child or by coldly withdrawing, then the physical sensations and the nascent feeling of anger that the child experiences may become further bound up with feelings of hopelessness. As the child grows older, the same physical sensations—a stomachache, for instance—can trigger feelings of anger or hopelessness—and leave a parent befuddled, completely unaware of how a deep-seated physical/emotional association might be the culprit and wondering, "Why the sudden change?" when just a moment ago their child seemed so happy.

How we respond to a child's emotions can lessen or heighten the associations that they form; and babies vary enormously in the amount of energy it takes from us to regulate these processes. The one thing that is now clear is that it is much easier to soothe or animate some babies than others. There are all sorts of factors involved: genetic, environmental, the effects of viruses or colic. But whatever a child's constitution, the important point remains the same at any age: Your child's positive emotions "fill the tank" with energy to manage ups and downs, so your shared delight adds to hers. Negative emotions drain energy, so when you can ease your child's negative emotions—not ignore or minimize them but help her through them—you dramatically reduce the load on her nervous system.

The "Three *R*'s" of Emotion Regulation

"Emotion regulation" is standardly defined as "monitoring, evaluating, and modifying one's emotions." In other words, children need to recognize when, for instance, they are overly anxious or angry, need to consider whether their emotion is appropriate to the situation, and if it is not, need to be able to calm themselves down. Whenever I read this definition to an audience of parents and ask how well their kids perform these various tasks, they guffaw. These skills are exactly what we all want our children to possess and exactly what we find so hard to instill.

I once listened to a mental-health specialist who was working in a school that had a large number of kids with "externalizing" and "internalizing" disorders—conduct or mood problems. She used a simplified "emotion vocabulary" chart to help them identify what they were feeling. The teachers would stop the students at various times of the day and ask them to point out where they were on the chart at that moment. The idea was that by being cued to tune in to their emotions the children would naturally become more aware of when they were anxious or angry and could then apply strategies to calm down (for instance, breathing deeply and counting to ten).

Her approach was like many widely used social-emotional learning (SEL) programs and techniques focusing on emotional intelligence and literacy. But it also shared the same limitations. Quite often the challenge for a child having trouble regulating his emotions is that he doesn't know—may even deny—that he is anxious or angry. Being put on the spot isn't helpful. It is also a strategy that can easily become overly intrusive and stressful for the child and that can create a power dynamic that skews the student's relationship with a teacher.

Most important, especially when a child is angry or distraught, is that left-brain processes such as language, analysis, and reflection might have gone offline as a result of all the adrenaline the child is pumping in the hyperaroused state. That is, the more flooded the child, the less capacity he has to monitor, evaluate, and modify his emotions. The very first thing the child needs to do is to come back to calm, and that must be a parent's (or teacher's) priority too. Help the child calm, not try to force him to monitor, evaluate, and modify what he's feeling.

Children need us to perform this regulating function for a remarkably long time. When they are young, they need us to do it constantly. Their emotional reactions are sudden and feel catastrophic—all-or-nothing—to them. But even when they are teens and young adults they come back to us for help when their emotions are overpowering. And what parents naturally find scary, perplexing, challenging, or frustrating is when they can't seem to help their kids calm down or cheer up. The child is so overwrought or angry that nothing that you say or do seems to help. This happens not because a child's "braking mechanism" is defective and certainly not because she isn't "trying hard enough" but because she is so aroused that she can't register what she or we are saying or doing.

No amount of exhorting a child to calm down will have this effect. You need to soothe before you try to "educate." Before we can help a child learn how to monitor, evaluate, and modify her emotions we need to focus on the "three *R*'s" of emotion regulation: *Recognize. Reduce. Restore.* Recognize the signs of escalating stress. Reduce the stress. Restore energy.

Emotions Aren't "All in the Head"

The Physical/Emotional Nexus

The processes of energy restoration and growth apply every bit as much to our emotional functioning as they do to our physiological functioning. In fact, restoration and growth in the biological and emotion domains are so intertwined that it is often difficult to distinguish between the two. A child who isn't getting enough sleep, sound nutrition, and physical activity isn't getting the fuel she needs to support healthy, stable emotional functioning. On the flip side, a child in chronic or extreme emotional distress is burning through energy that the brain and body need for healthy functioning overall, and at some point the emotional drain takes a toll on physical health.

Rosie's Bedroom Makeover—and Meltdown

Soon after we started working together, Marie reported on her latest challenge: Rosie's "bedroom makeover crisis." Every afternoon for several days in a row Rosie had rearranged the furniture in her room, but by evening she was in tears over the new arrangement. Marie was genuinely worried that this was turning into full-blown obsessive-compulsive disorder (OCD). Nothing that Marie said or did seemed to help. In fact, whatever she said or did just made things worse.

It seemed that Rosie's distress stemmed from more than just a fickle sense of decor, but there was no pattern of behavior that suggested something as extreme as OCD. What might other stressors be? Sibling rivalry with her older sister was a feature of her emotional life. As the younger sibling, Rosie had the smaller bedroom, something that she complained about frequently. Coupled with this was the fact that she had to go to bed an hour before her older sister and deeply resented being excluded from "all the fun" the family was having after she'd gone to bed. Rosie found it hard being the youngest in the family, but that was nothing new. Why this sudden emotional flare-up? *Why now?*

Self-Reg always begins with the biological, and when I asked Marie about Rosie's sleep, eating, physical activity, and general health, she immediately recognized other stressors to factor in. Most notably, Rosie was just getting over a bad bout of the flu. In fact, she had been vomiting the four previous nights before all this had started, meaning that she was in an exceptionally depleted physical state just before the crisis erupted. She had also missed school, so she was behind in her homework, and she had been absent from her circle of friends and felt out of sync.

The point here is simply that we must always bear in mind the physical/emotional nexus: the essential, core connection between the biological and emotion domains. Rosie's emotional stress was clearly a significant factor here, but it was not the only factor. Whatever mix of emotional stress and depleted energy triggered her meltdown, Rosie was essentially caught in a stress cycle in which her physical and emotional stress interacted with and intensified each other. In a situation like this, feelings of tension exacerbate the anxiety (or vice versa), which intensifies the tension, which intensifies the anxiety, and so on. Soon the whole system is spinning out.

When a child is overwhelmed by a catastrophic emotion, their arousal level skyrockets. Self-Reg paves the way for you to reengage, first by lowering your child's hyperarousal, beginning with her physical tension, just as you did when she was a baby. The more her physical arousal is reduced, the more her emotional arousal will start to subside, the result of interrupting the physical/emotional nexus. Only once a child's overall arousal is reduced can she begin to process the things you are desperate to tell her.

The facts of Rosie's birth order, her bedroom, and her bedtime weren't going to change, but reasoning with her over these facts of life was no way to help her calm herself and go to sleep. What Marie needed to do in the moment was ignore the emotional issue entirely and focus on the physical.

With the earlier sweatshirt success to draw from, and her new awareness of Rosie's stressors, Marie responded to Rosie's room-makeover meltdown with a gentle hug and light massage. No talking, no analyzing, just a head, shoulders, and back massage. Fifteen minutes was all it took. What I found most significant about this particular episode is that for the next few evenings Rosie herself asked Marie if she could have a massage. The two of them did eventually talk about her bedroom a couple of days later, but it turned out to be not nearly as big an issue as Marie had feared—and as Rosie had felt when she was tired and sick.

In the beginning Marie worked on helping Rosie learn how to focus not on what she was feeling emotionally but on becoming more aware of what she was feeling physically. This helped Rosie learn to recognize when she was overly tense and how to reduce that tension—when she had lost touch with her body and how to get back in touch. Marie would ask Rosie at the start of a massage if her arms felt stiff—like uncooked spaghetti—and then, after a couple of minutes, if they were starting to feel relaxed—like cooked noodles. This soon turned into a sort of game for the two of them, with Rosie telling her mom that she had "uncooked-spaghetti arms" when she was tense. As they did the Self-Reg steps together, this also gave Rosie a way to begin to help herself, a way to access the physical/emotional nexus and, with this simple Self-Reg skill, begin to get in touch with her emotions.

The three *R*'s—recognize, reduce, and restore—unfold naturally when you soothe first, as Rosie's story shows. When you and your child are calmly engaged, then you can set out together to identify sources of stress, take steps to reduce stress, identify what helps your child calm down, and learn how she can practice doing this for herself. The physical/emotional nexus is a universal access point for all of us, and this turned out to be a vital factor in Rosie's capacity to learn how to regulate her emotions. It was not the only factor, but it paved the way for Rosie's continued emotional growth, which could not proceed until she had significantly improved in her bodily self-awareness. As it turned out, Rosie's emotion regulation did indeed begin with a kind of "monitoring," but it was of her stress and tension, not her emotions.

Nurturing (or Inhibiting) Emotional Growth

Self-regulation in the biological domain can be summed up in a single line: A child shifts into physiological states that consume energy, then calms and recovers, restoring energy. The same is true in the emotion domain, where a child experiences strong emotions that consume enormous amounts of energy, then calms, recovers, and restores energy. The recovery phase is vital in the biological domain because it creates the optimal conditions for growth and healing. The same is true for the emotion domain.

The parent-child dynamic of the interbrain is crucial for emotional growth. It is not the sole engine of emotional growth, of course. Children naturally confront and explore their emotions through pretend play, peer interactions, the stories they read, and the stories they tell. Parents play a critical role in this process. Through our responses, unconscious as well as conscious, we enhance a child's emotional growth. And sometimes, unfortunately, we can hold back their emotional growth. When children broach emotional themes that make us uncomfortable—questions about life, death, sex, or aspects of our own behavior that we'd prefer to ignore—and we avoid the subject, they learn to avoid it too. If we engage them, are open to their questions, share from our experience and our own search for answers, they expand their emotional repertoire to include reflection and self-awareness.

A child stuck in a particular emotion will tend to respond reflexively to the thing she is scared of or angry about. It can be very frightening for a child or teen to find herself swept up in an emotional tsunami, and our fearful or angry response makes it that much harder for her to calm and find her emotional equilibrium. The more a child is gripped by fear or anger, the less she is able to engage with us or process what we are saying to help her deal with this challenge.

The critical step in nurturing a child's emotional growth is to maintain the fluid two-way communication of the interbrain, even through rough patches that threaten to disconnect you—*especially* in the rough patches. It is through these nurturing operations of the interbrain that a child's basic emotions can differentiate, broaden, and deepen and positive "secondary" emotions (courage, determination, hope, compassion) can develop. The deeper this base of emotional assets, the less effort is required to remain calm in stressful situations. But in this process a child can also acquire the sorts of negative secondary emotions that I mentioned (despair, envy, guilt, or helplessness), which render her even more emotionally fragile and vulnerable to anxiety. The two-way interbrain dialogue doesn't lie, and in Rosie's story Marie, in her own frustration, was communicating to Rosie that her behavior was annoying, which, far from helping, was like tossing gasoline onto Rosie's emotional bonfire. To help her daughter tease apart these complex feelings, Marie had to become aware of her own emotional undercurrents and how her reactions contributed to Rosie's emotional distress.

As a child grows, he starts to explore all sorts of different emotions, not just the ones that he finds exhilarating but also ones that he finds frightening. It is important that we be receptive to all his emotional overtures and don't shy away from the hard ones that make us uneasy. Just as we ourselves are mesmerized by movies that explore some dark and disturbing emotion, so too a child needs to feel safe exploring emotional themes that frighten him. We can provide this feeling of security only by remaining calm and engaged. This helps the child learn how to manage the emotions that he finds unsettling, rather than staying stuck in or regressing to an earlier phase of overwhelming physical and emotional reactions.

Illness and death, for instance, are common worries for children. Before their eyes grandparents grow older, sometimes ailing; aunts, uncles, young cousins, and others among family and friends may struggle with illness or die. They worry about others dying, perhaps you dying, and may become preoccupied with worry. The child's emotional stress may manifest itself in one particular domain—perhaps in stomachaches or anxiety—but regardless, they often bring their worries directly to you with their blunt questions or fretful concerns. Many such anxious children seem to respond well to self-regulating activities, which don't just distract them but that are regulating. Art has been shown to be especially powerful. And should the child choose to draw pictures with some sort of death theme, Mom and Dad need to tell him how beautiful the picture is, or maybe encourage him to explain it, and not be frightened by what they see or hear.

With each year of continued growth, children develop their capacity to think calmly and objectively about their emotions. They can start to understand the variety of situations related to their feelings of anger, fear, and sadness. As children explore these feelings in their pretend play, physical and emotional sensations bind tightly together in these psychodramas. Children who are calm have more details in their pretend play. There is more subtlety to their feelings and more situations that bring out those feelings. Conversely, children who are easily aroused are more tentative emotionally or display more anxious or aggressive themes in their pretend play.

As they become more reflective about their emotions, they begin to figure out why they are feeling so angry or frightened or sad. They begin to understand more of the subtlety involved in the gray areas of feelings and the give-and-take that peer relationships call for. At a young age a child might storm into the house shouting how much she hates her best friend for playing with another child at recess. By middle school she might respond to a perceived snub by reflecting, aloud or to herself, about why she feels so hurt.

All of these critical elements of a child's emotional growth—to identify emotions, develop tools for modulating emotions, think about his own or others' emotions, and understand where his emotions come from and why they feel a certain way—hinge on exploring emotions with you and trusted others in the safety of your relationship and the shared exchange of the interbrain. Without these formative experiences, a child's emotions stay locked in a catastrophic, all-or-nothing mode.

The Light of Day: Kids Need Emotional Openness and Safety

We humans are prone to repressing emotions that we find disturbing, in our children as much as in ourselves. But the secret to enhancing a child's emotional well-being is not to get her to avoid or suppress painful emotions but rather to expose them to the light of day. This is very difficult for a child. It is very difficult for all of us.

Children find strong negative emotions frightening and draining and, as we've seen, will try to bottle them up. The pressure builds until they reach the point where they lash out or shut down, at which point telling them to "use their words" isn't helpful because they are fleeing from the very emotion that they find frightening. What so often happens is that they regress into a prelinguistic state in which they are left speechless, or perhaps equipped to use only words that express a raw feeling of emotional pain, which typically only makes matters worse. How many times has a parent heard their raging child scream, "I hate you!" when, after the emotional storm has passed, they would never say or even think such a thing?

To help our children grow emotionally, we need to help them express what they're feeling and feel safe doing so. They need to expand their emotional vocabulary and reflectiveness and distinguish the different elements in their emotional responses. They have to learn how to identify their emotional triggers and, as they grow older, understand their emotional vulnerabilities. And they need to develop new emotions and learn how to deal with the new emotional challenges that are part of growing up.

Learning to Read the
Gauge—Together

Remember the car mechanic who came up to me after a Self-Reg talk and shared his epiphany that children's behaviors are like dashboard indicators of how their "engine" is running? Well, in many ways strong emotions *are* our indicator, letting us know when our engine is overheating or running on empty. One of the things that a child has to learn—in fact, what we all have to learn—is when a strong negative emotion is telling us that we're in a low-energy/high-tension state. It is quite remarkable how something that is frightening or irritating when we are low energy does not seem nearly so bothersome, perhaps doesn't even seem to be a problem at all, when we are in a high-energy/low-tension state.

Rather than teach them to suppress their strong emotions, we want children to recognize when these emotions serve as a signal that they are overstressed and need to recover. Once "scary" emotions are reframed in this way, by parent and child alike, they immediately become less frightening. Those angry explosions that we saw in Rosie were signals that, for varying reasons, she was overwrought and exhausted. In the following months her problems began to diminish as a result of seeing them as indicators that her tension needed to be reduced and her energy increased.

A child's learning to do this is always a two-person job. As your child's emotional mentor and partner, you can break an entrenched stress cycle. One of the most important lessons we can teach a child when we are cultivating emotion regulation is precisely this: to recognize the signs of emotional dysregulation when they are starting, before the feelings become so intense that the child is thrown into fight or flight or freeze, so that they can set to work on the five steps of Self-Reg.

Emotion regulation starts out, then, as dyadic—between two

people—and this remains a vital factor of healthy human functioning to the very end. We soothe our child by making her feel safe. Although this begins between parent and child, it becomes a feature of all other relationships, from friendships and peer groups to love and life partners. When the interbrain is functioning smoothly—what is called "goodness of fit"—it produces a shared feeling of safety and security. This is why it is such a stabilizing influence through emotional swings and expands and deepens through sharing each other's emotional differences. These are two sides of the same coin. Just as emotional swings are a staple of life, so too are moments of emotional discord. And just as it is the recovery from emotional swings that is essential to our individual well-being, so too is it how two partners, who have very different emotions, are able to find that common emotional ground that is critical for the strength of the interbrain.

A Child's Greatest Danger: Anger, Theirs or Ours?

We hear all the time that one of the greatest dangers a child faces is not being able to control his temper. All young children are thought to have trouble in this regard, some more than others, maybe for biological, family, or social reasons. The conventional thinking is that, whatever the cause, if a child gives in to his anger he's going to suffer, and there are plenty of studies to back this up. Research shows that such children are more likely to drop out of school early, engage in antisocial behavior, take drugs, harm themselves, or develop psychological and long-term physical problems. But to effectively address children's anger issues, it's essential that we separate cause and effect. Does a child's anger alone necessarily doom him to those consequences, or is our response to a child's anger a critical factor in his downward spiral?

The fact is that all of us—parents, teachers, even children—respond to someone's angry outbursts with anger of our own. When we feel angry, it is natural to project this onto the object of our anger—even when it is our own child. *He* is the one who is at fault. *He* is the one who "did it." He is the one who must submit and admit. And if he does not, and if the grim consequences alluded to above come about, then *he has only himself to blame*!

Of all the negative emotions, anger might be the hardest for parents and children to deal with. Children find anger especially draining and frightening and, as I said earlier, often will try to ignore or bottle it up. But the pressure builds until they reach the point where their anger is explosive. Parents often say that what makes their child's anger so scary is its unpredictability. At a parent meeting one evening, a mother described her son's angry outbursts: "It's zero to sixty," she said. "One second he's perfectly calm and the next moment he's ranting and raving."

Nobody really goes from zero to sixty—calm to furious—in an instant. A child's demeanor may change that fast, but that does not mean he has just gone from calm to furious. This is why it's imperative that we distinguish between the pressure-cooker "quiet"—liable to blow in an instant—and the self-regulated calm of emotional equilibrium. *In the explosive scenario, the child's tension has been building*, even though he doesn't show it, and what is most important, even though he doesn't *know* it. If that tension becomes too pitched, then something that has no effect on him when he's calm can set off an emotional explosion. This is why the child needs to recognize for himself the significance of the outburst. In other words, he needs to become aware of the physical state he was in leading up to the explosion.

Self-Reg tells us that a child's greatest danger is not, in fact, experiencing rage: That is a core part of the human condition. The child's greatest danger is if he is shamed for his feelings, blamed for a lack of self-control, and punished in ways that only make him more vulnerable to a wider range of negative emotions: feelings of helplessness, worthlessness, melancholy, or even self-hatred. All this and it brings the child not a whit closer to "controlling his temper."

Anger is not a *character weakness* that needs to be controlled. To be sure, a child has to have limits that he clearly understands. In fact, research has shown that having no limits is as great a stressor for a child as having limits that are too strict. But the goal of discipline is to help the child develop self-discipline, and *self-discipline comes from the child's positive, not his negative, emotions.* Self-discipline comes from his desire to become a certain sort of person and his belief that he can become that sort of person, not from fear that he will be shamed or punished for his actions.

Exposed to the Light of Day

Why would any child give in to rage when it is clear that this will lead to a bad end, make him a social pariah? Why would a child ever choose to remain emotionally distraught instead of calm and steady? Why see the difficulty in every opportunity when, as Churchill once said, it is so beneficial to see the opportunity in every difficulty? Why would a teen stay in bed all day with the curtains drawn? Why can't an anxious child "just let it go" or a glum child "just cheer up"?

The answer, as we've seen throughout this chapter, is that kids aren't *choosing* to be negative or contrary or just plain miserable. Believe it or not, the child whom you're exhorting to *calm down* actually wants to do just that; it's the *how* that leaves him flummoxed. Nor is the problem that he doesn't understand the costs of negative emotions. If that were the case, then we could just explain the consequences— again—and he'd switch off the anger, perk up, simmer down, stop fretting, *get a grip*.

Every parent I've ever talked with has realized, even if only intuitively, that resilience lies not in avoiding or repressing but in confronting and dealing with strong emotions. They've all tried in their own way to tackle their child's emotional problems head-on: to clear the air, get their child to open up about what's bothering her, or maybe just recognize that something is bothering her. And pretty much every one of them has found that persuasion was as ineffectual as logic as a response to emotional problems.

Self-Reg tells us not only why this is the case but also, more important, what to do about it. It teaches us to broaden our outlook: to look at the whole apparatus and not just one side of our child's physical/emotional seesaw. Because when one side is out of whack, so is the other, and we can't help our child learn how to regulate his emotional arousal without learning how to regulate his physical arousal.

Far from being an obstacle to your child's well-being, powerful emotions are the very secret to it. I'm not talking about just love and empathy or interest and curiosity but also the fears and vexations that are part of growing up. Even the anger and resentment that make your child and those around her miserable are mainsprings of development: all tied, inextricably and inseparably, to the physical. Expose this weird and scary behavior to the light of day and you'll discover that, like the monster in the attic, it's just a loose shutter banging in the wind.

SEVEN

Calm, Alert, and Learning

The Cognitive Domain

A wiry little guy of seven, Tyler didn't so much walk into a room as he dashed: into a room, out of a room, from thing to thing in a room, and from room to room. He was clumsy, constantly bumping into chairs and desks, even walls. He needed to touch and handle everything he saw, but only for a moment before he discarded it, more often than not simply tossing it onto the floor. Sit down to talk with him and he would pull out a handheld game device, and that was that. There was no way to draw him out of the game and into a conversation. His mother, Cynthia, explained that he never went anywhere without his electronic game. He even played it while he was walking or talking with someone. It was pretty much the only thing that would slow him down and keep his attention.

On the diagnostic checklist of behaviors describing attention disorders, "heightened distractibility" and "novelty seeking" are typically easy places to start. But it was difficult for Tyler's mom or others to describe his "heightened distractibility" in precise terms because he was never engaged in a task long enough to suggest that he was being distracted from it. It was even difficult to see his behavior as novelty seeking, since he barely seemed to be aware of the things he was see-ing or handling. Instead it was as if some deep need drove him to flit like a hummingbird from one stimulus to the next.

It wasn't just that he could never sit still. As he roamed around he seemed tense, more anxious than curious. And while he could stay glued to video games for hours on end, it was hard to tell if this truly was a show of concentration, which is an *active* mental state, or was "attentional capture"—when something grabs your attention by inter-rupting other processing. This kind of attention, even for a prolonged period, is considered a *passive* mental state. For Tyler, as for many children with attention issues, the barrage of rapidly changing images, loud noises, and bright colors deployed by these games keeps them glued but acts as a brain drain, providing brief but exhausting jolts of energy that are dysregulating—like junk food for the brain.

Tyler's hyperactive behavior as a toddler had been challenging enough at home. Just getting him to sit and finish breakfast or get ready for a trip to the grocery store had required epic patience and effort by his mother. But the situation had gone from bad to worse when he started school. Five years old and in kindergarten, Tyler's extreme inability to sit still and focus on a task, stand in line for recess, or play through a game or activity with classmates—something as simple as Simon Says or I Spy—made him hard to teach one on one and disruptive in group activities. All of this meant that he missed out on important learning opportunities.

Tyler was diagnosed with attention-deficit/hyperactivity disorder (ADHD) later that kindergarten year, and the following year he was placed on one of the psychostimulant drugs designed to improve at-tention. The medication helped a little with his behavior at school, Cynthia said, which was considered important for his social as well as his academic development. But he found it very hard to take the pills and he hated the taste of both the oral solution and the chewable tab-lets. They had tried a patch, but it was irritating and he would tear it off at the first chance. So just getting him to take the medication was a major battle, and the beneficial effects wore off by night, which made evenings harrowing for both of them. Cynthia was a single mom who worked high-pressure days as a legal secretary, but more challenging were evenings with Tyler, and the hardest part was bedtime. It could take her hours to get him settled. The nights that she got him to sleep by midnight were a minor triumph. And although she awoke in the morning exhausted, Tyler never seemed fazed by his lack of sleep.

Now three months into first grade, Tyler's situation had only become more distressing, for him and for his mother. The class had progressed to early reading, writing, and comprehension skills, and Tyler's inattention and impulsivity clearly held him back. His behavior now seemed an impenetrable wall that cut Tyler off from learning with the rest of his classmates or, his mother feared, from learning at all. Her concerns were justified and echo those of increasing numbers of parents who worry about what they—or their children's teachers—see as serious problems with attention. A child who can't pay attention can't learn, and a child who can't learn can't succeed.

Our clinical objective with Tyler would be to slow him down, help him get in touch with his body, help him experience and enjoy moments of calmness, and then learn how to manage this on his own. But our research focus when we work with children like Tyler is to see what, if anything, they can teach us about all children, not just those struggling with problems in the cognitive domain.

Digging Down to the Roots of the Cognitive Domain

"Cognition" is a very big word that covers an awful lot of territory in psychology. It refers to any of the mental processes involved in learning: things like attention, perception, memory, and problem solving. In fact, each of these covers an awful lot of territory in its own right. But Self-Reg stakes out a much smaller but essential claim: It is concerned with the common roots of these different cognitive processes and how constrictions in these roots can result in problems in one of the above aspects of learning.

The most frequent aspects of the cognitive domain that we see children and adolescents struggle with are:

- Attentiveness
- Ignoring distractions
- Delaying gratification
- Combining ideas
- Sequencing ideas
- Tolerating frustration
- Learning from mistakes
- Switching focus
- Seeing the relationships between causes and effects
- Thinking in abstract terms

It's natural, when you encounter any one of these problems, to think that you should be focusing on *that specific issue*. Say, for example, a child has trouble paying attention: It's tempting to think that he needs exercises to strengthen this capacity. But Self-Reg always asks: Why am I seeing this particular problem? What are the underlying factors? What can I do to strengthen the *roots* of cognition? This is important not just in children demonstrating one of the above problems but in all children. Even for a child who is an able learner, new challenges arise as schoolwork becomes more complex and the demands on attention grow. Pressure for academic success is fierce, and the social and emotional demands of school life only add to the stressors on a child.

A root system absorbs water and nutrients and serves to anchor the plant. Similarly, when we speak of the roots of cognition, we're referring to how the various senses take in and process different kinds of information, *internal* as well as *external*, and how these roots anchor or ground the child, in the sense of providing her with the feeling of security that is needed to be able to attend to the world. The reference to internal as well as external signals tells us that we're dealing not just with the five senses—sight, smell, taste, touch, and hearing—but also with internal sensors that tell the child what is going on inside his body, the position of his trunk, head, limbs, hands, and feet, changes in temperature and pressure, even an intuitive sense of time.

Pushing a child to master higher-order metacognitive skills—planning, self-monitoring, or evaluating their own learning—when there are constrictions in his sensory root system can be deeply frustrating for the child, his parents, and his teachers. Tyler is a case in point. The school, trying hard to help him, arranged for weekly executive function (EF) coaching sessions. The term "executive functions" refers to a number of different competencies involved in reasoning, problem solving, flexible thinking, planning and execution, and effective multitasking. If you have ever seen a child concentrate on learning the rules of a new game, shift handily from one task to another, build a LEGO model, or ignore your call to dinner while building a LEGO model, then you've witnessed executive functions in action.

EF coaching works on things like note taking, studying and analyzing a text, planning essays and preparing for tests, or time management. Such skills are invaluable and have proven to be a huge help for all sorts of children with learning deficits, reducing the stress of studying or writing essays and exams. But it didn't help Tyler, even though Cynthia would religiously go over his exercises with him every single night. The lessons never seemed to stick, and both of them came to dread their nightly sessions. The problem was that Tyler's challenges in the cognitive domain were much more rudimentary. As is the case in every domain of Self-Reg, we can't begin to work on a "higher" stage until a strong foundation has been laid. So before we could think about his heightened distractibility and impulsivity we had to work on his ability to take in and process different kinds of sensory information.

There are a number of reasons why a child might be having problems paying attention: biological, emotional, cognitive, psychological, social. A focus on executive function coaching helps some children, but educators often tell me that a large number of their students don't benefit. Why not? The big reason is that these programs or exercises presuppose a level of cognitive readiness that many children and even teens have not achieved. In other words, we need to nurture the roots before we worry about pruning the branches.

The Roots of Cognition

One of my favorite cartoons by Gary Larson in *The Far Side* compares "what we say to dogs" and "what they hear." It shows a man scolding his dog, Ginger, by name and in great verbal detail for her trash-can transgression. What the dog hears? Basically *blah, blah, blah, Ginger, blah, blah.* That is a useful way to start thinking about the roots of cognition.

In fact, a lot of children with attentional problems will hear not even "blah, blah, blah" but more like "blahblahblah"—a long, drawn-out stream of sound. So your simple instruction to "pick up your toys before you go out to play" becomes the garbled order to "pikupyrtoyzberoryugoutoplay." They may have trouble discerning the little bits of speech, like "ing" or "s" endings, where typically our voice drops. Or they can't tell if you're saying "cat," "bat," or "mat." Their difficulty is something like the trouble you would have differentiating subtle sounds in a foreign language that you didn't know. This wouldn't be because you weren't *paying attention* to what people were saying, although the more frustrated you became, the more likely you would be to tune out. There might be nothing wrong with your hearing at all, only that the auditory center of your brain wasn't familiar with the sounds. For some people, even in their own language, a problem in the way the auditory center in their brain processes speech sounds makes it harder for them to understand what's being said.

A big problem that Tyler had, again not uncommon, was with his internal sensors. He had a lot of trouble playing simple games like Simon Says and would quickly tire of them and quit. This made it seem that his problem was motivational: He couldn't be bothered to make the effort. But when we watched carefully, we could see that he was finding it hard to perform the motor sequences he was supposed to imitate.

Cynthia already was well aware of this simply from observing her son in everyday life, but she hadn't seen it as a part of a pattern until now. He'd been this way from an early age and still found it difficult to stand on one leg or stay on a balance board for more than a few seconds. He was awkward as he sat down or stood up and seemed to miss his body's cues for other simple things. He could be clearly shivering cold, yet she would have to tell him to put on a sweater. She had to stand over him to get him to eat even when she knew that he was hungry. As for going to bed, he never seemed to know when he was exhausted, even though it was so patently obvious to her.

For every child working on Self-Reg the starting point is to help him get comfortable in his own skin. For Tyler that meant playing games that helped him notice the messages coming in from his muscles and joints. He had trouble coordinating his actions and speech, so Cynthia played games with him that promoted this kind of awareness and worked on these processing challenges with him. Adaptations of timeless children's games such as Red Light/Green Light are effective because they're fun and rewarding for the child. At the same time they lead the child through an embodied experience of the cognitive processes they need to sequence their thoughts, movements, and vocal expression and confidently navigate their surrounding space. Games like these work on the *roots* of attention rather than the consequences of inattention.

Never assume that it is only young children who need to do this sort of work. Just because your hulking teenager is no longer a "child" doesn't mean he won't benefit from strengthening these brain-body connections. All of us do. In some instances teens have some subtle deficit in one of these roots that was never picked up, maybe because another one of their faculties—memory, for example—happened to be very strong and could compensate. But at some point the demands become too great for memory to handle, and that's why it's not uncommon to see a teenager who breezed through primary school suddenly develop an attentional problem in high school.

Revving the Cognitive Engine, Getting onto the Freeway of Life

Newborn babies have to make sense of the welter of "information" coming from inside as well as outside their bodies: sensations they've never experienced before. Biological restrictions in how they register or process different kinds of sensations, or sheer exhaustion, can make it even harder to make sense of what William James described as a "blooming, buzzing confusion."

To understand any child's challenges in the roots of the cognitive domain, especially children whose biology makes it hard for them to stay focused on a task, think of how it would feel to have to

- walk down a steep flight of stairs without holding on to a rail
- write a letter or play tennis with your "wrong" hand
- talk on a phone with such bad reception that you only heard parts of what the other person was saying

These are the sorts of processing issues that are a struggle for some children. For some it's a constant part of their day-to-day existence, and the effects often show up in attentional problems. When a child can't register or make sense of sensory stimuli, he feels a surge of anxiety, as any of us would, because he can't trust his senses and doesn't know what to expect.

How Does a Baby Start to Recognize Patterns?

Patterns make the world more predictable and less startling. The better a baby can recognize patterns, the less frightening and more engaging the world becomes. Babies constantly look and listen for patterns all around them. For example, a baby begins to hear not just sounds but the pauses between sounds and the way sounds are used. She begins to hear the words as distinct sounds—"stay" "out" "of" "the" "garbage"—and recognizes the connection between the loud voice, the scolding finger, and the facial expression when Daddy says this.

With pattern recognition comes the ability to know what you're feeling and to act in an intentional way on your environment. The child is able to tell others what she wants, or get her body to do what she wants—feed herself, pick up a toy, walk, stop, or go. These same cognitive roots enable her to start to figure out the relationships between causes and effects or recognize the connection between moods and behaviors, in herself as much as in her parents.

This growing ability to recognize patterns anchors the child by significantly reducing her stress, so that she stays in learning brain mode, open to and interested in the world around her. Children quickly shift to survival brain when they don't understand what they are experiencing or why people are acting the way they are, or when there's just too much for them to take in. So the roots of cognition aren't just *making sense* of the "blooming, buzzing confusion" but also, in so doing, creating the secure base that is needed to search for more complex patterns. So often a child who displays one of the above cognitive problems behaves this way because she doesn't have that secure base from which to attend to and explore the world around or, indeed, within. It may also be that the only way she can preserve a modicum of stability is by blocking out large parts of the information bombarding her senses.

But these roots don't develop all by themselves as the result, say, of some predetermined genetic program. A primary role of the inter-brain is to help the child in this process. You instinctively help a child who is having trouble sequencing his thoughts by simplifying the demands and supporting him in his problem-solving effort. This approach to learning, called "scaffolding," is essential for any kind of learning. But scaffolding starts very early in our efforts to nourish pattern recognition.

With a baby you prevent sensory overload as best you can, and when there is a "crash," you bring your baby back to a calm and stable state. You read her cues and modulate the intensity or the clarity of the stimuli you present. For example, we all change our vocalizations to find the pitch or volume that our infant seems to like best. This is the driving force behind "baby talk"—the way that parents in all cultures unconsciously adjust the way they speak to their infants in ways that help them recognize linguistic patterns. We accentuate the sound difference between "buh" and "puh" or exaggerate the different mouth shapes so that she can *see* as well as hear the difference. Combining visual with auditory information in this way is particularly beneficial for children who happen to be strong in one type of sensory processing but weak in another.

We support our children in so many ways as they learn to sit up or walk on their own. We "kiss the boo-boos" that are part of learning how to run on different terrains. We put training wheels on their bike; use a chair on the ice to help them learn how to skate or water wings to help them learn how to swim. We support them as they climb across the monkey bars. Perhaps the greatest mistake we can make is to assume that children need to struggle on their own—without our support—in learning how to pay attention. Every parent's dream is to see their child sitting quietly at the kitchen table finishing up their homework. But some children need a lot of help from us to reach this point.

The Taproot of Cognitive Problems

Arousal regulation is not just *another* root of cognition. It is the *taproot* that feeds all the smaller, lateral roots. Consider how much energy your infant is burning when she has trouble getting her hands or her mouth to do what she wants, or as she fights against gravity, which makes it so hard for her to sit up or walk. She also burns energy trying to figure out your actions, starting with the dizzying number of movements and sounds coming from your face.

Every child has some roots that are weaker than others. Some children find it hard to listen to a lecture or read a book, others, to master new math ideas or games on the playground. We all tend to shy away from the activities that we find overwhelming. "Weaknesses" are always more pronounced when you're tired and overstressed. The same holds true for children and adolescents. An awful lot of their cognitive problems may, in fact, simply be acts of avoidance. But there is a deeper issue here: The more stress a child is under, the more pronounced a problem in one of the roots becomes. As a result, the child's overall stress increases. So the child becomes enmeshed in a stress cycle at this rudimentary level of cognition, in which a problem recognizing patterns—perhaps the letters and words needed to read the simplest sentence in that first-grade primer—can cause stress, which adds to the energy drain, which then intensifies the experience of the original pattern recognition deficit, and so on.

Heightened stress also dampens or reduces sensory awareness. Even a child who ordinarily has no processing problem may find it hard to decipher speech sounds when he's under a lot of stress. For a child who does have a particular sensory hypersensitivity or a problem processing certain kinds of information, heightened stress can seriously deplete his reserves. If he has to spend too much energy trying to sit still, inhibit an impulse, or make sense of what he's seeing or hearing, there may not be enough left to work through a problem step by step. I once noticed that a young girl was distracted by the noise of the cooling fan on my desktop computer while she and I were working together on a math handout from her teacher. She was finding it almost impossible to pay attention to the math problem on the page in front of her, but the second I turned off the computer she was able to solve the question in a matter of minutes.

Working on the Physical Roots of Attention

For many children having problems paying attention, we start out not with exercises designed to reduce distractibility or improve planning and sequencing but by working on their body awareness, because this is where the ability to focus starts. All sorts of simple exercises and games can help young children develop this kind of awareness. For example, some games have them physically imitate animals (pretend you're an elephant, swinging your big trunk; pretend you're a vole, scurrying to safety) or modulate vocalizations (pretend you're a roaring lion; pretend you're a squeaky mouse) and speech patterns (talk as fast as you can; talk as slow as you can). Other activities involve hand movements (use sandpaper on a piece of wood; gently stroke a stuffed animal); tactile awareness (identify different kinds of substances while blindfolded); olfactory awareness (identify different types of essential oils by smell alone); or discriminating among different tastes (a version of Bertie Bott's Every Flavour Beans, without question most children's favorite).

The point of playing such games isn't simply to help the child *mas-*

ter the different kinds of movement or modulation in question. It is to help him *become aware* of his sensations as he does these things. Four basic ways to bring his attention to this internal experience:

- Slow things down (your speech, conversations and interactions with your child about everyday things, especially when you give instructions).
- Accentuate the intensity of certain kinds of stimuli—sound or visual, for instance—so that your child can fully register the sensation. Reduce the intensity of other stimuli that predictably trigger an alarm response in your child.
- Break ideas or instructions into smaller steps to allow your child to focus on one step or one piece of information at a time.
- Help your child recognize when a physical activity or a stimulating game helps him release tension and feel calmer. Ask your child if he feels like a robot (stiff or tense) or a rag doll (relaxed) afterward.

For a child with attention problems, especially one with significant deficits like Tyler's, it is particularly important to help him become aware of the sensory information coming from his proprioceptors— the sensory nerve endings in the muscles, tendons, joints, and inner ear that give him information about his position and movement. He needs us to slow down and accentuate the movements we want him to practice, and I mean *really* slow them down until he can feel the different parts of his body involved and the rhythm of what he is doing. And we have to do all this in a way that is fun, so that his alarm system isn't triggered.

A colleague once told me about a yoga clinic she had attended that perfectly illustrates how *slowing things down* strengthens this kind of body awareness. The pace of the class was extremely slow, with the emphasis on form rather than on trying to master new and difficult poses. Specifically, the instruction and movements focused on deepening awareness of the weight of the legs and their changing position through the movement, to focus attention on the tension in the muscles as they slowly worked against the pull of gravity. That is the proprioceptive faculty at work, but its importance to cognitive function is easy to overlook because it seems purely physical. She noted that by the end of the class she felt remarkably calm and light.

Astronauts have described how painful it is to return to earth: how reexperiencing the pull of gravity is like donning a heavy backpack or pushing a bike up a steep hill. Ordinarily we are so used to resisting the pull of gravity that we are oblivious to how many muscles we tense in order to maintain our upright posture. We have become so used to carrying the heavy backpack around wherever we go that we don't even notice it's there anymore. Even when just sitting, we tense muscles in our torso, upper back, shoulders, and neck to keep ourselves upright. But a baby first learning how to sit up fully experiences how much effort this takes, as does the crabby teenager who has to drag herself out of bed in the morning!

Two decades of research and several thousand years of meditation traditions support the positive effects of mindfulness on heart rate and other vitals that indicate a calming effect. But why? Part of the answer lies in the restorative effect of tuning in to our body, which releases the neurotransmitter acetylcholine, which not only lowers heart rate and promotes REM sleep but also is critical for sustained attention.

That is not to say that all kids with attentional problems tied to motor issues will enjoy doing "slo-mo" yoga; some perk up only when we do power yoga, and lots don't like any kind of yoga at all. So we're back to recognizing the importance of individual differences. The point isn't that there is a magic formula that will help your child develop his body awareness—only that the two of you need to figure this out together.

Anxious, Unfocused, and Unable to Learn

It has long been known that anxiety can seriously affect a child's ability to pay attention. This makes obvious sense from the perspective of Self-Reg: Heightened tension causes us to expend so much energy that little is left over to pay attention.

Attention is a full-body phenomenon involving the muscles as much as the mind. Watch a child immersed in a problem for a few minutes and you can see how her whole body is completely tensed as she concentrates. We describe a child as *working* on a problem: a highly significant metaphor, as the child is straining her muscles as much as her mind to solve the problem. I once heard a teacher tell his math class that it was "time for some heavy lifting," and I thought, as I watched the students clenching their jaws and furrowing their foreheads, that this really was an apt metaphor.

What's more, intense concentration can leave us anxious. I'm not simply referring to the anxiety created by thinking that you won't be able to solve a problem. I'm referring to the physiological effects of this full-body phenomenon. Whether we are in a state of low energy and high tension because of some emotional issue or because we've been concentrating so hard, the effects seem to be largely the same.

In our school-based Self-Reg work we use a general rule that children can concentrate for about the same number of minutes as their years in age. But there are, of course, always exceptions; some children can't concentrate anywhere near as long as you might expect, and some seem able to go on forever. But what all children have in common is that if they go past that point, whatever that is, you see the same sorts of emotional and cognitive problems that appear in children who have a kindled limbic system. They start to seem unmotivated to learn, uninterested in anything other than their video game, behaviors that adults can be quick to call "lazy."

Motivation Is One Thing, Energy Another

"Motivation" is one of those impossibly obscure words, generally defined as "the mental act that energizes, activates and directs behavior." But all this is really saying is that motivation is what motivates a child to act. Before we get too bogged down in the fruitless task of trying to define "motivation," the real point is that it's hard for a child to "energize" when he doesn't have any energy.

The link between energy and motivation is inextricable. The more "gas in the tank," the more motivated a child becomes. Low energy diminishes motivation. It's as simple as that. The more stresses on your child, the greater the energy drain and the less likely he is to stick to anything challenging. Physical stressors, as always, include illness or insufficient sleep, nutrition, or physical activity. Problems with friends or other social or emotional tension can undermine motivation. And then there are "cognitive stressors" unique to this domain.

In addition to the stress of not seeing patterns, a common cognitive stressor is asking a child to solve a problem before he has mastered the underlying skills or concepts. You wouldn't expect a child to read a chapter book before learning the alphabet, or to multiply and divide numbers before learning to add and subtract. At every stage of cognitive development, the scaffolding needs to be in place for a child to feel calm and confident in taking on the learning challenge. Presenting a child with cognitive demands before he is developmentally ready for them is a sure recipe for attentional problems. Other common cognitive stressors include piling on too much information or too many steps; not presenting the information clearly or, for that matter, in a way that the child finds interesting; or going through material too quickly—or too slowly.

We often find that children or adolescents demonstrating a serious lack of motivation are chronically hypoaroused. All too often they turn to things like video games or junk food to up-regulate themselves, but, for the reasons we'll look at in chapter 11 this leaves them even more drained and so even more unmotivated. That is not to say that when we do Self-Reg they will suddenly spring to life. But just reframing our view of the child's behavior has a powerful effect on his motivation because he picks up on our feelings about him, whether voiced or not, and there is still a tendency to see a child who doesn't appear to be interested in learning as lazy or undisciplined, an "underachiever."

Tyler was a classic case of a child whose tank was always empty, running on fumes to keep going. That is why he had all those problems—whether going to sleep or sitting still or paying attention. His parasympathetic nervous system just couldn't keep up with the demands that his sympathetic nervous system was making on it. But once Cynthia started doing Self-Reg with him—started figuring out why he was constantly burning adrenaline—she was able to reduce many of the stressors that were exacerbating his attentional problems, rather than just trying to cope with the symptoms. Especially important for Tyler was reducing the "visual noise" in his environment: The less clutter and the plainer the walls, the better he could pay attention.

There will, of course, always be times when a child isn't paying attention simply because he can't be bothered. So we need to learn how to recognize when this is the case, versus when his lack of attention is because his energy is low. Fear is certainly a way to force children and teens to buckle down even when they're running on empty, but it comes at a great cost to their mental and physical health. Fear causes them to dip deep into their reserves, with all the negative consequences we looked at in the preceding chapters: if not immediately, then later.

"Sit Up Straight and Concentrate!"

Our immediate inclination when a child is easily distracted may be to press him to *try harder*, when this may be the very opposite of what he needs. The self-control mantra tells the challenged child: "Sit still." "Stop fidgeting." "Be quiet." "Pay attention." In many cases what we should be saying is "Move around. Fidget some more. Hum to yourself. Close your eyes." Figure out what helps you to concentrate—and do it.

That starts, of course, with the child learning what helps him feel calm. All of the rest and recovery strategies we've looked at in the previous chapters apply in full force here: sleep, diet, exercise, and reducing environmental stressors. On top of this we need to explore "active" restorative strategies in the cognitive domain, ongoing ways of engaging attention that also reduce stress. These might include reading for pleasure, listening to music, cooking, bird-watching, or nature walks. But every child has to learn what helps *him* to concentrate, and sometimes what they come up with may strike us as the very opposite of what we think they should be doing.

Your child who says he needs to have the radio on when he does his homework may actually need the arousing effects of the music to up-regulate into the calmly alert and focused state necessary for getting the homework done. The child who insists on doing her homework lying on the couch may be unconsciously reducing the energy she must expend to keep her body upright; relaxed and alert, she's freeing more energy for concentration. The child who draws all the curtains and insists on doing his homework in low light may find visual stimulation draining.

What is critical for you as a parent is to recognize that you may have to let go of some of your assumptions—perhaps thinking that a child *should* sit up or have lots of light or have a quiet space to work. Maybe this is what works for you or what was required of you as a child, but it may not work that way for your child, or for each of your children the same way. What matters is what works for *this* child.

In everyday moments when stressors of any kind make it hard for you or your child to sustain attention, even just a few minutes meditating or focusing on the cold air coming into your nose and the warm air going out may be enough to revive focus. A mindfulness moment provides a brief restorative pause. But don't assume that because you've read that a lot of children benefit from this type of exercise, your child will, and that if he doesn't, then you have to force him to sit still and stop fidgeting so that he can meditate!

The Role of the Interbrain in Attention and Learning

We saw above how the interbrain plays a critical role in the child's development of pattern-recognition skills. But of course the interbrain is also essential for the sorts of executive functions mentioned earlier: for example, ignoring distractions, ordering your thoughts. And it's important to bear in mind that the interbrain dynamic applies to the child's interactions with all of the important adults in her life and her peers, not just her parents. One of the biggest challenges for children with attentional problems is that, so often, the interbrain contributes to rather than mitigates their problems, especially in the school setting. Teachers get anxious or angry. Coaches get frustrated. Other kids get impatient with them or simply lose interest in the classmate who is unable to comfortably engage with them or class activities.

The more anxious or frustrated the child becomes, the more irritated everyone with whom she's interacting tends to become. So the child experiences an escalating drain on her reserves as *others* add to her stress load when, as parents, teachers, coaches, or friends, we should have been helping her to deal with her stress. *The ability to pay attention is as much a function of the interbrain as the ability to regulate emotions. It's how we respond that is critical for how well children can attend.*

This is not simply a matter of taking extra time to teach a child metacognitive skills. Most important is whether we reduce the child's stress and the load on her senses to shift the energy/tension balance in favor of energy. For that to be possible, we have to try to put ourselves in the child's shoes, attempt to truly understand how that child *feels*.

Without this critical first step we can inadvertently add to the child's stress load, perhaps under the misguided assumption that we are actually helping her. For example, it was recently discovered that in many children with ADHD the parts of the brain that support sustained concentration grow more slowly. We are a long way from understanding cause and effect, but the research provides a further insight into how we can add to these children's stress by imposing the same cognitive demands on them as on typically developing children.

It has also been discovered that children with attention difficulties often operate on a faster time scale than typically developing children. I asked an adult friend of mine with ADHD about this, and she told me that when, as an adult, she finally starting taking medication for her ADHD, she suddenly felt everything "slow down." For the first time in her life she felt "in step with the rest of the world" and under so much less stress.

It might not be possible to figure out all the nuances of a child's cognitive makeup—not your own child, not any child. I'm still not sure I fully understand Tyler's needs. What I could understand was how stressed he felt, which is why he took refuge in his handheld game. So to help him we worked with his mom and the school staff to institute some calming routines. As surprising as it might sound, sometimes all Tyler needed to stay calm was just a reassuring voice or look—something his teachers found easier to deliver once they understood and saw the effect on him. For him this was a cue that he wasn't alone, that a caring adult was there to support him should he need it.

But I've stressed all along that the emphasis in self-regulation is on the *self*. Tyler's mom and his teachers were developing all sorts of effective techniques to regulate Tyler. How could they help him learn to do this on his own? This, ultimately, is every parent's question, especially around schoolwork: How do we get our kids to sit quietly at that kitchen table and do their homework without our having to stand over them to make sure the work gets done? To embrace and not run from the academic challenges that will keep growing larger as kids progress through primary, secondary, and postsecondary school? To resist the temptations and distractors that may *capture* attention, but at a significant cost to kids' ability to *pay* attention?

Being Quiet Versus Being Calm

For the child who is having problems paying attention, one of the most important things for him to become aware of is what's happening inside and around him. This means becoming aware of his physical state: Is he feeling hungry, thirsty, tired, hot? He also needs to become aware of when and why he is so drawn to playing a video game, for example. And he needs to become aware of how this leaves him feeling when he turns it off. It's equally important that he become aware of how he feels after the sorts of activities that refresh and restore energy.

There are many types of awareness: body awareness, emotional, visual-spatial, time, action, sensorimotor. The important thing is to slow things down so the child can attend to the feeling, the thought, the cause and effect. But maybe the most important awareness of all that the child needs to develop is *what it feels like to be calm*. As we saw in the previous chapter, quiet and calm are distinctly different biological states, yet all too often a child hears "calm down" as meaning "be quiet"—and the frustrated parent or teacher may mean it just that way. But the two states are not at all the same. A child can force himself to be quiet, even though he is all churned up inside. Calmness comes only from the pleasurable feeling of releasing the tension in our body and mind and being aware that this is happening. It is this combined physical, emotional, and cognitive state of calm that promotes restoration and growth, which in turn supports thought processes and learning.

One of the big benefits of a mindfulness meditation exercise is that it gets us to focus on a number of different sensations that we tend to tune out: things like the feeling of the floor against our feet, the atmosphere in the room, our own emotions. Ordinarily we are as oblivious to the world inside and around us as we are to the gravity backpack on our shoulders. Kids who have trouble paying attention are typically oblivious to what's going on inside and around them, often because as infants they never fully developed the capacity to find patterns—to bring chaos into coalescence. Children with significant attentional problems may have never experienced a sense of calm in the flow of information coming from different receptors; instead they may have become accustomed to internal chaos as their norm, and their behavior has mirrored that. Until they actually experience a state of calm, they can't know what it is. Once they have experienced it, the next step is to help them develop the self-awareness to recognize when they need to calm themselves and how to do it.

In our clinical work with children, and as we have introduced Self-Reg to parents and children through schools and community programs, we realized very early on that the biggest mistake we could make with such children was to rely too much on abstract words to help them in this process. You have to start off with very simple words and ideas that they can relate to (a gas tank empty or full or a computer that crashes when you try to run too many programs at once) or use props like Raggedy Ann and Buzz Lightyear dolls, asking if they feel floppy like Raggedy Ann or stiff like Buzz. Another hugely important discovery: Quite often a child needs to calm down a little before he becomes aware of the "pain in his tummy" or the "tingling in his arms and legs." When you ask a child who is in a low-energy/high-tension state what he is feeling in his body, you will usually get the answer "nothing." Perhaps surprisingly, the same point applies to older children and adolescents. They begin to calm down and then suddenly report something like a knot in their stomach that's "been there forever!"

When you do Self-Reg, you experiment with different techniques, watching your child's face and body to see what is having a calming effect. Tyler discovered that one thing he found calming was the tactile sensation when his mom gave him a firm back scratch or head massage. (He hated any kind of feathery touch.) The most important point of this was *for him to notice the effect* of the massage on the tension in his neck, shoulders, trunk, and legs. As they identified his stress triggers, reduced stressors where they could, and had him actively participate in his choices, the combination loosened that tether to his handheld game device. Without that body awareness he couldn't reach the last stage of Self-Reg: knowing when he needed to rest and recover and how to go about it.

The Importance of Feeling Safe

The most important element in helping any child or teen shift from survival brain to learning brain is that he feels safe and secure: physically, emotionally, and as a learner.

I am a big believer in the idea that kids need to spend a lot of time in nature to promote the development of these systems. But it was when I took a group of teenagers through the same woods that my kids have grown up in that I realized how much help some children need to feel safe and secure in nature. The teens I was with—boys and girls—were startled by things that my children would never have been bothered by, such as the sound of a squirrel chattering, a bird rustling in the bushes, the buzzing insects. They found the natural world both foreign and frightening. They moved gingerly over terrain that I was used to seeing my children race over. But then, my children had grown up in these woods. Lord knows how many times they had tripped and fallen down and come scurrying over to be lifted onto my shoulders. But in this way they had learned, from their own experience—no instruction necessary—how to adjust to the sensations coming from their feet and legs.

For these teens, climbing over a log, clambering down a rock, or walking through knee-high grasses where they couldn't see the ground made them anxious. Unsure of their footing, they were primed to be startled. They couldn't get out of survival brain mode and visibly sighed with relief when we finally got back to the parking lot. Far from being restorative, the walk had been an ordeal. When they got back to town, they immediately retreated to the closeted environment in which they felt safe, a world with artificial stimulation and barely any physical activity.

The reason animals can rest and recover in their burrows is precisely that that's where they feel most safe. Given a child's need for that same sense of security, this was perhaps the biggest lesson Tyler taught us: He was without a burrow! Not necessarily because his school wasn't a safe place or because there was no place at home for him to retreat when he needed to, but first and foremost because *he didn't feel safe in his own body*, and I suspect he never had.

Tyler Tunes In

This is why, to help Tyler, his mom and teachers started off with the sorts of very simple games and exercises described earlier. Sometimes something even more basic helped, such as having him feel the seat he was sitting on or the floor as he stood up. The goal was to make him aware of the information coming from his proprioceptors so that he was grounded: secure while he was just sitting or standing.

Breathing exercises that promote self-regulation seemed like a good idea to start with Tyler. They're simple and many teachers weave these calming moments into the school day with good outcomes. But focusing on breathing while sitting in a lotus position only made Tyler more agitated.

They tried other playful games that would develop his body awareness and eventually discovered that he loved to dance. When Tyler's attention began to wane on homework assignments, they would take a play break that included movement, sensory play—and salsa dancing! Cynthia and Tyler's teachers also took steps to eliminate extraneous visual distractions and noise that most of us might not notice but that triggered an alarm response for Tyler. Ultimately, though, Tyler's motivation to develop his self-awareness had to be entirely intrinsic. He had to learn how to track not just birdcalls or social cues but himself: his own bodily states and needs.

Just as the point of learning dance steps is to help the child become aware of his sensations as he is performing these actions, hands-on, step-by-step craft activities with you at the kitchen table have the same effect on the roots of attention. Tearing pictures and colors from magazine pages and pasting them down to create a collage or making homemade play dough from scratch (the measuring, mixing, hands-on mashing, and shaping) are not only creative activities. The Self-Reg science at work is that the activity helps attune the child's awareness to the internal sensory information that helps coordinate movement and position.

As in the mindfulness yoga class, the critical element is to slow down and accentuate the movements you want your child to practice, just as you would accentuate word sounds for children having trouble with language. *Really* slow the moves down until the child can feel the different parts of his body involved and the rhythm of each movement.

Tyler was, of course, a special case: a child born with a number of sensorimotor challenges that made it difficult for him to engage in the body awareness–building activities that every child naturally goes through. But the larger lesson Tyler taught us was that every child needs to be sure not just of his footing but of what is happening to him, especially within him. The more secure the child feels in new environments, the more he pays attention to what's going on inside and around him.

The Awakening of Awareness: Theirs—and Ours

By the time Tyler turned twelve he had made such great strides in his self-regulation and attention that he was able to discontinue his medication. Our intention had never been to get Tyler off his meds. But he had always hated the effects and was now old enough—and had developed the skills needed—to monitor his arousal states and recognize when he needed to take steps to calm himself.

I had one more important lesson to learn from Tyler, though, perhaps the most important lesson of all.

At one of our last sessions Tyler was moving restlessly about the room while I was talking, and, I confess, I became a little exasperated and blurted out: "What is the point of my trying to explain all this if you won't even look at me?" He then repeated word for word everything I had just said. He hadn't been like this in the beginning, but now he was taking in the world—just not in the way that I expected a thirteen-year-old to behave.

The better I got to know Tyler, the more I realized that we must never stop digging when we are working to understand a child—or ourselves! This point applies to how we interact with all children. We so automatically assume that children see the world through the same eyes that we do: not just that they process the same details but that they make the same judgments and have the same attitudes. If we give them a chance to describe their experience and we listen to what they say, we may discover that their view is completely different from our own. We may be surprised to discover how much we can learn from looking at the world through their eyes, rather than imposing our perception on them. But most important of all is that we actually see and value our children for who they are, rather than measuring them against some sort of personal or cultural standard.

The truth is that Tyler looks and acts differently from other kids his age. He walks a little pigeon-toed; wears his pants hiked a little too high; puts on the same shirt every single day; always has on a goofy hat that other kids make fun of but that he thinks is incredibly cool. He asks what sometimes sound like really weird questions, until you think about them. He doesn't much like the things that most kids his age do. He does have a few friends, although not many, and they seem to be as quirky as he is. Meeting new people is stressful for him; he is an absolute delight when he knows you and easily distressed when he doesn't.

The more I thought about him, the more I wondered: What exactly were we trying to accomplish? It was certainly not to make Tyler more like other kids: to change him, make him "more normal." No, what we wanted was for him to experience how it feels to be calm, alert, and learning. To know when he was tense and running on empty and how to recover, to learn when his alarm was sounding and how to turn it off on his own. All too often we confuse our needs with the child's: *We seek to make children like Tyler more manageable, rather than self-managing.*

I still think of Tyler as a hummingbird, full of restless energy. His "jags"—sudden obsessions that might last anywhere from a week to several months—reflect a child who is eager and able to learn. He is what I would call "intellectually omnivorous"—constantly discovering new appetites and devouring new interests. But he has become so much better at getting the restoration he needs, and as a result he is happier, smiling and cheerful much of the time.

Yes, he has his ups and downs (these days, far more ups than downs), and yes, he still finds certain social situations difficult. The biggest difference is that now he knows when he is becoming agitated and what to do to calm down.

The critical factor was the Self-Reg that Cynthia did at home with him. She practiced self-awareness exercises with him regularly and had to work hard at first to help him recognize when he was tired, hungry, cold, or even sick. The signs were obvious to her, but teaching Tyler to recognize these signs sometimes felt as if he were an infant all over again; and maybe that was the point. Maybe he hadn't ever fully mastered these important aspects of awareness, or maybe he had forgotten them. Perhaps his stress overload had somehow blunted what he had learned as an infant. Maybe he just needed us to see him and support him for what he is, rather than assail him for what he is not.

There was a time not so long ago when children were diagnosed with learning disorders when the real problem was that they couldn't hear the teacher or see the chalkboard. Of course their attention drifted. Of course they couldn't learn the way their classmates did. Fraught over failure, they might act out, and then their behavior became a problem. A correct diagnosis leading to the needed eyeglasses or hearing aid made all the difference. Looking back, it seems barbaric that we would have been harsh with such children or completely ignored them; but the situation is no different today in how we respond to children who are easily distracted or highly impulsive because of constrictions in their roots of attention.

EIGHT

A New Lens for Looking at Social Development

The Social Domain

It was a kindergarten class like all the others I had ever visited: noisy, happy, spilling over with exuberance. And a couple of kids who were mesmerizing to watch. I knew right away that the behavior of each of these children was telling me something important; it just took me a little while to figure out what that was.

The first was a little boy who never let go of his teacher's skirt when they were in the classroom. Wherever she went he tagged along, and she didn't even seem to notice his presence. When I mentioned this to her afterward she was surprised; he was such a fixture at her side that she hardly noticed anymore.

The second was a bossy little guy who seemed to have appointed himself second-in-command. I watched as he told other children that they were using the wrong colors, or how to hold their crayon, or when to put their coloring away. He never seemed to let up and be content with quietly doing his own work.

The third was a little girl sitting by herself in a corner reading a book. Or rather, pretending to read, saying whatever came into her head as she flipped through the pages. I watched as a teaching assistant came and stood over her and asked what the book was about. A look of panic flashed across the child's face, and as soon as she could, she buried herself in the book again.

It was fascinating to watch these very different children: the one so drawn to being close to an adult; the second assuming this role for himself; and the third shunning contact with an adult. As discreetly as I could, I tracked them over the course of the morning. One of the most interesting things I observed was when the children all gathered to sing. The teacher used an interactive whiteboard to flash the words of the songs on the screen, so the children weren't just getting the physiological benefits of singing but were also working on their reading skills. The children were really into it and shouting out which of their favorites they wanted to sing next. Except for these three little kids.

I wasn't sure if the problem was that they couldn't read or that it was a little too loud for them or that they just couldn't keep up with the pace; but whatever the problem, what was clear was that all three found the experience stressful. I could see both little boys mumbling words and every so often getting the right one—kind of the way I do when I'm singing the Canadian national anthem in French and don't want anyone around me to notice that I don't know all the words. Meanwhile, the little girl had shrunk into a corner, seemingly trying to make herself invisible. She sat there the whole time, staring at the screen, not making a sound, a strained look on her face.

At recess these three kids trotted outside with all the other children, but with none of their zest. The one little boy—the one who stuck so closely to his teacher's side—tried to join a bunch of other kids who were playing with a dirty sock that was lying on the ground. As far as I could tell, the game consisted of seeing who would be brave enough to touch the sock. One after another, the children would approach the sock and then tear away shrieking. This little guy tried to show that he was having as much fun as the others, but I suspected that he had no more idea than I did what the point of the game was.

The others were being silly, but he just looked awkward. What was most painful to see was that the others didn't pay the least bit of attention to him. It wasn't hard to understand why he was holding on to his teacher's skirt whenever he could; his social arousal must have been right through the roof.

The second little boy headed straight for the junior end of the playground to play with the four- and five-year-olds. They were building a fort; or rather, the younger kids were building a fort. He was issuing orders.

The little girl went off by herself to one of the swings, her head bent, slowly rocking back and forth. Seeing this, one of the teachers went up to her and led her by the hand to a group of other children who were playing tag. But as soon as the teacher left to go attend to a different child, the little girl made a beeline straight back to the swing. As far as I could tell, she didn't talk to one single child the entire recess, and when it was over she trooped silently back into the classroom. Her response to the social arousal she was feeling was to withdraw into herself, eschewing the support that she could have received from the adults around her or from other children as well.

All three of these children were having trouble coping with the social demands of kindergarten. Every parent worries about their child having good social skills: knowing what others are feeling and thinking; making friends; knowing when to come to them or go to the teacher for help. Even before they can walk we're taking them to the park or on playdates and trying to teach them these skills. But watching these three children, it was plain to see that something much more basic is involved.

Some kids master these skills so much more easily than others. That's puzzling when you consider that, as the interbrain shows us, the human brain comes into the world primed to hook up with other brains. But some kids can do this only with their parents and not with other kids; some can do it only with kids they know well; and some can't do it at all. What I wanted to understand was, of course, why this might be the case for these particular children but also, more important, what we could do to help. Simply telling the two little boys how important it was to look at and listen to what other children were doing wasn't going to help them learn how to fit in; and forcing the little girl to join a group wasn't going to have the slightest effect on her willingness to do so on her own.

The Glue of Connectedness: Neuroception

We need others. Our brains need other brains. Not just when we are babies but throughout our lives. But by the same token, other brains can be such a stress. How can one and the same phenomenon have such opposite effects? The answer lies in what the great American physiologist Steve Porges dubbed *neuroception*: a system deep in the brain for monitoring whether people and situations are safe or potentially dangerous.

I use a video that Steve sent me to give parents and teachers a glimpse of what neuroception looks like in action. Emerson, an eight-month-old boy, is watching his mom intently. He is smiling happily and making little chortling noses when she suddenly blows her nose. He is instantly alarmed. But this lasts only a moment; Mommy responds with soothing vocalizations and a big smile, which returns him to smiling and gurgling. But then she has to blow her nose again, and exactly the same scenario plays out. This sequence gets repeated four times, each with the same result, and then Mom blows her nose really hard and Emerson responds in a way that never fails to elicit loud laughs from the audience: a mixture of wide-eyed astonishment and fear. He jerks back so violently that, were it not for the harness on his high chair, he would topple right over. It's a powerful example of how strong the fight-or-flight response is in a baby who hasn't even learned to walk yet.

We experience just this sort of sequence of events with our babies all the time. There is no conscious judgment operating here: The baby's reaction is an automatic response governed by an alarm system housed in the middle of the brain. When this system registers danger, it sets off all those internal processes that we looked at in chapter 1 and external ones as well: His eyes and mouth open wide, and he raises his eyebrows, tenses his trunk, and flails his arms and legs. When the alarm system registers safety, it sends a message to contract the muscles around the eyes and cheeks, his body relaxes, and he laughs.

This is a critical function of the interbrain: to turn the alarm off. The frontal parts of the baby's brain that are growing most robustly in the early years of life house the systems that serve our ability to calm ourselves down: to tell ourselves after the fourth time that Mommy is only blowing her nose because she has a cold, or that the car alarm that keeps going off intermittently is just a car alarm that isn't working properly. It is the caregiver—the external brain—who has to play this role of turning off the alarm in the early years. The more gently and consistently she does this, the more the baby's "learning brain" stays active, so that the baby can process things like language and the meanings of facial expressions, not to mention colds and car alarms.

But neuroception cuts both ways: Just as the baby's expressions and movements are automatic, so too are Mom's. When I teach students about co-regulation, I show them a video clip of a mother and her baby son happily playing together: Their gestures, facial expressions, and emotions are finely attuned. But then the baby slaps Mommy a little too hard and she suddenly becomes angry and withdraws from the interaction. The baby instantly looks frightened and his body becomes rigid. Mommy sees this and looks deeply concerned, then instantly softens her gaze and leans in. The baby responds in kind: His body visibly relaxes and his smile returns.

Mommy's facial expressions are every bit as automatic throughout the sequence as her baby's. At the beginning both have pleased expressions—shining eyes and smiles. Through the sparkle in her eyes, the rhythm and pitch of her vocalizations, and the caresses that she gives, a caregiver serves as a vital source of arousal, up-regulating the baby to feed, play, learn. But then Mommy's nostrils flare and her brows furrow; baby's eyes and mouth open wide and his eyebrows rise; Mommy's eyebrows contract and her eyes narrow; and then both return to their pleased expressions, shining eyes, and mutual smiles. This remarkable micromanaged dance plays out on their faces as they move from mutual arousal to anger, fear, concern, and then back to happiness in a matter of just a few seconds.

Through their facial expressions, gestures, movements, posture, and vocalizations, they not only signal their feelings to each other but also trigger each other's feelings. At the beginning we see a shared emotion: Both are happy; then they shift into discordant emotional states—Mom is angry, baby is frightened; then it's baby's turn to be angry and Mom is frightened; and then they return to a shared state of relief mixed with happiness. Physiologically they go from optimal arousal to momentary hyperarousal and then back to calm.

It is hard to describe what is happening here in terms of "shared understanding"—this is a much more primitive co-regulatory process in which each responds automatically, both behaviorally and viscerally, to what the other is feeling. It is, in fact, the foundation on which mindreading—the ability to know what others are thinking or feeling from their body language—is built.

Neuroception is the glue that binds together not just the two individuals but the species as a whole. The system supports co-regulation and safety: *one's own, and that of another.* It activates internal processes to deal with a threat and external behaviors that signal when one is distressed. The system also activates internal responses when we observe someone in distress—our own limbic system resonates with theirs—and external behaviors that serve to soothe another who is in distress (we smile and offer comforting gazes or gestures). When this core system is operating smoothly, there is secure attachment or friendship; when it is obstructed or has too many glitches, this can have profound consequences for the child's social development.

Social Connectivity Begins in the Still Face Paradigm

Watching videos of the Still Face experiment is just like watching baby Emerson freaking out when his mother blows her nose. The Still Face experiment is very hard on the baby, but Tronick has shown that it is no less stressful for older children, and it turns out that it is just as hard on the mother. One of Tronick's research assistants conducted a variation of the Still Face in which she had college students play the role of either the infant or caregiver. The students who acted the part of the infant reported feeling anxious, frustrated, and even panicky; the students who acted the part of the unresponsive mother reported feeling distressed, anxious, and even ashamed.

But you don't need to run an experiment in a lab in order to understand how these students were feeling. How many of us have walked into our boss's office expecting to be congratulated for some fine piece of work we have done, only to be met by a scowl? Our brain puts us on high alert and we go instantly into fight or flight. Or think of how you feel if you are trying to negotiate a deal and the person opposite doesn't say a word. It's a common bargaining ploy: Make someone squirm and they'll start to talk too much or give away too much. There are even dating manuals out there that promote the fine art of emotional manipulation and passive-aggressive behavior: how to gain control by being nonresponsive if not outright hostile. But why should an angry or nonresponsive face make us squirm or lose self-control?

Of course, we don't all respond in the same way to these sorts of "social threats." Some of us will just laugh and shrug it off while others will look for someone's skirt to cling to or withdraw into a corner. Our individual responses are the product of our unique biological temperament together with the history of social encounters that began when we were infants, long before we got into kindergarten.

What we are looking at here is the effect of *social arousal*. Some adults find any form of interaction overly stressful: so much so that they shy away from any kind of social event, even with family and friends. Others crave the energy that they enjoy only in social settings. But regardless of where our "social arousability meter" is set, our neuroceptive system is constantly looking for safety. When it senses this, we feel calm and alert or relaxed as needed. When it senses a threat, we are left feeling tense, edgy, drained. In the latter case we might behave like an eight-month-old in the Still Face experiment and try to bring a nonresponsive or unsettling social partner back. When this fails, we can become apathetic and disorganized or find it difficult to look at, much less communicate with, the other person.

Perhaps the most fascinating thing about this system is how it monitors someone's body language—their tone of voice, gestures, facial expressions—*beneath the threshold of conscious awareness*. These social cues come in under the radar, so to speak. In fact, this unconscious monitoring system is far more important to how an interaction goes than the words that are exchanged. I was once in a meeting with a school principal who was eager to have her school join our Self-Reg initiative when a nine-year-old girl, Rachel, was brought to her office, in trouble for disrupting her class. Apparently this was something of an ongoing problem they'd been having with Rachel: She would act up and try to get the other children sitting at her table to do the same. They had cautioned her several times about this and changed her seating partners, but this was the second time that she had been sent to the principal's office.

What followed was a fascinating example of neuroception in action. The principal, very conscious of my presence—in fact, she introduced me to the little girl as a doctor who specialized in just her sort of problem—said all the right things: that she wanted to put this behavior behind them, help Rachel turn over a new leaf and become the sort of student her parents would be proud of. She even talked about hyperarousal and how the child needed to recognize when this was happening and what to do to calm herself down. The problem in all this, however, was that through her body language the principal was conveying a very different message. She was frowning, her voice was harsh, and she was drumming her fingers on her desk. I could see Rachel quailing at this nonverbal onslaught, and then she froze. It was clear to me that she hadn't processed much of what had been said to her: The color had drained from her face and she had to be prodded at the end to promise that she would stop behaving like this.

When the little girl left or, rather, fled from the office, the principal turned to me and, with a look of chagrin on her face, asked: "What am I supposed to do with a child like that?" I treated her question as a genuine request to brainstorm, rather than an emotive expression of the frustration and perhaps disappointment in herself that she was feeling. I said that the child seemed to be especially sensitive to tones of voice, facial expressions, and gestures and talked about how important it was to get her calmly focused and alert in order to begin to process what the principal had been trying to impart. And we explored why Rachel seemed to be having this problem: something that, we both soon recognized, wasn't just a consequence of poor social awareness and interpersonal skills but was tied to her problems in physical and emotional arousal. But the question on both our minds was how to promote her social comfort level.

The principal in question turned out to be a stunning example of how quickly our body language changes once we become aware of what we've been doing unconsciously. Overnight her interactions with Rachel were transformed. But it was not because she made a conscious effort to keep her hands in her lap; rather, it was because *she suddenly saw Rachel in a completely different light.* Where before she had found the little girl's behavior irritating, now she recognized how stressed the child was, and she immediately lowered her voice and her eyes.

"Social Animals" Need Social
Interaction—and Sometimes Fear It

Of course, there are also those who exploit the feelings of discomfort that we experience in Still Face–like encounters. Sadly, the person who intentionally manipulates this need that we all have is left not with the feelings of distress described by the undergraduates playing the role of nonresponsive caregiver but with a sense of power and control. But why should they have such an extremely self-centered impulse, which runs so contrary to the basic needs of social engagement? The answer to this question is complex and will ultimately take us, in the following chapter, deep into the prosocial domain. But the starting point lies in neuroception: in a stress-response system that has become tilted toward "fight."

The domineering individual has become habituated to seeing others as threats: The employee who has done well is going to ask for a raise; the businesswoman he is negotiating with is trying to take advantage of his weakness; the attractive woman at the bar is going to reject his advances. And just like an eight-month-old who becomes angry in the Still Face experiment, these individuals become aggressive. They strive to dominate as a way of coping with the anxiety that they habitually feel in social situations.

Conversely, the adult who is habitually submissive or who shies away from all social encounters isn't that way simply because she was born passive or is "congenitally shy." For whatever reason, strangers produce in her a surge of adrenaline that dictates a flight response that is easily pushed to freeze. Her need to withdraw isn't just emotional but also physiological: a defense mechanism to promote parasympathetic functioning.

These patterns can be hard to break, simply because they have become so entrenched. The dictatorial little boy whom I watched in the kindergarten class hadn't been born that way. I don't think that he was just acting out something he had experienced at home (although this might well have been a factor). Rather, he was confused about the subtle emotional currents swirling about him, and the more uncertain he felt, the more domineering he became. The little girl who bolted to the edge of the playground wasn't simply "socially anxious" but was seeking to reduce her stress in the only way she knew.

It's a phenomenon that helps us understand the great paradox of social interaction. We are indeed social animals: We come into the world with a brain that not just is receptive to but actually needs another brain in order to feel safe. The baby sends signals conveying a need for help; the caregiver responds with signals conveying the presence of that help. If a caregiver is unable to provide those signals—perhaps because she finds the infant's needs confusing—the result is likely to be hyperarousal across a number of domains: biological, emotion, cognitive, and social.

A young couple once shared with me their frantic upset because their nine-month-old baby son, Zack, had laughed when his mother had started to cry: "Does this mean," the father asked, "that our son has a sadistic streak?" As gently as I could, I explained that this was just an automatic reaction to Mom's crying, which had set off Zack's alarm system. It was a fear response, and it would be a few more years before Zack would begin to regulate his emotional responses. I could literally feel and not just see their tension release as they understood the point. The same is true for other automatic reactions, such as anger, although it's much harder for a lot of parents to understand that this too is just a primitive response to a perceived threat. I remember one mom in particular who got terribly upset when her baby daughter was angry; we had to help her see that she needed to stay calm herself and soften her response. The problem is that when a parent responds angrily to a baby's angry outbursts, this intensifies the child's neuroceptive sense of threat, which is what led to the anger display in the first place.

Social Threats Trigger Survival Brain and Fight-Flight-or-Freeze Response

If this sort of miscommunication becomes habitual, the child will shy away from what she most desperately needs when she is frightened: the calming presence of a caregiver or, at an older age, the calming presence of other children and adults. She will turn inward, into herself. That is what is really involved if we go into fight or flight: The brain has shifted from the most recent human evolutionary adaptation for dealing with threat, social engagement, to a much more primitive mechanism designed to protect an isolated animal: the so-called survival brain.

That is very much how it feels to be in fight or flight: on one's own, desperate to escape. It is extremely hard for children to use words to communicate when they are feeling this way, but we can help them by finding some nonverbal way for them to tell us when this happens. I remember one little girl, with the wonderful name of "Juniper" but known to all as Junebug, who would let Mommy and Daddy know when she was feeling overwhelmed by taking one of her dolls and putting it by itself in a corner of the dollhouse.

In fight or flight even the most benign of social acts can be interpreted as a threat. You remember Rosie of the evening meltdowns? One of the things she told me—several times, in fact—was that Mommy needed to stop yelling at her. But I had witnessed one of these occasions when Rosie got upset, and Mom hadn't even raised her voice, much less yelled. Yet that is how it felt to Rosie! And when she angrily told her mother to stop yelling, Marie did indeed raise her voice, because she was so frustrated and, for that matter, hurt by such an unjust accusation—in front of me, no less.

Instead of trying to reason with children who are experiencing this kind of negative bias or, what is much worse, discipline them, we have to bring them back to *the world of social engagement*, and for that to be possible we have to reestablish their sense of safety. The primary duty of the interbrain is *to make a child feel safe*. And it bears repeating that this is true for a very long time. It applies to life in general, not simply the dynamics of child rearing. But it is especially true for child rearing.

If it was simply about the pleasantness of feeling safe in social interactions, we might leave the issue at that: Sometimes you're going to feel comfortable and sometimes you're not, and that's life. But we've already seen how much more is involved here than just a subjective experience: Social arousal has a powerful effect on all the other domains of self-regulation. When a child feels threatened, the result can be sympathetic flooding (anger and aggression, flight or desertion) or parasympathetic flooding (withdrawal, paralysis). Such dysregulation can have a profound effect on her tension, emotions, and self-awareness. The restorative state that she experiences when she feels safe is more than just pleasurable. It is the state in which learning and growth can occur. In this case the growth is social: the skills that enable a child to deal with increasingly complex social challenges.

Anthropologists from Mars

So far we have looked at the importance of being calmly focused and alert for the processes of biological, emotional, and cognitive restoration and growth; but it turns out that it is every bit as important for the process of social growth. There is an analogy here to the recovery phase that is so important after a hard workout. Every gym rat knows that the most important part of a workout is the recovery phase afterward. Muscles grow only when they're challenged a bit past their comfort zone, then given a chance to repair. Something similar is true for social growth. We need a chance to think about social situations that we found challenging. But for far too many kids today, the fact that social media requires them to be always "on" means that there isn't enough downtime to think about when and why they felt threatened, which is essential for social growth. To the extent that their socializing is reduced to texts and screens, they also miss out on important aspects of face-to-face social engagement, in which the nuances of body language and facial expression, tone of voice, the rhythm of verbal exchanges, and physical context are so vital to social engagement and social learning and growth.

Indeed, it is somewhat misleading even to distinguish among biological, emotional, cognitive, and social growth, for all are inextricably tied together, really just different aspects of self-regulation. When a child feels safe, she enjoys interaction and can attend for longer periods to her caregiver or others. The more she pays attention, the more she begins to identify social patterns. This pattern recognition is quite literally being wired into her brain, enabling her to anticipate what someone is going to do from the look on their face or the sound or gesture that they make. And it enables her to express her own wishes and desires: wishes and desires that grow more complex as her social development and communication skills grow.

Another powerful video that we use for teaching purposes shows one of the dads we worked with lying on a bed with his baby son. The two of them are playing that time-honored game of making funny faces at each other. Both are taking intense pleasure in this activity, but after less than a minute the baby tires and turns his head away. Recognizing his son's need to take a break, the father relaxes and patiently waits for him to return, which he does after little more than thirty seconds. Then the two of them are right back at it, howling in delight at each other's antics.

Then we contrast this wonderful little pas de deux with a video of the two of them made just two months earlier, when they had first come to see us. They are engaged in the identical activity. But this time Dad responds intrusively when his son turns away. He badly wants to keep the interaction going, despite his son's clear message that he needs a break. As we watch, the baby becomes more and more agitated. But maybe the most poignant part of the whole sequence is the look on Dad's face as this transpires: You can easily read his feelings of rejection.

When they first came in, the two of them had a lot of trouble being in sync with each other, which was hard on both of them. We needed to get them into sync, so as to promote the wiring of the baby's social brain. As the baby's brain matures, he will not just be able to tolerate longer episodes of such engagement but will crave them. By following his son's lead and adjusting the amount of stimulation to the child's comfort level, the father was doing so much more than just spending a few quality minutes with his baby.

The micromanaged dance I described above would be getting ever more complex. This isn't a maturational or hardwired phenomenon but a learned behavior: the consequence of engaging in longer and more complex interactions. The child learns what to expect from certain facial expressions, vocalizations, gestures, and, indeed, words. The child is moving from box step to tango, and the skills that she is acquiring—mindreading, "mind displaying" (learning how to *show* what we're feeling through facial expressions and gestures), and language skills, for example—will enable her to dance with an ever larger number of partners.

Neuroception creates the safety zone where such social growth is possible. The process operating here is similar to and, in fact, inextricably tied to the child's emotional growth.

If for whatever reason a child finds social engagement difficult, this learning process will be diminished. The child will find herself overwhelmed by situations that outstrip her social abilities, and she will likely respond aggressively to or withdraw from such situations. Such a response then further compounds her social deficits, for she needs to engage in more complex interactions in order to develop more sophisticated mind-reading and mind-displaying skills.

The problem for such a child is that the social expectations on her are growing exponentially but she can't keep up. She can't "read" what strangers are feeling from their faces or has trouble following conversational twists and turns. She doesn't understand why what she said or did elicited a fear or anger or amused response on the face of the person she was engaging with. Everyone in the group seems to be on the same page except her; everyone laughs at the joke except her. This is the world that Temple Grandin painted when she described herself as feeling like "an anthropologist from Mars." It's a feeling that many children experience, and instead of being gently guided into social understanding, they are met with harsh and even punitive responses that send them into a heightened state of social anxiety.

This is precisely what was happening with Rachel, that little girl I sat with in the principal's office. She was having trouble processing the subtle emotional currents that swept through the class. The teacher would say something and everybody except her would laugh. Then, to cover this up, she would clown around. She had learned that by being silly she could get some of the other kids to be silly and in this way feel part of the group. But you could see that she was in a chronic state of social arousal, which was exacerbated by getting into trouble so much.

It is a state that many kids get used to: a state that many of us have gotten used to. In many cases the child will develop coping skills and perhaps even go on to shine in some endeavor, which can serve as its own coping strategy. This, in fact, is a reason why many adults who have chronic social arousal excel at their work: It is a way of functioning successfully in an environment in which one feels ill at ease. The anxiety is always there, however, like a constant hum in the background. And the effects of chronic social arousal are all too clear: the problems sleeping or eating, physical ailments with no clear cause, relationship problems, a general sense of malaise, or worse.

James: Tracing Growth in the Social Domain

The instant you meet James you like him. He's such an attractive sixteen-year-old. He's six feet tall, has a shock of brown hair and brown eyes, is lean and muscular, and seems "comfortable in his own skin," as my grandmother used to say about my friends. He looks you in the eye, shakes your hand firmly, tells you what a pleasure it is to meet you, listens attentively. He's the sort of person who immediately makes you feel comfortable, who inspires confidence. It's hard to believe that this attractive young man was once a fretful, agitated infant, a fussy toddler who couldn't cope with day care, a hyperactive schoolboy who couldn't make friends, couldn't keep it together when he got frustrated, and basically couldn't stay out of trouble.

From the earliest age James had been desperate to have playmates yet didn't know how to behave with other children. Mom described how she had tried to start him off playing with just one child and had invited a mom friend and her son over for an afternoon playdate. But the session ended with James, then three years old, hitting the other child quite hard on the back and mother and son fleeing from the house, leaving James bereft for hours.

James's early years were filled with this sort of incident. Mom tried scouts, and after the third meeting the troop leader asked her to hold James back for a year or two, explaining, "He's not ready yet." The same thing happened at the Y summer camp and even at one of the most advanced day cares in the city, although there he lasted around a month before the director advised that James should "get some help." Kindergarten, in Mom's words, "was a disaster from the get-go."

Yet on his own James could be a very sweet child, eager to

please, compliant in just about everything (except turning off the TV!). Put him with other kids, however, and he seemed to fall apart. Within minutes he could be yelling or pushing or worse. Unfortunately, the adult response to this behavior, repeated over and over, was to become exasperated: to insist that he be excluded from social activities, depriving him of the very experiences that he most needed to develop in this domain; or, worse still, to punish, even shame him. It was what happened in grade three, however, that drove the family to seek our help. He had been sent to the school psychologist because of a fight on the playground that he had started, for no apparent reason. This was the third time this had happened in the past month, and the psychologist said that if this behavior wasn't curbed, it could lead to "a full-blown conduct disorder."

The first thing that his parents, Sharon and Dave, did after this meeting was rush home and read as much as they could about "conduct disorder" on the Internet. The more they read—the fact that such children are at a heightened risk of dropping out of school early, taking drugs, ending up in the justice system, suffering from some mental illness—the more alarmed they became. They arranged for our clinical team to meet with them in the hope that perhaps we could "figure out a way to give him a different future," as Dave grimly remarked.

Really the only thing that stood out was that James had a lot of trouble mindreading, or registering nonverbal cues. There weren't any sensory challenges that we could identify: only a nine-year-old who didn't seem to notice the subtle messages that we send one another through our gestures or tone of voice. This would certainly explain why James found social interactions stressful. Imagine being in a foreign country where you neither knew the spoken language nor understood people's body language: You'd be uncertain about their intentions, out of step with what was going on around you, in a state of high alert.

James was clearly having trouble understanding other children's intentions and, as a result, was often anxious around other kids. Some children become very withdrawn in this situation; some become unresponsive; some flee from social situations; some become hyperactive or hyperreactive. In some cases they become performers, trying to "entertain" the other children without having to actually engage with them. Or, as in James's case, they can at different times be all of the above.

He found school especially difficult, which is hardly surprising considering that it is such an intense social environment. He would tend to shut down in class and become aggressive on the playground. This might be attributed to the fact that he was being teased rather mercilessly. The other children had figured out that they could get him to explode and then watch him get into trouble. Sometimes he bolted, which resulted one day in a call from the school principal complaining that she didn't have the manpower to keep an eye on him. As Sharon told me, it wasn't a friendly or solicitous call: The principal was clearly angry with this child who "was unable to control himself." Further, the principal's angry tone only made Sharon feel more like a failure. "I felt like I was being yelled at for being such a terrible parent."

In home videos taken when James was a baby we were able to see some of the range of behavior that his parents saw, and what we saw were two very different children: the one who was generally calm when he was playing with his parents; but another who looked lost and struggling to join in the fun at social events, like a birthday party or a Thanksgiving gathering. It was especially interesting to see how Sharon and Dave interacted with James in my office: They spoke softly and slowly, didn't gesture or smile too much, and waited very patiently whenever he paused before answering a question. There was a graceful rhythm among the three of them that reminded me of a waltz. It was clear that even in those earliest days, before they had sought our help, Sharon and Dave had begun to learn intuitively to tone down their nonverbal cues in order to keep James engaged. I noticed that James quickly became overwhelmed if one of our staff was too animated with him. And this, I suspected, explained what was going on at school. Too many kids, too many emotional currents swirling about, and multiperson interactions that were too fast for him to process, let alone grasp the effects of his clumsy attempts to join in.

Of all the different kinds of "threats" that children have to cope with, particularly difficult is not knowing what someone is going to do next, what they're supposed to do next, or even why everyone is laughing. This was likely the reason why James was getting into a lot of fights. Trying to reason with him when this happened was pointless. He would report that the other kid had started it, had hit him first. The teacher, who had seen exactly what had happened, would naturally be exasperated. This meant that, on top of everything else, James was constantly being accused of lying to avoid getting into trouble.

No doubt there was an element of truth in this that, if you think about it, makes pretty good sense. But what no one had ever considered was that he was describing exactly what he perceived! He may not have been "making things up" to keep from getting into trouble: He may have been reporting the situation exactly as he had experienced it. One of the big problems with the distortions produced by negative bias is that even though the child's version of events may bear little resemblance to reality, it is very much how the child experienced the event. With a kindled alarm, even the most innocuous of behaviors is perceived as a threat. A child gives a playful push and the hyperaroused child whacks him back because he experienced this as an attack. Or a teacher tells him to wait his turn and he starts crying because, in his mind, he has just been yelled at and his teacher hates him.

Of all the challenges that young James was dealing with, his greatest was simply that he was getting into trouble all the time at school. He was regularly put on detention during lunch hour or recess; on a couple of occasions he was suspended; and in third grade he was even expelled for two days. Word got around that he was a troublemaker, and this framed teachers' perceptions and expectations of him. Without realizing it, they would have a grim look on their face when they saw him, no matter what it was that he was doing. Whenever there was any sort of commotion in the classroom, James would be the first to be singled out.

Each year seemed to get a little worse, but it was not until grade five that he really started to fall apart. Hardly a day went by when he wasn't sent to stand by himself in the hall or down to the principal's office. He would wake up every morning dreading going to school and come home at the end of each day an emotional wreck. As a result, Sharon and Dave decided to try something bold, and the following year they moved him to one of the schools involved in our Self-Reg initiatives—the national drive to incorporate Self-Reg into all aspects of education for children, teachers and administrators, and parents. At the new school James found a new community of children and teachers and a sympathetic principal who was determined to help this little boy. She seemed to intuitively understand him. The principal suggested that James work with an educational assistant, and what unfolded over his sixth year was nothing short of amazing.

The educational assistant, Mr. Tela, was one of the gentlest and most patient people I have ever met. Right from the start he adopted the attitude that he would help James learn at whatever pace he was comfortable with, but for that to be possible James had to trust him. He would never yell, never pressure, and though there would be limits, they'd be enforced in a way that James clearly understood. Perhaps most important, he was naturally just like Sharon and Dave: spoke quietly and slowly, didn't gesture or gesticulate or move about too much, was very patient.

The teachers were all apprised of what was happening, and it was agreed that James would be allowed to leave the class whenever Mr. Tela felt the need. In the beginning this happened regularly: James and Mr. Tela would quietly get up and walk around the school, just chilling, until James was ready to go back. Just knowing that he had this freedom had a wonderfully calming effect, and his need to leave the class got less and less and had completely disappeared by Christmas, as had the oppositional outbursts with his teachers.

In their schoolwork Mr. Tela started by finding what James was really interested in, which turned out to be World War II. In short order James was reading voraciously and had become fascinated with history. Next would be the big challenge: math. With a variety of math games it turned out that his anxiety was the big reason why James had had so much trouble in math; in his mind it was better to not even try than to try and fail. But soon he was ready to tackle math too. James's confidence was growing by leaps and bounds. Within a remarkably short time—and I do mean remarkable—he had not just reached grade level across the board but was even starting to excel. How was all this possible?

The answer was that Mr. Tela made him feel safe, and the safer he felt, the better he could pay attention in class. But soon something even more remarkable started to happen: James began to build relationships. He was starting to be a part of the class, working well with the other children. What had appeared to be a problem in poor social skills was, in fact, a function of a much larger neuroceptive challenge. He had rarely experienced with his teachers the kind of nurturing social engagement that he had with his parents, and the heightened anxiety that he felt in school then led him to see threats where none were actually present.

The problem was that in school he had been yelled at too much, had gotten into trouble too often and been forced to apologize or concede that he was guilty of some infraction without really understanding what he had done wrong. What he *had* learned was that saying "I'm sorry" or "I won't do it again" would end the attack, yet this response only seemed to confirm in his teachers' eyes that he was indeed guilty. Yet he really didn't understand why people got so mad at him. So the whole system had become locked in a negative cycle, and that was the real reason why he had been heading toward a conduct disorder: not that he wasn't capable of learning social skills but that he was consistently treated as if he were refusing to make the effort required to control his behavior.

Mr. Tela called me one day and we brainstormed together how he might take James a little further in his social development. We decided that he would accompany James to basketball practice, even going onto the court as an assistant coach; and stay with James during recess, available if he should be needed but not hovering. I went to see for myself what was happening, and what I saw took me straight back to the three little kids in kindergarten. A bunch of boys were playing a game they had made up: a combination of baseball, soccer, and rugby. I'm sure that James had as much trouble under-standing the rules as I did, and after a while he gave up. When he had been a little boy and this sort of thing happened, he would retreat to the periphery of the playground and become engrossed in an insect or a stone. But this time I saw him go up to Mr. Tela and tell him something, then walk away. Throughout the recess I saw him move away from Mr. Tela to join a group of kids and then come back to ask or tell him something. I realized that what I was seeing was exactly the same thing as with the little boy who kept holding on to his teacher's skirt.

The more he experienced the calming effect of social engage-ment with Mr. Tela when he most needed it (which, for James, was in class and during recess) the more he could pay attention—to the other kids as much as to his teacher. He began to acquire the very social skills that had seemed to be beyond his reach. Everyone—his parents, his teachers, and his fellow students—commented on it. This did not happen instantly. There was no "magic moment" when he suddenly became like all the other kids. But slowly and surely the changes were happening, and the black moments when Sharon and Dave feared he would one day succumb to the dreaded "conduct disorder" were starting to become less and less frequent.

When we saw James at sixteen, we asked Sharon and Dave if there had been a moment when they suddenly realized that, instead of the dire future that had been painted for them, they had a glimpse of what sort of adult James might become. Both answered immedi-ately: It was when he was chosen to be the captain of his basketball team in his junior year in high school. This was big for what it said about his skills in basketball, but even more important was that this was the first time that he had received positive affirmation from an adult outside the family. It was also something that all the kids on the team respected, which was important for his self-esteem, which had always suffered.

There is no doubt that basketball was a big factor in helping James overcome his negative bias. The kid loved to play. He loved everything about the game: the challenge, the practice ethic, the camaraderie, and the payoff. He'd walk down the street bouncing a ball and spend hours on the driveway practicing his jump shot, and he spent one entire summer with his right hand bound up in a tensor bandage so that he'd be forced to learn how to "go left." He dreams now of playing pro one day and he may have a shot at it: Who knows? Whatever his eventual career path, James is such an engaging, well-adjusted, and well-rounded kid that he has all the qualities that set him up for success in adult life.

A child's natural interests often become a path for discovering the inner motivation that supports development of self-regulation across domains. Basketball was regulating for James in all five of our domains. A team wins only when it co-regulates, and the better his skills became, the more James attended to what everyone else was doing, not just in terms of what was happening on the court but off the court as well. He became increasingly good at engaging in and sustaining smooth social interactions. My feeling was that in no small part this was because of all the social-skills training he was getting in the locker room, going to restaurants together, traveling on the team bus, hanging out between games at tournaments.

James's story is a reminder of the "systems" interrelatedness of the five domains and the fact we need to look at each one and at all of them together when we're working on behavior in a particular domain. As James's social skills grew, his emotion regulation improved; the less anxious he felt in social situations, the more his social skills grew. The better his mindreading, the less draining he found social interactions. The less anxiety he felt, the better he paid attention: to what was going on inside him as much as around him. Even his self-discipline was improving. One of the more touching stories Sharon told me was of when he decided not to join the other kids in the hotel pool at a tournament but to go to bed early so that he could be fully rested for the game the next day. It may seem a little thing, but not for a child who throughout his childhood had characteristically become extremely hyperaroused when around other hyperaroused kids. For him now to have the self-awareness and self-regulation skills to make a choice that showed that he knew what was best for him—this was a huge step forward.

Self-Reg Creates the Scaffolding for Positive Social Engagement

Self-regulation in the social domain is essentially concerned with neuroception and the development of the social engagement system. The challenge: Social interaction can be a stressor in its own right, yet social engagement constitutes the child's first line of defense for dealing with stress. Self-Reg helps us see how parents—and later teachers—can help a child navigate this tension.

The fundamental unit of early child development is the dyad—the parent and child or caregiver and child—and the operations of the interbrain, which applies to *all* aspects of a child's development, and for an awful lot longer than we ever imagined. We are talking decades here, not weeks or months, and we are talking a developmental process that occurs step by step, with lots of stalled periods and backward steps. It is how we, the higher-order brain in the child's life, respond to that child's needs that shapes his or her trajectory.

Recall the mismatch we saw with Tyler in the previous chapter, between the kinds of interactions that he needed in order to develop his executive functions and the kinds of interactions that he was experiencing. He needed calming responses from those around him, not pressure to sit still or try harder, since that registers as threatening. The same point applied to James. *James did not need social skills in order to develop social engagement; he needed social engagement in order to develop social skills.*

We all want our children to be socially successful. For this to happen they have to be able to read nonverbal cues, and some children need a bit more help here—and endless patience! In the end all children can learn how to read social cues and the social milieu. It's never too late to learn to mindread, provided they are calm and alert. So we need to read a child's signs of heightened social arousal, like clinging to a teacher's skirt; identify when his alarm is going off and, when we see this happening, lessen his arousal by pacing interactions to suit his comfort level; help him learn to recognize when he is starting to become anxious in social situations; and help him develop self-regulating strategies that enable him to stay socially engaged. For a child can acquire the mindreading skills that he needs only in natural interactions; and he can engage in such natural interactions only when he feels safe.

NINE

The Better Self

Empathy and the Prosocial Domain

My son's hockey team was on its way to another victory in a season full of them, and Sasha, eleven years old at the time, was leading the way with goals. In the closing seconds he had the chance for a final tap-in to end the game with a flourish, but instead he passed to a trailing teammate so the boy could get on the board. How could Sasha have passed up the chance for this elegant, effortless final goal? I asked him that on the drive home, no doubt with a tinge of annoyance in my voice, and his answer, given a little stridently, still rings in my ears: "How the team does is more important than how I do, Dad."

Every single child is born with this capacity for selfless behavior and consideration for the well-being of others. Wired from the womb for it, in fact. It shows in spontaneous acts of caring or comforting from even the youngest child—a hug, a touch, a shared treat or toy. Research shows that infants can perceive and react to someone else's distress. As children grow, you hope that yours will be the one who shares easily, who thinks to comfort a friend or welcome the new kid. The one who can see beyond himself to the bigger picture and pitch in to help others. These acts seem simple enough. Yet our experiences demonstrate over and over again that making these choices is not always easy.

Prosocial" is one of those jargony terms that social scientists love to create. Experts debate its meaning, and as a parent you can live a lifetime and never need to use it. But as the antonym of "antisocial," "prosocial" stands for important aspects of what it means to be human—empathetic, generous, caring, and unselfish—someone of good character. We want our children to have those core qualities deep set, and we worry when we see any sign that suggests they don't. Few parents want their child to grow up to be ruthless, exploitive, or purely self-serving.

The wide range of antisocial behavior in children is a scary prospect, especially when we've seen the tragic outcomes in the extremes of teen shooters and cyberbullying. But in the everyday realm more familiar social cruelty and lack of regard for others is also disturbing: aggression and bullying, narcissism, and manipulative behavior that, though not violent, shows a chilling lack of conscience.

Even a child's simple lapses in consideration sometimes trigger an angry response, or concern if they come too often. These fears about character and conscience have particular power in our view of a child's development. No other developmental domain is so loosely defined and so highly charged with moral implication. Most parents can come to terms with a child's social, emotional, or learning challenges, but they have a deeper, more visceral response when it comes to matters of character. Yet recent neuroscience research shows that children described as having "character problems," from insensitive or hurtful behavior toward others to lying, cheating, or stealing, frequently reveal a pattern of poor arousal regulation, in particular regulation of their emotions. The effects of impulsivity, poorly managed negative emotions, inattentiveness, and gaps in social intelligence all emerge center stage in the prosocial domain.

Marshmallows: For One or for All?

More profoundly than any other, the prosocial domain is intrinsically stressful for your child because it invariably involves conflicts between what he feels or wants and what another child or group of others feels or wants. The classical view, which some still hold today, is that the child will never make this transition from self-serving to empathetic and considerate of others unless forced to do so; that children must be trained to exercise willpower and self-control over self-serving impulses. But does that mean that the fifth and final domain in the Self-Reg model is, after all, simply that of self-control?

Instead of looking at this fifth domain as being about building a child's self-control, Self-Reg frames prosocial development as a matter of developing capabilities for empathetic connection that are present in every single child right from the start. As we saw in the previous chapter on the social domain, we are a species that hungers for social connection from the moment of birth. We require it to survive and we need this prosocial piece to thrive.

In other words, rather than "How do we turn our child into a decent human being?" the better question is "How do we nurture our child's natural inclination to be caring and empathetic?" Clearly there are children, even very young ones, who have all sorts of moments when they don't demonstrate this tendency. Self-Reg enables us to understand not just when and why this is happening but also, more important, what to do about it.

We Are Social Creatures with a Propensity to Care

The idea that a child has to learn—be forced, if necessary—to suppress his "base instincts" to become a decent human being was seventeenth-century English philosopher Thomas Hobbes's point when he wrote that were humans allowed to revert to natural instincts, there would be "no arts, no letters, no society and which is worst of all, continual fear and danger of violent death, and the life of man, solitary, poor, nasty, brutish, and short." To survive their own brutish nature, such thought suggests, humans are forced to band together under the rule of law, and those who fail to comply must either be forced to do so or be banished or incarcerated. But force instills only fear, not empathy. Empathy *is* natural to our species and can grow only naturally, as a function of the interbrain's two-way empathic exchange.

The crux of Self-Reg is that we are social beings, and to be such is to be born with a brain that *demands* empathy. The work of evolutionary biologists tells us that empathy is present in all of the higher primates. It is a core part of our biological heritage. A growing body of research on empathy in young children shows this clearly, and most parents and early-childhood caregivers have seen some version of a child's caring response at home. In our lab and clinic we see it routinely in interactions between young children—including infants—and their parents.

Clearly there are biological as well as social reasons that a child's natural capacity for empathy can fail to thrive and in its place uncaring tendencies arise—behavior we interpret as greedy, selfish, unfeeling, or mean. But equally clearly there are biological mechanisms that in the right circumstances can lead to a child of good conscience, integrity, and compassion, capable of putting others' needs ahead of her own: the "better self" most of us aspire to be. Indeed, all signs indicate that antisocial behavior is the *anomaly*, not the norm; otherwise our species could never have made it to this point.

A New Outlook on Empathy

Prosocial development rests first and foremost upon a child's experience of empathy. Being loved, even when you're behaving in a beastly fashion, is such an important point that it ranks as one of the governing principles of Self-Reg. Just as a child learns how to self-regulate by being regulated, so too a child develops empathy by experiencing empathy. The capacity is inborn in all of us, but it is by experiencing empathy that a child's capacity for it blossoms.

Rachel was sent to the principal's office for being disruptive in class and froze in fear at the principal's scolding. Once that happened, fear became the only lesson Rachel took from the principal's response. It was an opportunity missed, not only for Rachel to have learned something more constructive but also for her to have experienced an empathetic response that would have reached deeper to cultivate her own capacity for self-awareness and an awareness of others' needs.

Much more is involved in true empathy than just responding sympathetically when a child is upset. It involves a deeper understanding, which has to be embodied and not just cerebral. The adult has to tap into her own experience of what it feels like to be in that state of upset and then try to figure out why the child is upset and how to help. The child herself will rarely know that she is being outrageously self-centered, let alone be able to describe the reasons why she is behaving this way. That is our job.

We have to stop looking at empathy solely in terms of what is going on inside the child, as a function of "character," perhaps, or "temperament." *True empathy is a two-way phenomenon: dyadic.* The interbrain encompasses both partners' experiences and has to regulate their *shared* emotional states. When a child is in distress, we become distressed, and it is up to our higher-order brain to try to figure out the causes and assuage them.

A Child's Developmental Journey
from Helpless to Helper

In the late fifteenth century *The Summoning of Everyman*, a morality play, was a blockbuster that told the story of the journey we are all called upon to make over the course of our lifetime as we struggle to resist various temptations. But the journey—and the struggle—could easily describe that of Everychild on the developmental journey from one pole of the interbrain to the other: the journey from coddled infant to thoughtful friend and someday parent; from having all of one's needs met to meeting the needs of others; from being *the one who is regulated* to being *the one who regulates*.

This journey along the interbrain can be arduous, over the rocks and crevasses of urges and impulses that can tempt us into unbridled selfishness, and it doesn't proceed in a straight path. Children can be empathetic in one instant but not the next, or empathetic with one person but not another. It's a meandering route with all sorts of detours and slippages along the way, and we have to recognize that it is natural for a child to regress to a self-centered state, especially under excessive stress. In many ways this is the defining feature of our primitive defense mechanisms.

As a parent you've likely experienced this uneven journey yourself. You know how difficult caring for an infant can be and yet how profoundly rewarding it can also be. It's the nature of parenthood. Parents and caregivers, in the role of "external brain" regulating the baby, are rewarded for their efforts with the release of neurotransmitters that trigger feelings of pleasure, calmness, and energy. In 2006 scientists found that the very act of giving activates the same part of the brain that releases these feel-good neurotransmitters, a phenomenon referred to as "helper's high." Other research has shown that helper's high is associated with health benefits for the helper. It turns out that "givers" are much happier and healthier than "nongivers," not just for psychological but also for biological reasons. These positive feelings come from the mesolimbic system, which, it seems, was designed to reward us for—and indeed push us into—prosocial acts. That is, we have a brain that does not just "demand" empathy but is designed to benefit others and to benefit from that mutual exchange.

A large body of scientific literature examining "social support" shows quite conclusively that the more socially connected we are, the better our mental as well as physical health. A number of factors are involved, psychological as well as biological. What is particularly noteworthy is that social support has been shown to lower blood pressure and heart rate, reduce levels of cortisol (the stress hormone), and improve immune system functioning. It has even been shown that people with more social support have a lower susceptibility to the common cold.

If helping makes us feel happier and healthier, what, then, would keep someone from responding to others in helpful, caring ways? Take the example of an overwrought caregiver: Why do some caregivers shun or even harm their babies? The answer to this question is the same one we've considered in every chapter of the book so far. The problem lies in stress overload. A caregiver who cannot cope with her own stress finds her baby's distress more than she can bear and, more to the point, something that she cannot understand or withstand. Oxytocin is just not enough to prevent her from going into fight or flight.

Just as a caregiver in extreme distress may find her baby overwhelming, so too some children find another person's distress overwhelming. This underscores the fundamental inquiry at the heart of Self-Reg in the prosocial domain: to identify why this expanded, empathetic social connection is comfortable for some children, difficult for others, and so difficult for some children that they turn away from this path.

Stress and the Undoing of the Social Brain—and Prosocial Behavior

A child may find this developmental journey hard going for many reasons. Some children are born with a biology that leaves them drained and more susceptible to limbic arousal. For others something may have happened—an earlier experience or a history of hard feelings with someone—that has kindled their alarm. Either way, they are chronically hyperaroused, and in this state desires and impulses intensify while social and self-awareness declines. When this happens, the child finds it impossible to share or sympathize or, indeed, even communicate. She might become overly sensitive to the point that she finds internal and external signals insufferable or her sensitivity becomes so blunted that she is numb to her own body's cues and bewildered by the actions of those around her. In this state she may find someone else's arousal so stressful that it triggers fight or flight.

In other words, yet another range of stressors unique to the prosocial domain add considerably to the list of biological, emotional, cognitive, and social stressors that we have looked at in the preceding chapters. *Being exposed to someone else's stress or being expected to put someone else's needs ahead of one's own is a stressor, sometimes acute.* It is hardly surprising that a child who is chronically in a low-energy/high-tension state should find this particular source of internal tension so taxing. It requires an enormous amount of energy to give to someone else who is dysregulated.

Just as being in fight or flight restricts the operations of our metabolic and immune systems and impedes the systems in the social brain that support mindreading and communication, it also shuts down the very systems that enable us to experience empathy. By this I mean not only being affected by what someone else is feeling but also being aware that we're affected this way. When this happens, ancient systems take over and run the show. For a stressed-out parent these primitive systems, which predate the social brain, can perceive a bawling baby as a threat or trigger the same response to a child whose uncaring behavior upsets us.

The child is caught in the same stress-induced cycle, reacting to the supposed "threat" that another child presents and the additional threat of the adult's angry reaction.

His behavior is the consequence of the twofold effect of excessive stress: First, the excessive stress inflames negative limbic impulses, triggering fight or flight. Second, it reduces his prefrontal inhibitory and social mindreading capacities. Not only does he turn a deaf ear to you, but also his survival brain has shut down these other systems. For any of us the instinct when we go into fight or flight is to shy away from social support, retreat to some "burrow," and then try to restore in isolation.

Self-regulatory problems in the prosocial domain are often revealed in a child's difficulty joining with others in one-on-one and larger-group social interactions; or in his being drawn to a group that cultivates undesirable qualities. Trouble in the prosocial domain is often a sign of trouble in another domain. Often, however, the child's behavior is due to an autonomic nervous system that has been overloaded by any number of causes.

So we arrive at the full five-domain stress cycle:

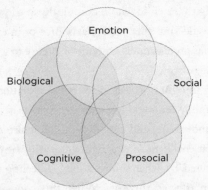

The Multiplier Effect: Five-Domain Stress Cycle

For Everychild the journey from "me" to "we" on the interbrain is not simply cognitive, a matter of coming to understand what other people are thinking and feeling, or grasping that he'll be banished from the group if he doesn't learn to control his impulses. The development of true empathy and its expression in the prosocial domain depends first and foremost on self-regulation: learning how to stay calm in the face of someone else's stress. That is, for the interbrain to deepen and grow, *a child has to learn how to stay regulated as he is exposed to someone else's distress.*

It Takes Two: Empathy Develops from Me-You to Me-We

Children's capacity to experience deeper levels of empathy is innate but does not develop on its own. That is the role of the interbrain. Long before a child's world of connections expands, he learns his first lessons in empathetic exchange through interactions with his parents or caregiver. This makes the way in which we respond to his lack of empathy critical, especially when he expresses that he's overwhelmed through aggressive behavior or fleeing (mentally, if not physically).

Parents instantly react angrily to their child's lack of empathy: This is an ancient response, lodged in a part of the brain that doesn't stop to distinguish between *my child* and *a stranger.* The problem for a child is that his brain does the same thing—interprets our angry or negative response as a threat. Worse still, it is his parent, trusted caregiver, or teacher who now presents the threat. But if parents or other adults consistently chastise a child for his lack of empathy, shouting when they should soothe, escalating when they should down-regulate, this can over time turn a child away from caring and toward antisocial behavior. This negative trajectory can start remarkably early, in some cases even before a child can walk.

Peace and Safety: Basic Needs for Self-Regulation, Growth, and Empathy

Language and the roots of our everyday expressions reveal telling aspects of our species as social beings—and prosocial beings. The way we greet someone—with a warm "hello," a smile, a handshake, or a hug, for instance—can communicate a peaceful intention and the desire to evoke the same feeling in the other, *a joint feeling of safety*. These social conventions signaling safety or threat aren't unique to humans, but they are a reminder of the deep human need for a shared sense of safety. Empathy is what makes this possible.

In the Hobbesian view of humankind's brutish nature, empathy is what neuroscientists call an *experience-dependent* phenomenon. The idea is that a child is by nature purely self-centered and that by nurturing and disciplining your child you are changing the natural wiring of his brain in the manner that is deemed socially desirable: superimposing prosocial circuits on a brain designed to think only of itself. Self-Reg sees empathy as what neuroscientists call an *experience-expectant* trait. That is, your child's brain is primed for empathy, which develops more broadly and deeply as a result of nurturing child-rearing practices that have been passed down from one generation to the next over the course of human evolution.

The connection between empathy and self-regulation goes deeper still. Your child isn't just biologically predisposed to be but actually *needs* to be empathetic to self-regulate. This isn't simply a case of his needing others to recognize and respond to his distress. Every bit as important is his need to help others. But sometimes the need for empathy from others becomes so great that it overrides, even obstructs the instinct to help others.

Our need to feel safe with others is so great that it even governs our responses to our own children, even when they are babies. I've seen caregivers get angry with an infant who had suddenly gotten angry with them. It's an automatic, visceral response, a sudden burst, utterly irrational, in which the parent may shut down, storm out, shout, or in extreme cases try to hurt the child. Then the child-blaming mind-set takes over and they tell themselves that it was all the child's fault, that he needed to have shown more self-control or that he's unusually selfish or spoiled and that they're doing this only for the child's own good.

A large part of the problem is that our amygdala is automatically aroused by someone else's anger or stressful behavior. We react this way not simply because our amygdala has been suddenly aroused but because our social brain—and the child's expanding prosocial brain—*needs* safety messages from others.

The journey along the interbrain involves learning how to cope with the feelings of fear or anger that others arouse in us: learning how to cope with their fear or anger as well as our own. To smile when a stranger looks grim; to soothe when our child is screaming; to counterregulate—for instance, slow down and soften our speech or gestures—when he needs to down-regulate. In the sudden burst of anger we regress to a purely self-centered state in which empathy shuts down. All we are aware of is *our* distress, *our* needs.

When my children were young, if they did or said something particularly hurtful, I would explode in a storm of parental invectives: "How could you say that?" On and on it would go until my wife would gently—or perhaps not so gently—encourage me to go to another room and calm down. There I would sit, stewing in my anger until my prefrontal cortex came back online and I could begin to ponder what on earth that had all been about. As soon as I calmed down, I could go back and attend lovingly to my children, who by this point had progressed to flooded, their whole body and face expressing fury or fear, the breakdown of social engagement complete.

As we saw in earlier chapters with Marie and her daughter Rosie, what Rosie needed to feel calm was her mom's soothing touch, a purely empathetic response. Not so much words; often no words at all. Instead, an arm around the shoulder, a gentle touch or back rub: simple soothing. This is the absolute core of empathy: pure right brain–to–right brain communication in which we let our child *feel* that we aren't abandoning her in her time of need. When we do this, we're activating positive memories lodged deep in her limbic systems of times when she was a baby and it was Mommy's or Daddy's reassuring touch or voice that took away the fear. A child not only is calmed this way but, once calmed, will seek to reengage and eventually to extend empathy as well as receive it.

Empathy Needs an Empathetic Environment in Which to Grow

The little boy whom I mentioned in the introduction to this book, whose father and grandfather before him had been described as "bad to the core," certainly showed all the signs of following in the family tradition of problems in the prosocial domain. He had already been suspended from school twice for hitting other children and he was only in kindergarten. He was a big kid, quite capable of intimidating his teacher and classmates alike. For obvious reasons, there was cause for concern.

I once attended a lecture in which the speaker tried to prove that idea of genetic destiny. We were shown a video of a three-year-old viciously pummeling his baby brother. It was just the sort of behavior that would make you feel that at least some kids are "born bad," and that if we don't knock this predilection out of them while they're still young, then the path ahead of them inevitably leads to antisocial misfortune. But it is just this response that I find so worrying, because it leads to the very outcome that we're trying to prevent.

As I watched the video, I wondered what might have brought on the attack. Had it been something as simple as resentment over the amount of attention the new baby was getting? It might have been that his brother had invaded his personal space and, lacking the words to express his anger, he had lashed out. High levels of stress and anxiety from other sources, as we've seen, also can trigger this kind of behavior.

Or had he just been hyperaroused? All I was left with, then, were questions. Lots of them. The one thing I felt certain about, based on extensive research and clinical experience, was that there was not some sort of innate, atavistic urge to hurt. The problem, however, is that such an urge can certainly take root, depending on how others— especially adults—respond to the child's outbursts. If a child is consistently threatened or, far worse, hurt physically or emotionally, he can easily come to associate doing the same to someone weaker with a perverted feeling of pleasure. Some research suggests that there may be a dopamine sensitization process involved in chronic acts of bullying, leading to more and more aggressive acts to get the same neurochemical "reward." Violent video games are worrisome for that reason, as is pornography, in that they continually ramp up the novelty factor, solely in order to keep the dopamine flowing.

Bullying has become of increasing concern, rightly so, and schools throughout the United States and Canada have responded with "safe school" initiatives. Protecting the innocent from bullying is not just a natural human response but a necessary one. Bullying hurts everyone; not just the victim but the bully and the witnesses as well. The danger, however, is that when schools and communities create primarily punitive "zero tolerance" policies on bullying, the intended ban doesn't address the roots of the problem. It only further isolates the offending child and fails to create a climate that is grounded in empathy and the opportunity for growth, an environment that benefits every child: the bully as much as the bullied.

The Canadian Broadcasting Corporation's excellent 2004 documentary *Children Full of Life* showed just what an antibullying climate should look like. It tells the story of Toshiro Kanamori, a teacher in Japan who helps his fourth-grade students express deeply suppressed emotions and support one another in this sometimes painful process. It is a profoundly moving depiction of the power of group empathy and how an adult needs to create the climate in which children can help one another feel emotionally as well as physically safe. What is especially striking in this fourth-grade class is that, as our Self-Reg schools initiative has found in every school and every grade level, *every one of the children* needs this experience: not just the ones whose emotional problems stand out.

The Point of It All: Prosocial Growth

Like all the other domains, prosocial self-regulation is about *growth*. In the prosocial domain we naturally—and rightly—think in terms of the cultivation of internal moral qualities. But for such growth to be possible the child's interbrain has to grow, and that means that the child has to feel safe with an ever-enlarging group of peers as well as adults.

The developmental journey your child makes is one from the closeted and cosseted security of your family into the larger sphere of human interactions: friends, classmates, community, society, and today, as a result of technology, the global village. But your child's interbrain can grow only if she feels safe and secure in these larger and more complex social settings. This means building trusting and supportive relationships with others. It means recognizing and responding to the hopes and worries of others, and it means caring for all the members of the group she is a part of, no matter how large that group, and not just about what is on the plate in front of her.

Self-regulation is the essential component, the means by which your child is able to shift effectively from the me-centered moment to the we-centered one. Calm and engaged, she can more comfortably connect with others, read their cues, recognize their needs, and not just delay gratification of personal desires but override them, if need be, to respond to the needs of others. That is the more relevant marsh-mallow task: to refrain from eating the treat in front of you so that someone else can have one; and, quite remarkably, it has been shown that even rats and monkeys can pass this test.

If your child is struggling with physical distractions, anxious about school or family tensions, upset over a tiff with a friend, or overwhelmed by academic demands, he is going to find it hard to focus on the big picture and others' needs. When your child is exhausted and as a result has become highly irritable and irritating, what he or she needs is to lie down and restore, not to be harangued or punished. The same is true for antisocial behavior. Yes, he needs to be told that what he did was wrong, and why—firmly but patiently and, most important, *when he is receptive.*

Typically that means guiding the child to a quiet environment where he can down-regulate. Not, I hasten to add, a "time-out." We are talking about a space where he feels safe and secure; for only then will he be able to down-regulate. And don't be in a rush to talk about what happened. Sometimes you may have to wait twenty-four hours before the child is ready. What's more, you need to recognize that it can be extremely difficult for a child to understand, let alone explain, "what happened."

The more adept your child is at self-regulating in the other domains, the more practiced she will become at co-regulating with other children, reading and responding effectively to their needs, and the more energy she'll have for thinking beyond herself and caring about the group. Kids don't need endless instruction on this. They need experience and practice learning to listen, contribute ideas, help out, and respect others. At home as well, this is how children learn that an idea matters, that it exists in real life. In this case the idea that matters is empathy and how we treat other people. That can include friends, family members, new kids at school, teachers, or strangers we encounter in everyday life. Genuine empathy is all-inclusive. Everyone counts, and no one is undeserving.

As a parent you can give your child the language for it. You can model it, live it, and talk about it as a value that's important to you. Make no mistake about it, prosocial growth is driven by the values a child has developed, not, for instance, by self-serving acts of strategic altruism designed to pad a college résumé. Nothing turns a child cynical faster than the hypocrisy of community service done to gain a competitive edge or make themselves (or you) look good. Kids aren't fooled, but they are always open to the genuine experience of empathy, and it registers deeply at any age.

"Win at All Costs" Is Too High a Cost

The episode at the hockey game that opened this chapter, when I got so upset that Sasha didn't grab his easy goal, continued to niggle away at me. How could I have gotten it so completely wrong? It's a cop-out to say that, like so many other hockey parents, I got a little carried away in the heat of the moment. The question is why. *Why do we become so worked up, to the point that we may actually be impeding our child's prosocial growth?*

So much of children's lives have become ultracompetitive. They have to compete against one another in everything they do: school, sports, music, art, social status—online and off. Over and over the message they hear is that you succeed only by beating someone else out. And the competition begins ridiculously early, with parents' ambitious expectations beginning before a child even enters school. The negative effects of this chronic competitive pressure are worrisome. Recent research shows that excessive focus on maximizing accomplishment and status can impede empathy development and prosocial growth. In particular, "privileged but pressured" adolescents who internalize performance as a core value—without a context of loving, supportive parents, empathy, and prosocial values—show higher rates of depression and other mental health problems, drug and alcohol use, and markers of antisocial behavior.

For most of our evolutionary existence, parents, then community, served as a buffer against the stresses encountered by children and adolescents. Parents remain a child's first and most potent partners in the transition the child must make from the parent-child dyad to the expanding interbrain attuned to the larger collective "we." But if a parent's behavior has the opposite effect—dramatically intensifying the stress load on the child—then the child faces an even greater challenge to healthy social and prosocial engagement. If he then behaves in ways that express his struggle but that we misunderstand and attribute to bad character or bad genes, we have abandoned him to the very isolation and suffering we had hoped to steer him away from.

Remember that the "switch" in the brain that can take us from excessive rumination or distraction to more expansive awareness puts our "better self"—our most empathetic self—just a few deep belly breaths away. You can practice consciously "flipping the switch," and teach your child to do the same, to be aware of the tension in your muscles, your breathing, and your other responses, especially in a moment when you feel stress spike. This simple Self-Reg practice to reduce the stress, calm ourselves, and restore in the moment enables us to reengage with others and perhaps help them do the same. The night of my overbearing behavior after the hockey game, my son's words brought me up short. When I reflected on my own state of mind at the time, I realized that I had been overstressed, and this was likely one of the reasons I had been too personally involved in my son's accomplishments on the ice, to the point where I had become oblivious of his needs. Even in the heat of competition, empathy has a place, and my son knew that. I had forgotten.

Our Children Teach Us and Turn to Us

We often gravitate in our thoughts and conversations to the things that bother us, especially about our kids. But when I ask parents to recall moments when they were touched or moved by their child's capacity to show them the world through fresh eyes, perhaps challenge a jaded view with moral clarity, many have had that experience. It may have been in a quiet bedtime conversation, or on a walk, or in a moment when their child helped them break out of an old, unhelpful pattern and see new possibilities. Children are like an aeolian harp, resonating to the slightest emotional currents that they pick up from us.

One day when my daughter Sammi was six, we were walking down a street and a panhandler approached us, asking if we could spare any change for him to go get a meal. I smiled but shook my head, muttered "no," and continued walking. We hadn't gone a dozen paces when my daughter stopped me and, with her hands on her hips, asked: "Why did you say that, Daddy? You know you have lots of change in your pockets." I explained how he would just take whatever I gave him and go spend it on drink, and I really didn't want to be responsible for doing him even more harm. "But, Daddy," she objected, "have you forgotten all about Luke Bryan?!"

That summer the two of us had been listening to Bryan's new album, *Tailgates & Tanlines*, and we had decided that our favorite song was "You Don't Know Jack." The title plays on how we often don't have a clue—don't know "jack squat"—about the reality of life for others, especially when we reduce them to stereotypes. In this case the song tells the story of a panhandler's miserable, shame- and pain-filled life, estranged from his wife and children, all too aware of what his drinking has cost him and his loved ones and feeling the judgment of others as they walk past. Others like me.

As we walked past the panhandler on our own street corner, his hat on the sidewalk for donations and my muttered "no" hanging in the air, my daughter turned to me and said: "*You don't know jack*, Dad. Maybe he really does just want to go get a burger." I was utterly stunned by this remark. Whether or not she was right, the lesson I was giving her *with my own behavior* was so much more profound than any lectures I might give her on the importance of empathy or any of the programs I'd looked at that are designed to enhance a child's human development. So I gave her a five-dollar bill and told her to go put it in his hat. She stood waiting until he wasn't looking, tucked the bill into the hatband, and darted away before he had even noticed.

Our children provide us with a wonderful opportunity to reach the highest levels of human development. Through them we can experience an entirely new level of emotional and reflective functioning. It's not just a case of providing for them or protecting them. Through their eyes we can begin to see those areas of ourselves where we too must grow. So when we talk about the importance of prosocial growth, this encompasses our own as much as our children's; indeed, the two are inextricably tied together. We help each other master the next stages in our human development. They learn about empathy, generosity, and kindness from us, and we from them.

All for One and One for All: Marshmallows and More

We could easily have spent this entire chapter wrestling with the definition of "prosocial"; in fact, that is exactly what philosophers have been doing for the past two thousand years, and scientists too now. But intuitively we all know what "prosocial" means, and we want to help our children cultivate this empathetic inner self. The four components of "calmly focused and alert" that we've looked at so far—the first four domains—are incomplete without this piece. To be calm is not just to be relaxed, aware, and enjoying being in that state; maybe most important of all is this fifth element: the prosocial.

A teacher shared a story from her school's Self-Reg initiative of a day when she planned to re-create the marshmallow task for her second-grade class. She had the marshmallows out and was ready to set things up when she was suddenly called to the office. She placed the plate of marshmallows in the middle of a table and told the children not to touch them while she was gone. The kids all gathered around the table, staring at the mesmerizing treats, but rather than grabbing them they began to help one another resist the temptation. One little boy was finding this just a little too challenging, and he was trying desperately to grab the plate. Rather than allowing this or, for that matter, ganging up on him, the children all pitched in to help. They encouraged him, distracted him, and then, what was most remarkable of all, cheered him on when he was able to resist. When the teacher returned to the classroom, there was the plate of marshmallows, fully intact, a group of beaming children, and an excited little boy who couldn't wait to share his self-regulation success story with her. More to the point regarding prosocial behavior was the way these children supported one another in their aim for a common goal, stepping up that effort for the one among them who needed the most help.

This is perhaps the ultimate shift involved in the Self-Reg view of prosocial behavior. Far from being a journey of learning how to "control his inner nature," the journey the child must make is more accurately one through which he learns how to cater to his innermost needs—which includes responding to the needs of others. The social-support research is clear: We restore best when we are socially connected. Self-Reg helps us turn off our child's alarm and teach him how to do this himself. This is ultimately why it is so important to help them acquire the desire and skills to develop close and meaningful friendships. We rest and restore in the company of others, who in turn find true peace in our presence. The benefits are indeed here and now: for self and other, individual and group.

PART III

Teens, Temptations, and Parents Under Pressure

TEN

The Power and Perils
of Adolescence

My hosts wanted to give me a "real taste of Texas," so they had arranged for me to see a high school football game on the Friday night after my last master class of the week. David W. Carter High School was playing Justin F. Kimball High School in Dallas: a rivalry, they told me, that people came from miles around to see. I was intrigued: Here were teenagers—fast, strong, disciplined, and extremely fit. This was all about teens pitted against teens. There were still adults involved, guiding and supervising them (in fact, yelling at them) both on and off the field. But the adults were separated from the players they were coaching, both physically and figuratively, wearing polo shirts rather than team uniforms and observing the game from the relative safety of the sidelines.

The players took the most outrageous risks, displaying astonishing skills for their age. They acted largely on impulse—the result of hours of training, to be sure, but impulse nonetheless. They pushed themselves physically beyond what any might have been capable of on his own and managed to channel all that physical aggression (for the most part) within the accepted rules of the game.

They were totally wrapped up in one another, completely focused on the shared goal of winning the game. And something a little more subtle: When one of them made a mistake, another would try to cover for him. Once, when a player misjudged a play and his error resulted in a touchdown for the other team, his teammates patted him on the back and the helmet and uttered words of encouragement. In other words, their intuitive response was to spur him on to renewed effort rather than to chastise him.

The halftime show was every bit as mesmerizing. The David W. Carter Marching Band took to the field and performed several musical dance numbers with stunning skill and exuberance. The cheerleading squad showed the same energy and precision in their own teamwork. The effect was contagious, as much for the spectators in the stands as for the kids on the field.

Finally, it was interesting to observe how the stands full of adults as well as classmates cheered the teams on, every bit as bound up in winning the game as the teenagers on the field and doing their own part to up-regulate their proxy heroes and, for that matter, themselves. This was so much more than a football game, as anyone who's ever witnessed one knows well. This was primal stuff.

There isn't a more iconic modern spectacle than a high school football game. Yet as quintessentially contemporary as it is, it affords an insight into something far more ancient. As I'll explain in this chapter, adolescence is in many ways an evolutionary puzzle, a pronounced period of biological as well as social transformation and instability. If you're the parent of a teenager, you might be thinking that adolescence evolved only to test your endurance. But there has to be something more to this unique phase of human development, given that nature decided to stick with the experiment.

Anywhere in the world you go, adolescents drive, support, and nurture one another when engaged in pursuit of a shared goal. It is a reminder that in evolutionary terms adolescence must serve a purpose. As it happens, the great early human migration into Asia and Europe— the so-called exodus from Africa—that began with *H. erectus* is said by some primatologists to have coincided with the first fossil evidence of adolescence. One line of reasoning suggests that the two events were closely connected. Adolescents, driven by their restlessness, their capacity to endure prolonged states of depletion, and the biological changes affecting their risk assessment—and misassessment—led the way. Perhaps the adults cheered them on like the parents at the Carter-versus-Kimball football game.

As it happens, there is a striking difference between the ways adolescents and adults assess the balance between potential rewards and risks. One can easily imagine that *H. erectus* parents might have been reluctant to move, preferring to make the best of where they were despite dwindling food sources. But the teens—were they, as some paleoanthropologists have speculated, the bold adventurers who searched for new lands? Who experimented with new foods and developed new tools to extract those foods? Who acted as sentries while their parents slept?

However you cut it, adolescence constitutes a unique phase in human development, dramatically different from the childhood dependency that precedes it and the often more settled adult life that follows. It is a time of unparalleled richness and potential peril. It is this latter, darker side of adolescence that has become a major concern in recent years, and it is here where Self-Reg has an especially important role to play.

A Time of Torment and Turmoil: For What Purpose?

Angie sat slumped in the chair, barely talking. She was a small kid for her age, fourteen, but despite her slouched demeanor she was dressed nicely and it was clear that she cared about her appearance. Her school and family history indicated she had a lot going for her, a smart kid from a stable, loving family—the sort of kid who you'd think would face the day with some modicum of confidence and optimism. Not so. Getting to the office had taken a herculean effort for Angie. It wasn't just coming to see us that she found difficult. Everything about every day felt that way. Every day she'd wake up hoping that this day was going to be different; but it hardly ever was. She found that just getting out of bed—let alone searching for new lands—was a battle against inertia, as were getting dressed and eating breakfast. She had some close friends, she told me, but most days didn't feel up to getting in touch with them. She couldn't say why all of this was so hard, only that she felt this way almost every single day.

In that regard Angie is not alone. Not by a long shot.

In February of 2013, for example, the Toronto District School Board, the largest of its kind in Canada, released the findings of its 2011–12 Student Census, which was the largest ever conducted in Canada and the first time anyone had looked specifically at the prevalence of anxiety. Almost 90 percent of all Toronto students in grades seven through twelve—more than 103,000 students in total—took part in the survey, and what they reported sent shock waves around the country.

More than half the students in grades seven and eight (58 percent) reported that they felt tired for no reason or had difficulty concentrating (56 percent); an astonishing 76 percent of the students in grades nine through twelve reported having these problems. Forty percent of all students in grades seven and eight and 66 percent of all students in grades nine through twelve reported feeling under a lot of stress. And most worrying of all, 63 percent of all students in grades seven and eight and 72 percent of all high school students said they felt nervous or anxious often or all the time.

This statistical profile tells us how kids see themselves—how they interpret their feelings in familiar terms on a survey—but not necessarily how they actually *are*. Many have never actually experienced "calm" but don't know it. Kids often don't know exactly what they're feeling or can't explain why they feel so bad but will start to self-medicate, dosing themselves with over-the-counter medications for headaches, gut problems, or sleeplessness. For others, chronic anxiety leads them to self-medicate with alcohol or other substances, and the problems only compound. The result is growing alarm among parents and educators about what they see as rising tides of serious adolescent physical and mental health problems.

In my work around the United States and throughout Canada, teachers and administrators tell me that they see increasing numbers of teens with serious mood problems, and we've seen a similar trend just in calls to the clinic, with more and more contact from parents with a child like Angie. They live with teens who are struggling—*deeply struggling*—with anxiety or depression. And "depression," in the words of Philip W. Gold, a research chief at NIH, "like autoimmunity, represents a dysregulated adaptive response: a stress response that has gone awry."

We see similar increases in the number of teens having trouble with anger control and antisocial behavior; mindless risky behavior; drug, alcohol, gambling, and pornography addictions; intentional self-harm; eating disorders; sleep disorders; body image disorders. It's as if what the German Romantics described as a period of "storm and stress" has intensified tenfold, transforming adolescence for many into a time of "torment and turmoil."

Every one of these psychological and behavioral problems is, to return to our metaphor, the sign of an engine running on empty. That's not to say that exhausted energy reserves are the cause of these diverse problems. In many cases it's the opposite. Social, emotional, or learning problems are the hidden stressors that deplete energy reserves. But whatever the cause, in each of these conditions a teen is in a chronic state of low energy coupled with exceedingly high tension—an energy/tension ratio that is seriously out of balance. The brain's natural reaction to being in this state may, in fact, exacerbate the problem, telling the teen not to move at all when maybe that's what she needs most; or telling him to keep moving when what he needs is to rest.

But why is this happening to so many teens? Of course, to some degree it is happening to *all* teens, if only because the profound changes of adolescence are inherently demanding and draining, and the transition from childhood to adulthood requires them to recalibrate from parent-centered regulation to peer co-regulation and self-regulation. As we saw earlier, if adolescence serves some evolutionary purpose, then to understand why so many are suffering so much today we can look for clues in what amounts to a fundamental clash between the modern world and a biology forged in the Pleistocene. A "mismatch," as Peter Gluckman calls it, that is creating such undue stresses on our teens that it's showing up in a massive wave of health problems, both mental and physical.

Ancient Adolescence Offers Clues About Today's Teens

Adolescence begins around the age of ten to twelve with a prepubertal brain explosion: a period of robust neural growth, synaptic pruning, myelination, and rewiring. In other words, a major brain overhaul. It's nature's way of completely changing the way your child's brain has been working, slowing some things down, speeding others up. This isn't just a case of doing some spring housekeeping—this is an out-and-out reorganization.

The brain grows at an astonishing rate in the early years of life. By the age of six and a half, it will have completed 95 percent of its growth. During this time the child's core sensory, motor, communicative, emotional, social, and cognitive processes all become firmly established and integrated. By the end of this phase of childhood, around the age of seven, the brain is in a highly stable state. So why, after maintaining this state for two or three years more, should nature have decided it was time to suddenly render it unstable again? It's a bit like, having finally finished a large jigsaw puzzle, nature decided to toss the pieces into a bag and start all over again.

This is not the only biological aspect of adolescence that is puzzling. In most mammals there is a seamless transition from childhood to adulthood, and puberty is marked by an actual *decline* in growth rate to reach the stable maintenance level that characterizes adulthood. The opposite happens in humans. Our adolescence is marked by a rapid growth spurt, as every parent of a teen knows only too well. Girls, boys, shapes, sizes, senses, and sensibilities—everything is suddenly turbocharged.

This growth spurt is tied to the cascade of sex hormones unleashed at puberty, something that we all know and take for granted but that also is puzzling. Sex hormones are present from birth, so why not have the slow and gradual increase seen in most other mammals? Why throw human adolescents into chaos by suddenly blitzing them with estrogen and androgens? Why the big changes in muscle-to-fat metabolism? Is this nature's way of having teens pump up before the big game? The brain's energy efficiency also changes. Wouldn't it have made sense to start this a lot earlier? And why the change in melatonin transcription, which alters adolescent sleep patterns dramatically? Why the periods of extreme restlessness followed by total collapse? Maybe most puzzling of all: Why the critical changes in the brain's "reward system," which has such a profound impact on adolescent risk taking?

The answer to all these questions is that adolescence marks the cost our species has to pay for the advantage conferred by secondary altriciality—that uniquely long period of complete dependency in infancy, when brain growth is so significant. Let me explain.

Adolescence marks the transition from one mode of social functioning into quite a different one: in essence, a shift from the parent-dominant mode of childhood to the peer-peer organization of adolescence. A teen comes to rely much more heavily on his friends than his parents during this phase of his journey along the interbrain.

This is an important reason why the adolescent becomes so much more susceptible to peer influence. The child is forced to transition from the narrow and protected confines of his family into the real world of his community, where he must now both compete and cooperate for the rest of his life. There comes a point when prolonged childhood has to end if the child is to become an independent and self-sufficient adult, and with that critical goal it would make sense that the prepubertal brain explosion was nature's way of forcing your child out of the house!

As we all know, the transition into adolescence is also marked by heightened risk taking. The neural systems needed to regulate these risky impulses are still growing slowly. The result is, to borrow a particularly apt description, an adolescent brain akin to a Formula 1 race car without an experienced driver at the wheel. But in fact the analogy goes even deeper. Like a teenaged driver with a bunch of other teens in the car, the teen has a brain that is easily distracted and pushes him to drive way too fast and way too far, without a speed or a fuel gauge or, for that matter, side or rearview mirrors. To make matters worse, he doesn't like to listen to his driving instructor nagging him to check his blind spot before he changes lanes.

Talking—and Not Talking—to Our Teens

The furthest thing from my mind as I talked with Angie—and certainly the last thing that I would have said to her—was that she needed to "pull up her socks" and make a greater effort to get on with her life. Angie was fighting a battle—her term—every day just to get out of bed. She was already making an extraordinary effort just trying to accomplish the most basic of daily tasks. What she desperately needed was to be making less, not more of an effort to get up in the morning. Nor would she have benefited in the least from an explanation of how irrational her fears were or how she really was a kid who had everything going for her. In fact, that is pretty much exactly what her parents had tried, to no avail.

Our tendency with our teens—maybe especially with our teens because we are sure they're old enough to understand—is to *explain*, to get them to see how irrational they're being or that they need to do such-and-such to feel better. That might be your instinct with Self-Reg as well—to try to *tell* them what self-regulation is and why it's so important for them to refill their tank. But there's just one problem. They may be going through a giant developmental step forward, but the effects of heightened stress are exactly the same as when they were kids. The same prefrontal systems are shutting down when they go into fight or flight or freeze. When this happens, they are every bit as incapable of processing what you're saying as they were when they were children. And they are just as liable to go into limbic hyperarousal if you try too hard to press home a point—maybe even more so.

There are some very real modern stressors that account for the epidemic of anxiety that we're seeing in teens. But before we can start to talk to them about these, and try to get them to recognize the effects of that stress, we need to help them to *do* the five steps of Self-Reg. What's most important for teenagers is that *they* go through the five steps on their own. That is, *they* need to recognize the significance of things like having trouble getting out of bed or losing control at night; *they* have to figure out what their stressors are and then how to reduce them; they have to learn—or relearn—what it feels like to be calm, and figure out what they find soothing and restorative.

What makes all this especially difficult for parents today is that teens are exposed to multiple stressors that neither they nor we recognize as such. Making matters considerably harder, they will often insist that these stressors are nothing of the sort! But the first step for parents, even as their teen is trying to push them aside, is to help them refill their tank, because no message is going to get through while they're running on empty. And there are some pretty powerful reasons why teens are prone to be in this state.

The Making of a Teenage Gas Guzzler

As every parent knows, a surge in caloric intake begins at puberty. An active fourteen-year-old may need as much as twice as many calories as an active eight-year-old. This sharp increase in energy needs is obviously closely related to, but is not solely a function of, the growth spurt and (ideally) increased activity levels. Another critical factor accounts for the way teens are burning so much energy.

Adolescence heralds a period of *dramatically increased sensitivity to stress*. We see significant changes in the limbic system and the HPA (hypothalamic-pituitary-adrenal) pathway—that part of the neuroendocrine system that controls reactions to stress and regulates internal processes—all marked by either reduced or higher levels of cortisol. It is as if the teen's neuroceptive system were being recalibrated, and it's not just the amygdala that is involved. There is heightened sensitivity to environmental stressors—visual, auditory, olfactory, tactile—and, most important of all, social stressors.

The social stressors are especially acute. Recent studies have shown that teens display heightened sensitivity to "negative affect cues" (a frown, grimace, or sharp tone of voice) and, if that weren't enough, a heightened bias for perceiving signals as negative, even when they're not. Significantly, teens do worse on emotion-recognition tasks than they did when they performed the same tasks as children. As teens they tend to read neutral facial expressions as threatening. The more tired they become, the more likely they are to register even the most benign facial expression or tone of voice as a threat.

Why is this so serious? Because it means that your teenager's alarm is much more sensitive, and in some teens becomes hair-trigger sensitive. The teen's amygdala is like a smoke alarm that goes off when all you're doing is boiling water. And every time the alarm goes off, tension surges and energy consumption spikes. Furthermore, sleep deprivation exacerbates stress reactivity and negative bias considerably, and we see a very sharp decline in sleep in most teenagers today.

A sixteen-year-old still needs around nine hours of sleep a night, possibly more. Remarkably few are now getting that much consistently. Sleep deprivation also has a profound impact on the striatal system, a part of the brain that is strongly associated with reward-related decision making. The sleep-deprived adolescent is prone to take greater risks and be less concerned with possible negative consequences—until they happen! Then the teen's stress goes right through the roof, leading to behaviors that boggle any rational mind.

No Teen Is an Island: Clubs, Cliques, and the Safety of Social Connection

What sorts of things can your teen do to recover from being in a prolonged "ergotropic" state, in which stress is burning vast amounts of energy? Increased physical activity, yoga, music and drama ensembles, and adventure programs have all been shown to be highly restorative. But they are most beneficial when they're done in small groups. There is an evolutionary dynamic operating here as well. Early humans lived in communities of one hundred to two hundred individuals, so when adolescents grouped together to play, travel, or hunt, their numbers would have been small, which is a critical factor in enabling them to feel safe and secure.

Think of what it feels like to be in a high school setting with a couple of hundred kids in your grade and maybe a couple of thousand in the school—enough to make you feel invisible, all alone.

At D. W. Carter, where I spent the day and attended the football game, as at most schools the football team stood out as a distinctive group, even in a student body of more than 1,800. All the players wore either a T-shirt or a sweatshirt with a picture of a cowboy riding a bucking bronco. When I stopped three of them walking together and asked them about the design, they explained that it was the team's name—the Cowboys—a symbol that was obviously a source of pride, and their team shirts another, earned and respected by the entire community, school and beyond. But more was involved here than just self-esteem. Their social identity was a source of security.

This is in the nature of our species and of adolescents in particular. Teens need small-group activities built around a shared goal that requires dedication, sacrifice, and something greater than self-gratification. They must experience failure as well as success together if they are to develop resilience. But they must experience success as well as failure together if they are to develop the drive to keep going in the face of adversity. A personal sense of identity does not come from a group that does not itself have a strong identity. For that to develop there has to be something encouraging, challenging, and indeed inspiring the group.

The big worry is that many teens are opting out of traditional group activities that require skill, practice, and dedication in favor of "surrogate" group experiences—online gaming, for instance—with artificial and in many ways trivial "skills." Teens who have spent countless hours mastering some online game are the new Internet "stars." Just recently I was talking to a group of teenage boys at the end of the school day who told me they each had to go to their own homes to play together. When I looked puzzled, they explained how they would link up on Skype to play either with or against one another in an online game. On its own this is perfectly harmless, even lots of fun. The trouble arises when these activities become the teen's main mode of peer interaction.

More than a hundred years ago the biologist Jacques Loeb discovered why insects make the arduous climb to the top of a tree, where all their food is located. For a long time biologists had thought that insects must have a survival instinct to search for food. But what Loeb discovered was that they have photoreceptors that draw them to where there is the most light—the top of plants—where, coincidentally, food is most plentiful. In the case of adolescents drawn to video games or social media, the products developed to feed off their sensation seeking and social needs do not lead them to a rich food source and, as we'll see in the following chapter, may in fact be further starving them.

Team sports show this phenomenon of the adolescent social engagement and support system in high relief but, of course, not every teen needs to be, or can be, an athlete. Since the beginning of time, there has to have been room for the thinker, artist, inventor, storyteller, poet, scientist, business magnate, and aspiring politician—and, of course, these "personae" are by no means mutually exclusive. The point is not that teens should never play video games or go on Facebook but the detrimental effect these things can have on your teen's stress level when taken to excess.

When your teen is part of a group—whether it is a bunch of surfers, a rock band, a congressman's campaign team, or any other—you need to establish whether his involvement is actually increasing rather than reducing his stress level. The same point applies to video games or social media. Some parents value how the gaming activity helps their teen achieve some measure of connectedness with peers; other parents see troubling signs of overuse and resort to desperate measures to break what they regard as a dangerous addiction.

In the case of gaming addiction we see a number of associated health problems (backaches, headaches, eye strain, carpel tunnel syndrome); heightened aggression or problems with interpersonal skills; and both attentional and motivational problems at school. Excessive social media use has been linked to feelings of exclusion, a pressure to be entertaining, paranoia, envy of others' lifestyle, and depression. Far from enhancing the feeling of safety and security, excessive video gaming or time spent on social media is having the opposite effect. What teens need from one another is not simply to be entertained: They need peers to help them deal with their stress.

Anxiety has long been regarded as a sort of weakness, which greatly intensifies the problem. I saw this in Angie, who, in addition to all the physiological stress she was experiencing, internalized her distress as a sign of a deep character flaw, which only added to her anxiety. "Why," she asked through tears at the end of our first meeting, "am I so pathetic?" But what she had to learn, what all teens have to learn, is that weakness has nothing to do with why they are feeling so anxious or depressed.

In children anxiety is a sign of excessive strain on the autonomic nervous system, and it is no different in the case of teens. Heightened anxiety is an incontrovertible sign of chronic limbic arousal, the result of too great a stress load (often involving all five domains) coupled with the absence of the sorts of social activities that, from the dawn of adolescence, have helped teenagers reduce their tension and recover from their exhaustion. Your role as a regulating parent doesn't disappear, but as your teen makes the journey along the interbrain, her peers become a critical factor in turning off her kindled alarm, in some ways much as you did when she was young. Despite its merits, social media simply wasn't playing this role for Angie, just as it doesn't for so many of the teens struggling with social anxiety.

Real "Face Time" Is Essential to Strengthen Teens' Social Support

Social engagement, the brain's first line for dealing with stress, requires "proximal" interaction: touches, looks, a sympathetic ear, and soothing vocalizations. Our need for proximal interaction stays with us to the end of life, which is why seniors do so much better when they are part of a social group. "Distal" interaction, such as by telephone or social media, satisfies some of the need for feeling connected, but it cannot replace the benefits of proximal interaction. It cannot promote the sort of secure attachment that teens need from one another in order to navigate the biological as well as social changes they're undergoing.

The concern is that despite the remarkable potential for learning and personal development that modern technology has created, certain aspects of the media may be contributing to the high levels of anxiety in teens. It is certainly a significant reason why so many teens aren't getting enough sleep. Research also shows cause for concern that their eating patterns are affected, further contributing to the need for stimulus-rich sensations that overload an already overworked autonomic nervous system.

Other stressors include the intense competition that confronts teens in just about every aspect of their lives. Beyond traditional pressures for grades and popularity, the pressure to prove themselves often comes down to performance measures that are tougher than ever to meet: highly selective schools, social media "fame," and material success.

With the best of intentions, or perhaps excessive ambition, we have in many cases created a high school experience that ignores the most basic developmental needs of children and adolescents in favor of perfectionistic performance measures that are both unwise and unsustainable. This last trend is particularly disturbing. Recently I was asked if we could bring Self-Reg into a Far Eastern country that is most noted for the number of top-level scientists and engineers that it turns out. The reason for the inquiry? The government has become deeply alarmed about the explosion of mental health problems among the country's teens.

Mismatch Theory Says Eat Real, Sleep More, and Go for a Walk!

The basic principle of Gluckman's mismatch theory, mentioned earlier and expounded in *Mismatch: Why Our World No Longer Fits Our Bodies*, is that the greater the mismatch between our biology and our environment, the greater the stress and the greater the cost to our internal systems, even though we develop strategies for surviving in inhospitable environments. Our stressed-out adolescents are the quintessential poster children for mismatch theory as it applies to self-regulation and the five domains—from what they eat to how they sleep and what they do, or don't do, in their waking hours.

Let's start with what's on their plates—or in their fast-food cartons. The shape of our teeth tells us that our ancestors spent a significant amount of time chewing things like tubers and tough meat. Chewing actually has a self-regulating effect, because it causes the release of calming neurochemicals, which no doubt is why chewing gum is so popular in the teen market, with chewing tobacco making inroads too. This generation of teens eats primarily highly processed foods that require minimal chewing and deliver dubious nutritional returns. Health advocates have fought hard to put junk food on the chopping block for reasons we've all heard, including the prevalence of obesity and increase in diabetes and other chronic health problems in adolescence. Now research shows that junk food disrupts the mechanisms for arousal regulation—a systemic threat affecting all five domains—so yes, diet belongs high on the mismatch list.

It's pretty much impossible to speculate about primitive sleep patterns, given the great variability that we see in hunter-gatherer populations today. But the one thing we do know is that the invention of the electric lightbulb and, more recently, blue-lit screens, has had a profound impact on sleep patterns. What data we have in this area indicates that the average teenager is getting one to two hours less sleep a night than just a decade ago, and I'd be surprised if this doesn't apply to your teen as well.

Of all the mismatches, however, top honors belong to the *lack of movement.* Whether or not teens played a major role in the ancient exodus from Africa, what we can infer with some certainty is that they moved a lot during the day, an awful lot. In fact, studies of modern hunting-gathering groups have recorded what from a modern, urban perspective seems like an astonishing amount of walking—between thirty thousand and forty thousand steps a day. Some years ago I did some work in Madagascar, and on one of my trips I was driven from one end of the island to the other through the interior. All along the way we passed teens walking up and down the mountainous highways, most of them laden with goods their families sold at the market in town or returning with supplies they had purchased there. These towns were typically ten to fifteen miles away from their mountaintop villages! They did this trip, both ways, almost every day—most of them barefoot or wearing flip-flops!

Walking is extremely important for stress reduction in teens, and not just because the more time spent walking, the less time spent gaming or on social media. Walking is highly beneficial for their cardiovascular fitness and muscle and bone strength. It promotes the elimination of waste products in the tissues and the release of tension. It releases endorphins and has an inhibiting effect on the neurons that fire when they are anxious. They get the benefits of sunshine, fresh air, and the sounds and sights of nature. And a rhythmic stride induces a meditative, autohypnotic state that promotes creativity as well as restoration. Plus it gives their feet a nice gentle massage!

We know that sitting too much is a factor in the obesity epidemic among teens; just as significant is the effect of a sedentary lifestyle on mood. Angie, like so many of the teens who struggle with mood problems, was stuck in sedentary mode, and she needed help to get moving and make physical activity a normal part of her day. Many schools are taking this seriously, and some of the most effective practices I've seen in the high schools doing Self-Reg is to build small amounts of movement right into the lesson. For example, moving students to different sides of the room depending on their answer to a question. Many teachers use periodic cues for students to stand and stretch or do a calming breath. We've seen fantastic results in our Spark Self-Reg initiative, which places stationary bikes at the back of a classroom for students to use if and when they feel the need. Parents tell me that devices like Wii Fit or Wii Dance have helped their teens get moving, or volunteer activities that aren't focused on fitness but involve some level of physical activity to get the job done.

Helping Teens Get to Know Themselves

Walking and then more vigorous forms of exercise are really just a way to kick-start the Self-Reg process. But to truly *self*-regulate, the teen has to be the one who identifies her stressors across all five domains. *She* has to know what kinds of activities bring her back to being calmly focused and alert and what kinds of situations to avoid or prepare for. Most important, she has to be the one who realizes when her tank is empty or she is getting really tense. At least in the beginning, this is where teens most need their parents' help.

Adolescents have a tendency to fixate on the emotional state they're in without reflecting on their physical state. Strong negative feelings can be so overpowering that teens don't recognize the connection between their physical and emotional state, let alone the more complex connection between their present energy depletion/tension imbalance and subsequent emotional state.

It does no good to exhort a teen to exercise greater self-control when he's struggling with intrusive thoughts or has a strong negative bias, spends excessive hours in front of a screen, or is drawn to addictive substances or mindless thrill seeking. Even if we teach teens adaptive coping strategies or place them in a situation that requires some sort of collaborative problem-solving response, they are unlikely to master or use these new cognitive or social skills if they have poor self-awareness.

A prominent theme throughout the scientific literature on adolescence today is that we have seriously underestimated the duration of childhood. The research on the teenage brain tells us how poorly equipped teens are to make decisions or assess risks. Hence we need to ensure that they continue to receive the sort of adult guidance needed to compensate for their still-underdeveloped executive functions. This point is important in that it asks us to reframe adolescent risk taking, to understand the biological factors involved in sensation seeking, and to be more understanding of the processing limitations teens are under that may lead them into more hazardous forms of risk taking. This new understanding of the adolescent brain has stimulated the popular conversation, and that's a great start. Now we need to see how it all comes together—neurology, biology, cognition, social behavior, and emotion regulation—to drive the stress cycle so we can give kids the tools they need to manage this Formula 1 racing engine.

Giving adolescents the tools—but *not attempting to do the job for them*—is essential. From an evolutionary point of view this is an important distinction for parents to remember as they transition from being the parent of an infant and young child to their role as parent of an adolescent. After all, nature could hardly have afforded a species that needed close parental monitoring for twenty to twenty-five years, if only because she couldn't count on parents to last that long!

This is not to say that increasingly diligent attention by parents and schools aimed at moderating adolescent risk taking are misplaced, but only that the need for it may be distinctly modern—made necessary by a contemporary environment that calls for greater adult guidance and instruction because of the proliferation of dysregulating influences.

The challenge for parents comes in stepping up parental guidance as needed to help the teen safely navigate today's world while stepping back enough to let the adolescent's natural developmental processes progress as we've considered in this chapter. After all, initiation rites around the world suggest that puberty has long been understood as marking a fairly abrupt transition from dependence to independence, with all the responsibilities that this entails. We have to be careful that we don't, in a well-intentioned response to modern risks, adopt a parenting style that runs counter to the most basic developmental needs of the adolescent brain.

Nyx

The fifteen-year-old girl who came in to see us certainly made a striking entrance. She was dressed all in black, with short spiky hair and studs in her ears, eyebrows, and nose. But it wasn't the clothes or the piercings that caught our attention. It was the sadness and anger that she exuded. She had taken a goth name for herself: one that was resonant of darkness and chaos. She refused to respond to her given name, "Mary Catherine." "Nyx" was now the only name that she would go by, and you could hear the catch in her mother's voice every time she uttered it.

Mom told us several times that she couldn't understand what had happened to the little girl who had once liked nothing more than to dress up like a princess and spend hours at a time playing with her dolls. According to Mom, she had been the perfect baby. She slept through the night almost from the start and she rarely cried. She would lie contentedly in her cot all day, feeling the different textures on her bumper pads. A friend had told her how important it is to stimulate a baby's senses, so Mom had hung a colorful mobile over the crib that the baby just loved to stare at and then, when she was a little older, had bought one of those activity mats designed for the same purpose. Her baby would lie on her back and stare at the various things hanging down for hours at a time or rub her hands over the different textures.

Mom and Dad both worked hard to interact with their baby daughter, but they agreed that she seemed happiest when she was left alone. She would typically smile and laugh when they made silly faces or sang silly songs, but, they said, she was "just one of those babies who liked to be by herself." So more and more they left her alone, reluctant, as Mom put it, to "intrude into her personal space."

Mom had studied the developmental milestones chart religiously, always a bit anxious about her daughter's development. She was a little slower to sit up and to start crawling than the chart showed, and a little slower to babble or respond to her name and start talking. But a trip to the pediatrician always ended with the reassurance, "Don't worry, some kids just take a bit longer." And sure enough, it did take a bit longer, but there was never any question of a serious motor or language delay.

The one slight lingering concern was that the little girl had no desire to play with other children. At preschool she preferred to play by herself, and in primary school she never joined in the ruckus during recess but always sat by herself in a corner. She never went to birthday parties and shunned the idea of having her own birthday party. Naturally withdrawn herself, Mom remarked: "She must have inherited my temperament!"

Mom had tried to get her interested in ballet class. They started when she was three, and she seemed happy enough to put on her leotard, tights, and tutu. She loved it when the teacher gave the kids ribbons or wands to wave about. But in the second year there always seemed to be some reason she couldn't go to ballet class that day: a stomachache, a sore throat. And somehow ballet seemed to just sort of die out on its own, without anyone's ever consciously deciding to give it up.

Still eager to get her more socially involved, Mom and Dad tried a number of other after-school activities. But nothing seemed to work: not soccer or tae kwon do or music—not even art class. She would go submissively enough once or twice, but then the same pattern always repeated itself and the terrible stomachache or sore throat suddenly came back. Eventually Mom and Dad decided that since she was so happy on her own, it was cruel to try to force her to do something that she clearly didn't enjoy.

As far as Mom and Dad could tell, she didn't have a single real friend. In fact, despite their fairly constant urging, she refused any kind of social involvement, constantly complaining that her peers were "shallow" and "pathetic." She would lock herself in her room for hours at a time, listening to music and writing poems or essays she kept to herself. In fact, it was becoming increasingly difficult to communicate with her. She had become a devoted follower of the English rock band Bauhaus and would listen to their albums on an iPod at seemingly all hours of the day.

Another cause of concern was that she had started to put on a good deal of weight. She had always been slightly pudgy, but now she was becoming seriously overweight. And for the first time in her life she had developed a sleep problem. She would sleep four to five hours several nights in a row and then "catch up" with a marathon sleep of twelve hours or more. Sometimes her parents weren't sure whether she had slept the previous night at all. She became even more distant, even more difficult to engage in conversation or get to join them for dinner. If pressed she would insist that she was feeling "fine," but her actions and her mood said otherwise.

Her parents knew so little about what was going in her life that it was only from a third party that they learned that Nyx had posted a poem on her Facebook wall about cutting herself. They immediately arranged for her to see a psychotherapist, who reported that Nyx was very anxious, that she was struggling with some serious anger issues, directed as much at herself as at others, and that she had started cutting because it was "the only time that she felt alive."

The therapist was careful to stress that she did not feel that Nyx was in any way suicidal. In her words, "She is not mentally ill; but neither is she mentally healthy." This is one of the more profound statements I have heard and applicable to so many teens today: perhaps far more than we are willing to recognize.

It was on a recommendation from the therapist, who was familiar with our work in self-regulation, that Mom and Dad brought Nyx in to see us. The therapist thought that Nyx was in a chronic state of hypoarousal—low energy, low interest—and hoped that we might be able to help identify some of the stressors she was struggling with and suggest Self-Reg strategies. The full evaluation showed that Nyx had a number of sensory hyposensitivities that meant she needed a little more of some stimuli—light, sound, touch, and even taste—to feel "right." This could well be the reason she had been so drawn to visual and tactile stimulation as a baby and why, as a teen, she was glued to her iPod and drawn to high-calorie foods that used salt to enhance sweetness or MSG to stimulate the glutamate receptors. But in addition it seemed clear that Nyx was struggling with profound social stressors.

The years she had spent growing up mostly alone had deprived her of the critical experiences necessary to learn how to mindread—to know what others are thinking from their gestures, eyes, posture, tones of voice. She also had not developed her capacity to empathize with others, to understand what friends were feeling. Here too we suspected that these deficits had begun quite early, that what her parents had regarded as signs of a baby who was "happiest when left alone" were, in fact, the signs of a baby who needed extra wooing in order to entice her to enter into those countless everyday two-way interactions that develop the parent-child interbrain and the foundation of these mindreading and prosocial skills.

But Nyx's problem wasn't simply a consequence of having trouble picking up the subtle signs of the effect of her actions or utterances on others; she also found it hard to regulate her strong emotions. Mom reported that as a small child Nyx was never angry; on those rare occasions when she did start to lose her temper, she would invariably go sit in a dark quiet space until she had calmed down. As a teenager, if she was confronted with someone else's strong anxiety or distress, she became overwhelmed by her own feelings of anxiety or distress and would shut down.

This limited ability to express and modulate her strong emotions, coupled with her feelings of numbness and loneliness, imposed a terrible cost on her: not just emotionally and socially but physiologically, contributing to her sleep problems and triggering her appetite for junk food under stress. In short, she was caught in a stress cycle where all these different stressors were impinging on and exacerbating her problems in self-regulation.

At the end of the day Nyx's need for peer interaction was every bit as great as that of any other teenager. What she lacked were the social skills needed to build meaningful relationships. She turned to an online goth community to satisfy this deep need, but the problem for her was that this didn't provide the regulating effects of traditional activity that brings peers together.

Nyx needed help in several different domains. She obviously had to develop better sleep and eating habits, and she needed to engage in activities that would help her develop socially and prosocially. But as she and her parents began to work with Self-Reg, it was important to be very mindful of the points about the adolescent brain that we've looked at in this chapter, in particular the need to be part of a small group engaged in some shared goal.

Of all the factors involved in the progress that Nyx made once she started doing Self-Reg, possibly the most significant was joining the school choir. The physical act of singing has a highly regulating effect on the nervous system, and from the moment she tried it Nyx found the experience exhilarating. It turned out that she had a lovely soprano voice, so here was an activity in which she could begin to shine. Perhaps most important was that now she was involved in a group activity that introduced her to others with a similar interest. Her sociability and enthusiasm for singing together was a sign of just how strong her desire had been all along to be part of a group.

Now a vibrant young adult, she still sometimes goes to her parents when she needs to talk about something that she's finding stressful—as most of us would hope of our twentysomethings. But she has a much deeper understanding of her physiological needs and emotional vulnerabilities and, at this point in her life as a college junior, she is in a state that can quite legitimately be described as "mentally healthy." She has all sorts of friends, and not just from choir. She takes good care of herself and takes pride in herself. Perhaps most telling of all, she chooses to go by her given name, "Mary Catherine."

ELEVEN

More

*Desire, Dopamine, and the Surprising
Biology of Boredom (the Reward System)*

The boys were in grade seven, and some had serious behavior, mood, and attention problems. Their teacher, Mrs. W, a passionate and experienced educator, was under strain. "I've always had to deal with one or two children in a classroom who have a lot of trouble settling," she said, "but this is more extreme than anything I've ever seen before—they're really affecting the rest of the class." My visit was early on a Monday morning, and many of the boys had spent the weekend together playing *Call of Duty*, a violent video game. They had slept very little, one not at all.

After learning that every one of them played soccer, lacrosse, or hockey, I asked how they felt after a game, and one blurted out: "I feel really calm." That last word took me aback: how it feels to be successfully self-regulating. Many children cannot even name a time they have felt calm. When I surveyed the rest of the boys, every one said the same sort of thing. But when I asked, "And how did you feel this morning when you had to get up to go to school?" They each admitted, "I felt really crappy." They knew how differently each activity made them feel, but when I asked, "Would you rather play hockey or soccer outside, or *Call of Duty*?" every single voice, in unison, rang out: "Stay inside and play *Call of Duty*!" This was interesting but more than a little depressing. Why would they choose crappy over great?

The flip side to this story is Jane, our neat and composed receptionist, who returned from a week away on spring break with her husband and two sons absolutely frazzled. It turned out they'd been forced to cancel their plans to get away, but to keep her kids happy she had gotten them a subscription to Netflix for the week. "It certainly kept them quiet," she said. Nevertheless, that morning both kids had complained bitterly about how boring spring break had been. She didn't get it. She had let them watch whatever they wanted whenever they wanted, and they had always been so engrossed. How could they say they had been bored?

Many parents are asking that very same question. Part of the answer could be that children are so overstimulated today that they are no longer capable of entertaining themselves; they haven't developed the sort of creativity and resourcefulness that come from traditional imaginative play. For thousands of years children played the ancient Indian board game of Snakes and Ladders together, played games like tag or hide-and-seek together, sorted through boxes to play dress-up or find building blocks. With modern video and online games, the physical interaction and conversation of face-to-face play are lost. Typically the child plays against the computer, not another child. Self-Reg helps us understand this loss of human interaction in an entirely new light.

The Surprising Biology of Boredom

There isn't a parent reading this book who hasn't heard her child complain, "I'm bored." We treat such statements as if children were describing their mental state—that they're restless and can't find anything interesting to do. But their statement isn't really a description at all. It's more like an animal call—what philosophers call an *avowal*—in this case a primitive expression of agitation. Children could simply make that whining noise that is boredom's universal signature without any words at all, and we'd instantly know what they're feeling; in fact, this would probably be a lot less misleading for us.

Studies have shown how overstimulation produces boredom, and Self-Reg tells us why. When we induce boredom with an activity that overstimulates a child, her cortisol shoots up. This happens because the adrenaline-stimulating activity—for instance, an online war game—causes the child to dip into her energy reserves. This increases her cortisol, the stress hormone. The higher level of cortisol sharpens her awareness of physiological and emotional distress. "Boredom" involves a distinctive and uncomfortable physical feeling that comes from having too much cortisol in the bloodstream.

When the source of the stimulation is turned off, the mammalian and reptilian brains may respond to this imbalance with an abrupt swing from hyper- into hypoarousal. This is an ancient neural mechanism designed to halt energy drain and promote recovery. But children find this sudden shift a further acute stressor, sort of what it feels like if you slam on the brakes too hard.

What all this means is that we need to apply the first step of Self-Reg and reframe the utterance "I'm bored," which simply signifies, "I feel yucky." That's why they whine. This is the natural expression of heightened stress brought about by the "entertaining" activity. If we don't understand this point we'll mistakenly think that our child needs further stimulation and end up doing precisely the opposite of what is called for—inadvertently adding to his stress load when what we really need to do is reduce it. We need to bring the hypoaroused child back to calm, not have him shoot back up to hyper.

How the Reward System Works

If you've taken a look at the now-classic digital games like *Candy Crush* or *Angry Birds* (or perhaps been hooked on them yourself) or any of the many other such mind-numbing "exciting" pastimes that keep us transfixed without complaint, the logical question that presents itself is one science has taken seriously: If there isn't anything particularly interesting about it, what keeps us glued to it for so long?

Neuroscientists found the answer to that question back in the late 1990s. We knew, of course, that games trigger adrenaline; that was the whole point. But scientists had become interested in the effects of video games on the brain's reward system. They discovered that these games cause dopamine levels to double. That's a major finding, and the explanation was a breakthrough in addiction science.

The games trigger the release of opioids, the neurohormones that make us feel good. There are a number of reasons why games have this effect. It's not just the brain's natural response to winning something (even when the reward in question is utterly inane). The game's bells and whistles—the bright colors and lights and sudden loud noises that accompany hitting a target (or being hit)—add to the effect. And then dopamine—the source of craving—surges, driving the brain to get another hit of opioid, and another, and another.

This is the neurochemical reward system: the interaction between opioids and dopamine. It is simple by nature's design, which was intended for purposes of survival: find a food source that provides energy and then make the experience of eating that food pleasurable. (The same point applies, in a big way, to sex; nature wanted to make sure that we procreate!) The opioids released are psychoactive chemicals that produce pleasant sensations and relief from pain or stress. Opioids bind to receptors that are scattered throughout the nervous system and the gastrointestinal tract. They work by giving us a shot of energy while inhibiting the firing of neurons that are activated by pain, stress, or anxiety. That's one of the reasons why they make us feel so much better.

Opioids are present in breast milk, which is an important factor in promoting both feeding and attachment. They are produced by exercise and even released by touch, by being cuddled or stroked—all good things. Later, once an opioid becomes associated with a reward—say, eating some ice cream—and especially when it happens quickly, the midbrain releases dopamine, which fires up the nucleus accumbens in the ventral striatum, driving us to seek out that reward and making us feel anxious until this craving has been sated. In fact, what we call "anxiety" is really just a state of sustained fear or hypervigilance (marked by rapid pulse, shallow breathing, sweating, dilated pupils, sensory hypersensitivities), which keeps us alert, ready to protect ourselves or chase after the reward.

Dopamine is released when we just think about a reward, or when we encounter a stimulus that we associate with a reward. The brain releases other neuromodulators that promote alertness and arousal (norepinephrine), regulate how we process information (serotonin), and promote recovery (acetylcholine). Dopamine is critical to behavior insofar as it creates yearning and desire. But too much of it results in the feelings of dissatisfaction and restlessness that Jane saw in her kids.

When the Thrill Is Gone: Hooked on *More*

The better something feels, the more we want of it, until its impact lessens and it no longer produces that pleasurable response. This, in turn, drives us to seek out more, or something even more pleasurable. Activating the reward system creates an overpowering desire to play a game over and over or watch movie after movie, driving out all thoughts of engaging in less opioid- and dopamine-intense experiences like reading or playing a card or board game.

Violence-themed role-playing or first-person-shooter games are habituating children to a heightened level of arousal that renders more sedate games not just boring but even unpleasant. Modern films aimed at kids are the same. You may have noticed these movies are getting louder and more violent, with ever less attention paid to the human dimension of plots and character development. That's intentional. These films are designed to activate the neural "sweet spot" and are tested in focus-group screenings that use galvanic skin response, EKG, or even fMRI so that the creators can calibrate sensory stimulation for the desired effect. It's pretty hard to sit through *Fantasia* once your brain has habituated to *Transformers*.

There is some evidence that high-intensity role-playing games may offer some fine-motor and even cognitive benefits. But at the heart of the matter is a primitive system in the brain burning so much energy that it leaves the child desperately in need of instant energy. Violent movies work the same way on the brain. When the poet-philosopher Samuel Coleridge talked in 1817 about the "willing suspension of disbelief," in which a reader suspends rational judgment about aspects of a story, what he was partly alluding to was what we now understand as the operations of the limbic system—the prefrontal cortex going off-line under this kind of stress. Your poor mammalian brain responds to the hero's peril by sending a message to the reptilian brain to get your own heart rate racing. Swelling music and bursts of light and color add to the effect. And since you're not going anywhere, none of this built-up tension gets released. I once got talked into taking my kids to one of these movies, and when it was over, I didn't so much walk out as totter into the lobby, exhausted from the limbic marathon I'd just run. All around me were food kiosks selling things that ordinarily I never touch, but now my craving for a Big Gulp was uncontrollable.

No coincidence there. Junk food falls into the same rewards category as violent games and movies. What is most remarkable about junk food is how it is designed to stimulate dopamine. To get the dopamine receptors firing, the "foods" (so processed and artificial they hardly qualify as such) have to maximize opioid release. In fact, this happens to some degree with natural foods too: sugar, wheat, milk, even meat. But junk food, or so-called hyperpalatable foods, take this phenomenon to a much higher level.

To create a hyperpalatable food, technicians experiment with various combinations of fat, sugar, and salt, as well as odors, appearance, complex combinations, and texture, to reach a "bliss point" where opioid release is maximized. This stimulates the production of dopamine, which is what drives craving and drives up sales. And from a food producer's point of view, the neat thing about opioid release is that the effect wears off, but not the dopamine that keeps the craving strong.

It is only because video-game designers, movie producers, and food scientists have become so good at what they do that neuroscientists and public-health officials have become so concerned about the effects of superstimulants. The problem is that the "dopaminergic spike" is so powerful that it hijacks the autonomic nervous system. It bypasses the brain's natural signals for rest and restoration or satiation, so the child keeps playing or eating well past the point of natural cessation.

It's not simply the opioid-dopamine circuit that's the problem but the fact that the game or food leaves the child *more depleted* than when he started, hence more in need of another opioid hit. Not all children are affected in the same way by superstimulants, and even for those children who do in some sense get "hooked," the effects are much less serious than those of, say, alcohol or drugs. Yet they are of concern, not just because the habit might be fostering a tendency to experiment with more serious, chemically enhanced opioids as the child grows older but because of the much more immediate effect on the child's mood, behavior, and health.

Perhaps the biggest problem, however, is how superstimulants interfere with those natural activities that reduce stress. For example, munching on potato chips or a candy bar not only has none of the long-lasting self-regulatory benefits of munching on an apple (which are a function of both the chewing and the apple's slow-release form of energy) but can also kill the child's inclination to eat an apple.

There is the further worry that, when carried to excess, potato chips and soft drinks may actually increase the child's stress load. For example, because the hypothalamus responds to an elevated level of salt in the bloodstream by trying to flush it out, a surprising number of children and adolescents are dehydrated, and this results in a deficiency in several important minerals that influence our ability to think clearly. A sudden rush of energy followed by the equally sudden energy crash can also play havoc with arousal regulation and the capacity to think clearly. So the child who eats too much of these foods or spends too much time playing these games may be diminishing his capacity to think about what he's eating or doing. The more a child gets hooked on these products, the more he wants the very things that have put him in this state in the first place. Far from a generation of satisfied, stimulated children, the result is just the opposite: stimulated, unsatisfied—indeed unsatisfiable—children.

Taming the Beast: Tuning In to Cues Helps a Child Take Charge

The associations that drive cravings are not simply with a pleasure that we experienced when we ate or did something but with the physical and emotional state we were in when we formed this "stimulus-reward" association. All four factors are vitally interconnected: the physical, the emotional, the opioid, and the dopamine. When a child is in the same state of exhaustion or anxiety that he was in the first time he ate the chips (or played the stimulating game), his limbic system suddenly reminds him of the effect they had the last time he felt this way.

In fact, we see the same phenomenon with drugs and alcohol and other true addictions. For decades parents were bombarded with the message that the addictive element in drugs is so powerful that a single exposure is enough to hook a vulnerable teen. But we now know after years of careful research that what makes a teen vulnerable is not some sort of overpowering chemical reaction over which the brain has no control but the teen's *physical and emotional state* that drove him to seek some chemical way to suppress his feelings. What's more, studies show that the way to effectively control a teen's drug use is not to try to make drugs inaccessible (which in all likelihood is impossible) but to address the stress overload that drives him to try to suppress his acute distress in such a dangerously maladaptive way.

Self-Reg's emphasis on self-awareness, learning to tune in to internal cues, helps a child develop mindful attention to physical and emotional states that may otherwise slip into an unhealthy stimulus-reward pattern. So often this step signals a turnaround, as Jonah's story illustrates.

Jonah

Jonah was nine when he and his parents came to see us. He walked into my office that first day a bit of a sad sack, munching on potato chips yet clearly oblivious to what he was doing. Jonah was overweight but not obese; more worrying was that he just didn't look healthy. His skin had a sort of pallor and he had a noticeably strained look on his face. But what really brought home that there might be a problem here was when he finished the bag of chips and then pulled a chocolate bar out of his pocket.

His family had come to see us because Jonah was having a lot of trouble paying attention in school. He wasn't particularly hyperactive, just very inattentive. It wasn't that he disturbed anyone else or focused on something of his own choosing. He just seemed to be in a sort of funk all the time. His teacher reported to his parents that she had to stand "almost right on top of him" and call his name out loudly to get his attention. She suggested that he see a psychologist to "work on his motivation," because "if he doesn't start applying himself, he's going to have all sorts of trouble when he gets into the higher grades." We could all see that this was true.

Learning to apply himself was clearly not much on Jonah's mind as he munched chips through our conversation. It was hard to tell what, in fact, was on his mind other than the next chip. He seemed to be on automatic pilot, not just unaware of *what* he was eating but unaware *that* he was eating. He popped one chip after another into his mouth without pause. The crinkle of the empty sack was his cue to quit.

This was no different from the situation for many of us these days and for many, if not most, kids. Junk food is certainly a significant contributing factor to one of the biggest epidemics that we see in children today (other than obesity), and that is an epidemic of "mindlessness"—not just being unaware of what is going on inside or around them but often being unaware of what they are doing. One look at Jonah told us that this mindlessness—about eating and in general—was a problem for him.

As part of our work with Jonah, we taught him to recognize that when he had the desire for chips or a candy bar, this was his body's way of telling him that he was depleted. But we didn't start with a lecture about nutrition, energy needs for a kid his age, and the need to replenish energy and not become depleted. Rather, at the end of the first session I asked him if he could do one thing for me. I wanted to know what happened in Mom's car when she ran out of gas. Mom agreed to let the tank run down and made sure he was in the car when the fuel light came on.

Jonah came back the next week excited to tell me what happened: A red light had gone on, and he had found out from his dad that this was because there was a float inside the gas tank, and when it dropped down too low it caused a light on the dashboard to go on. So then I asked him, did he have anything similar in his gas tank that, when he was really low on fuel, triggered some sort of signal? He thought hard about this for a while and finally gave up and implored me to answer the question for him. Instead I asked him if the little voice inside his head telling him to go get some potato chips or a candy bar might be just such a signal. He thought hard about this for a moment and then broke out in a big smile when he saw the connection.

There was still a lot of work ahead, helping Jonah to understand what his personal stressors were and how stress drains energy we need for other things—like paying attention in class or paying attention to the food we eat—and exploring much more effective ways to respond to stressed-out feelings than reaching for junk food and tuning out through the school day. But this initial "aha moment" was profoundly important for changing his trajectory. It represented a critical first step, that of developing the *self-awareness* needed to regulate himself. The aim was not to get him to inhibit these cravings. They were the product of some strong associations formed deep in the amygdala, orbital frontal cortex, and nucleus accumbens, the parts of the brain that integrate emotions, emotional behavior, and motivation. The aim was to get him to recognize the "meaning" of these cravings.

Redirecting Calls to the Emergency Response System

We are all, children and adults alike, drawn to superstimulants when we're overstressed. Traditionally, we have sought to battle these cravings by encouraging children to exercise more self-control. But struggling against these manipulated desires is highly energy expensive and extremely taxing in its own right. These are battles that we all invariably lose the moment we enter them, for the more energy we expend trying to inhibit a powerful impulse, the more likely we are to succumb either at that moment or shortly afterward. Hence the rebound effect that frequently follows a seemingly successful diet.

The Self-Reg alternative is to tackle the roots of these impulses so one doesn't enter the battle in the first place. This is not a case of educating our children about the dangers of superstimulants. Self-Reg tells us that we shouldn't be looking at this issue in *cognitive* terms at all—lectures about the dangers of superstimulants fall on deaf ears when craving calls. This is first and foremost biological and emotional, a matter of energy expenditure and recovery. You don't reason with an aroused limbic system; you soothe it, to quell one of its most primitive and hardwired functions.

The limbic system serves not just as an alarm but as an "emergency response system"—ERS for short—for when your tank is empty. The ERS searches its memory to identify what served in the past to soothe and provide rapid energy. Eating a doughnut may make perfect sense, because it's not just being soothed that has been associated with this experience but also fast energy release. Moreover, resisting the doughnut in these circumstances takes only more effortful control—is a further significant energy "expense"—making us that much more vulnerable, if not to the doughnut, then to some other reward that promises instant relief and energy. (As it happens, exactly the same is true for alcohol or drugs.)

The more hyper- or hypoaroused a child is, the more the brain's ERS stays on high alert. In this state the child is driven to consume calorie-dense rather than nutrient-dense foods. One of the most fascinating things we have seen in our work with overweight children is that when they become calmly focused and alert they crave water, fruit, or yogurt after physical activities. That's because the brain has a priority list of needs to be met, and beyond its basic requirement for energy it also sends out the message to meet the body's need for fluids or vitamins and minerals or slow-release carbohydrates. In a crisis it will take the junk calories to burn, but when calm, it prefers higher-quality fuel for optimal health.

So doughnuts and fresh fruit are both options, but—and this is an important "but"—the goal of Self-Reg is not to try to suppress old associations and fond memories of doughnuts but instead to create new, positive ones. The biggest lesson we've learned is that you don't accomplish this goal by trying to persuade a child or teenager to stop eating or playing something that isn't good for them (good luck with that!). It's a case of getting kids to recognize how they feel when they do something that reduces their tension and tops up their energy. Once their ERS goes back on standby, cravings quickly change. Now when the need for energy spikes, the hypothalamus searches its memory for favorite sources and finds the healthier option.

Lights, Action, Excess: Stressors Surround the "Urbanized Generation"

Time spent in nature plays a vital role in self-regulation, particularly when children have positive experiences and associations that register as a reward when the overstressed limbic system goes searching for one. Imagine your child preferring a walk outdoors, or just relaxing under a tree, to yet another hour on a screen game. Imagine her older, with deep, sustaining memories of childhood in which nature was—

and now remains—a source of calm, joy, or solace to return to when the stresses of the day become oppressive and the urge for a quick fix spikes.

Nurturing children's relationship with nature has become increasingly challenging as their lives have become increasingly "urbanized" in many ways—from bright lights and crowded environments to the "always on" social media and their online lives. An estimated 50 percent of children globally (projected to increase to 66 percent by mid-century), and 81 percent in the United States and Canada, live in urban or suburban environments. Even those who live in more rural settings are often spending hours a day on computer games or social media. In a sense they are an urbanized generation no matter where they live, and the ubiquitous stressors of sleep deprivation, artificial lights, frantic activity, crowds, traffic or industrial noise, and in some cases poverty and chronic hardship all take a toll.

A flurry of scientific papers in the past few years have looked at urbanization as a major cause of the increased stress in children and adults. Identifying and understanding the effects of these cumulative stressors may also help us understand the effects on the reward system that put children at additional risk.

For example, sleep deprivation affects the amygdala, and scientists worry that the amount of nocturnal light present in cities could be disrupting this mechanism. Similar concerns have arisen over the light emitted by computer and other digital screens. Why? Once again we return to the role of the hypothalamus as the brain's master control system. Or rather, a small, wing-shaped structure within the hypothalamus, the *suprachiasmatic nucleus* (SCN), which regulates the body's circadian rhythm. The SCN responds to internal signals by producing neurochemicals that keep the body close to, but not exactly on, a twenty-four-hour cycle, and it requires external cues—principally light—to keep to the twenty-four-hour schedule. But the deeper point is that the cycle and the mechanism are integral parts of arousal regulation and the reward system.

The hypothalamus responds to fatigue just as it does to something startling: by raising arousal, which causes the amygdala to sound the alarm and search through its store of fear-based memories for instant forms of self-soothing. Or it sets in play systems for scanning the environment for potential threats, which, if the arousal is strong enough, the subject will see everywhere. All the noise, the sudden eruption of shouting or violence, the traffic and pollution, lights up the amygdala, with all the psychological, cognitive, and behavioral consequences that we've looked at in his book.

The reason that stress associated with city living has suddenly became such a hot topic again—and the reason why I became interested in this issue—was not the insane traffic congestion that we see in every city around the world: It was a paper that Andreas Meyer-Lindenberg's lab published in 2011, linking urbanization to heightened activation in the amygdala and the anterior cingulate cortex (ACC).

These were precisely the systems that we were studying in young children with autism. What we saw in the kids we treated was that as we reduced their arousal, the parts of the brain used to think, choose, reappraise, etc., were lighting up: in essence, taking charge of their thought, mood, and behavior. Meyer-Lindenberg suggested that urbanization seemed to be producing something very similar to what we had observed in children before they started treatment.

It's important to bear in mind that more than one thing can cause the amygdala to become hyperaroused—stressors from across all domains and a wide range of health and developmental complications. Maybe for many of us the urban setting does lead to poor sleep: a result of too much light, noise, and overall stimulation. Unfortunately, there haven't been many rigorous studies comparing rural and urban sleep patterns, but the few that have been done suggest a difference in both the amount and the quality of sleep, although no doubt technology and children's "always on" media habits are rapidly erasing this.

For many children the stress of their home environment renders self-regulation extremely difficult. The work of Gary Evans and

Jeanne Brooks-Gunn at the Stanford University and Harvard Kennedy School Collaboration for Poverty Research, along with the scientists connected with the National Science Council in Washington, has shown that the effect of "toxic stress"—pollution, noise, crowding, poor housing, inadequate school buildings, schools and neighborhoods with high turnover, family conflict, and exposure to violence and crime—on a child's stress reactivity can be severe and long-lasting.

TWELVE

Parents Under Pressure

Where Do We Go from Here?

Parents are under extraordinary pressure today, and it isn't much easier for you to stay calmly focused and alert than it is for your child. I'm referring not to personal problems but solely to the stresses associated with parenting. I could make a long list here of the different ways our children stress us, and you'd no doubt be well ahead of me with a list of your own. But there are five fundamental stressors for parents that are hot buttons for their own self-regulation problems:

(1) Socializing your child

You spend countless hours, day after day, year after year, trying to teach your child the rules of "acceptable" behavior. Settle down! Brush your teeth! Don't grab! Wait your turn! Share! Be nice! Say you're sorry! If it were easy to socialize your child—"normalize" him, as some have said—and you never had to repeat a lesson, there would be no such thing as a tired, exasperated parent. But the world is full of tired, exasperated parents. From preschool to high school prom, all too often you find yourself locked in a battle: Your child doesn't want to do what you want him to do or doesn't understand what you want him to do or finds it difficult to do what you want him to do or simply forgets what he was supposed to be doing.

No matter how you cut it, the socialization process is stressful—for your child and for you. Some children present more of a challenge than others due to temperament, or perhaps because they have special developmental needs or chronic health issues. Or you may have to deal with other difficult circumstances—illness, workplace or family complications, or financial hardship. Yet there's something different today about the pressure of socializing a child. Children as young as three are now being suspended from preschool for their "inappropriate" language or behavior. We've already seen how this attitude is based on the confusion of self-control with self-regulation and the harm this can have on children. But overhanging all these factors is a climate of zero tolerance, in which parents are constantly on edge that their child may do or say something deemed "unacceptable" and, most concerning, that the consequences will be severe. Children and adolescents are largely oblivious to this, like a three-year-old who thinks nothing of wandering into the street, but for parents this ongoing task of socialization has become more high-stakes than ever.

(2) Shared anxiety

Parents' stress levels are often high not because they are annoyed by what their child is saying or doing but because they want so badly to protect their children and, when their children are struggling, to help or soothe them. In a fascinating "parental empathy" study that we did in our lab, our director of neuroscience, Jim Stieben, looked at parents' empathic response in terms of brain activity when they watched their child engaged in a frustrating task. The task that he designed promised the child a reward if he could accumulate so many points; then, just when the child was about to "win," the game suddenly became impossible and the child lost many of his accumulated points. (Don't worry: Jim made sure that they all recouped their points so that every child got his reward at the end!) The parents' neurological reaction to the stress was clear on the scans (with sudden, intense activity in the ventral side of the ACC).

It is a part of the functioning of the interbrain that we need to take very seriously: how closely tied we are to our children's emotional swings and challenges. The better we can stay calm and alert, the faster they will return to being calm and alert, which in turn will help us stay calm, which in turn . . . You get the picture.

(3) Competitive parenting

Make no mistake about it: This competitiveness is a huge stressor on parents, not just on their kids. It's a big reason why some parents behave irrationally at Little League or soccer games or berate their child after a game for his lackluster performance. The same is true for a child's academic, social, or other accomplishments. It's become parents' status that's on the line, not their child's: their ambitions, their bragging rights, or, as is so often the case, their bitter disappointment.

(4) Navigating your way through the sea of superstimulants

We now know that superstimulants should be seen as physiological stressors that, when carried to excess, can trigger a stress cycle. Having a chronically overstressed child is a huge stressor on a parent. But this pales in comparison with the stress of trying to wean your child from a superstimulant.

Unfortunately there is no single solution, no one way to protect your child from the junk food, games, and other superstimulants that have become ubiquitous, and this anxiety adds to parental stress considerably. You can try outright banning the game or the food or whatever has hooked your child, but prohibition didn't work for the government and it rarely works for us. This is especially so as children get older. Instead we need to divert rather than try to subvert. We need to weaken the appeal of the superstimulants by redirecting our children into something regulating that they find even more appealing.

Figuring out how to do that is every parent's dilemma today, made that much more stressful by the proliferation of superstimulants in so many aspects of your child's life. We need to set limits and explain why they're there, and that process in itself is stressful because it typically devolves into an adversarial one. And today when kids argue, "But everyone else is doing it," the "everybody" may be the huge online culture that is, indeed, defining standards for kids.

(5) Moving beyond labels that oversimplify and don't solve the problem

We hear all the time that the key to successful parenting is adopting the right "parenting style." This idea is based on work that was done in the late 1960s by the developmental psychologist Diana Baumrind. Ever since, scientists have tended to categorize parenting behaviors into one of four basic styles: "authoritative," "authoritarian," "permissive," and "uninvolved."

But there are problems with this taxonomy. One is that whatever parenting style you might identify as generally characteristic of you—from easygoing mentor to boot-camp disciplinarian—no single parenting style guarantees stress-free parenting or ideal outcomes. What's more, we rarely conform to a single type of parenting style: Different challenges or stages in our child's life—or our own—may bring out different sides of our personality or communication style with our child. In fact, we are rarely all that conscious of our parenting as a chosen "style." More often than not we simply parent the way that we were parented. But the biggest problem in focusing on parenting styles is the missing variable in this equation: *the child*.

The truth is these classic "parenting styles" are just grooves that we settle into for all sorts of reasons. When things aren't going well, the real issue is not that we've bought in to a parenting style that isn't working or has been shown to have undesirable consequences. The issue is that certain factors have pushed us into this negative pattern. Simply telling "permissive" parents that if they keep it up their children are more likely to be aggressive when they grow older only adds to a stress load that is often the reason they have become permissive in the first place. They're exhausted, depleted; they have no energy left for the struggle to control their kids, as they've been led to believe they must do. What's needed is to go beyond these labels and work on the causes.

I n the moment, stress invariably changes the way we respond to our child. It might be stress directly related to your child's behavior or situation, but it might just as easily be stressors from work, people, or situations having nothing to do with your child. The five-domain model is applicable to all of us, and if you're running on empty, then the drain affects your self-regulation in all of the domains, and stress involving your child will register all the more. The result is as stressful for your child as it is for you. You know the vicious cycle: You grow more and more insistent, then either blow up in anger or give up and withdraw. The better you can keep yourself calmly focused and engaged with your child, the more likely he will learn whatever it is that you want him to learn, as well as think through the consequences of his actions, deal with his emotions, persevere in a task, and cope with frustration.

This doesn't require a personality makeover or even willpower on your part. The more you practice regulating yourself to a calm, composed state, the better you'll feel instantly and the more competent you'll come to feel as a parent. In that calmer state your intuitive "sixth sense" kicks into high gear and you naturally become more finely attuned to your child's arousal. You'll also grow more attuned to the effects of your own behavior and that of others on your child, and you'll find the calm, ready response to match. In moments that might otherwise be dysregulating for both of you, you'll be better able to maintain your equilibrium and help your child do the same.

Finding What Works

Self-Reg helps you learn how to read the early indicators of when your child is slipping into hypo- or hyperarousal and helps your child develop that self-awareness too. Nonetheless, there is endless variability in the idiosyncratic ways that children signal when they're under too much stress. As we've seen, some kids become hyper, others withdraw. They also vary in their responses to your attempts to up- or down-regulate them. The more you work with your child to develop self-regulation, the more familiar those early signs will become for both of you. Every child is unique in what he or she finds soothing or distressing, and children can vary dramatically in their responses, even within the span of a few minutes.

There are some valuable lessons here for Self-Reg. Are you listening to your child with your eyes as well as your ears? Are you working with your child on his clock or your own? Are you teaching your child to be independent or dependent; to be resilient or spiritless; to be confident or submissive? Are you aiding your child on his path to self-discovery or impeding him? Most important of all, are you helping your child to become the master of her destiny or are you still looking for compliance?

Lessons Learned: Ten Ways to See the Signs and Develop the Habit of Self-Reg

1. Look for Patterns

The sign that a child is becoming overaroused can be as subtle as a change in facial complexion or tone of voice, a distinctive facial expression, or maybe no facial expressions at all. So we have to learn when they are telling us, through their body and their speech, that their stress is too great.

2. Keep Your Eyes on the Target

The focus of Self-Reg has to be on self-regulation itself, not some secondary or specific problem that may have arisen from or been exacerbated by an excessive stress load. Self-Reg enables you to shift from a behavioral "control and correct" mind-set, or simply trying to extinguish a behavior, to a more fundamental connection with your child to understand his behavior and together strengthen self-regulation. Once Self-Reg starts to take hold, so many problems with behavior, learning, socialization, and communication resolve on their own. The goal is to help children learn Self-Reg skills and strategies so that they develop their capacity to self-regulate, especially under pressure. To take a simple example, we don't just want to see children going to bed at the proper time; we want to see them looking forward to going to sleep.

3. Proceed Gradually

Doing Self-Reg with your child always involves a learning curve, sometimes steep, and every curve looks a little different. But something exciting always happens: When you proceed slowly and steadily, the direction of the curve always begins to shift. Your child will start to have longer periods of feeling calm and staying engaged. Don't look for some dramatic change but rather for subtle signs that the trajectory is shifting.

This is the big driver behind our trial-and-error approach: trying to figure out from the gains you are seeing, however small, what is working and why and, just as important, what is not working and why.

4. Get Excited When Your Child Begins to Initiate

As soon as you see your child starting to initiate and not just respond to your overtures, you know that his brain is transitioning from relying on primitive mechanisms for dealing with stress (fight or flight or freeze) to social engagement. Your child rushing to show or tell you something, your teenager collapsing on the couch and telling you, unprompted, about her day: These are the sorts of everyday signs of optimal regulation that we don't ever want to take for granted.

5. Expect the Unexpected

If there is one thing that working with children on their Self-Reg teaches you, it is humility. You can have the best reasons in the world for the predictions that you make, only to have the child completely defy your expectations. Again we come back to the overarching importance of seeing Self-Reg as a process: one in which we learn as much from the children as they learn from us. There are so many ways in which one learns to expect the unexpected, but there seem to be a few basic rules operating here:

- What works beautifully for one child may have the opposite effect on another, even though the two seemed to have very similar needs.
- Invariably, something that has worked beautifully stops working.
- Sometimes something works, but for none of the reasons you expected.
- Sometimes something doesn't work for reasons that you'll never understand.
- All too often what you love they'll hate, and vice versa.

- Sometimes what you thought was working was actually making things worse.
- And sometimes something that you were sure wasn't working turns out to be terrific: It just took awhile.

6. Be Wary of Using Big Words

We tend to skip over so much when we rely too much on language. You might not think that "calm" is a big word, but what makes it "big" is not the number of letters it contains but the number of elements. In this respect "calm" is a very big word, for it contains three distinct components: physical, cognitive, and emotional. The physical element is the sensation of a slow heart rate, deep and relaxed breathing, and loose or completely relaxed muscles. The cognitive element is being aware of these physical sensations and what's going on around you. And the emotional is actually enjoying this state. This is what is meant by an "embodied understanding" of "calm"—not just being able to define or even use the word correctly but associating these clusters of sensations, emotions, and awareness with the word. I'm continually amazed by how few of the children and teens we see truly understand the meaning of "calm." Most of them seem to think that it just means "quiet."

7. Don't Go Too Metacognitive

Whenever we do Self-Reg with a child, regardless of the child's age, we have to try very hard to find ways of presenting the information so that he or she can fully grasp it. What this means is that we have to try to communicate at the child's developmental level, which involves all five domains. This applies just as much to a teenager as to a young child.

Where this gets tricky is when a child is at a high level in one domain but a relatively low level in another. For example, your child might be at a high level of cognitive development but a lower level of social and emotional functioning (the stereotype of the brainy kid who is socially awkward and distraught when interactions go poorly). Even within domains we might encounter striking disparities. For example, a child might be at a high level of abstract reasoning yet a low level of self-awareness. This is what we saw with Steven: He was able to process *what* his parents were saying, and he could use the word "calm" correctly, even define it if asked. Yet he didn't have an embodied understanding of what the word meant: He didn't know what calmness felt like. His understanding of the meaning of "calm" was a bit like that of someone who can define but doesn't really understand a word in a foreign language.

This can be a challenge for parents. It is natural for us to think that we can always explain what we mean—even if we have to use simpler language or talk louder! But for children and, indeed, teens to be able to do Self-Reg they have to know what big words like "hypoaroused," "hyperaroused," and "calm" feel like. They have to understand the difference between feeling "drowsy" and "hypoaroused," or "energized" and "hyper." And, of course, they have to know how pleasant it feels to be calm.

8. Remember That It Is Never Too Early to Start Doing Self-Reg—or Too Late

One of the questions I'm most often asked is when you should start doing Self-Reg. The answer is, of course, the second you put down this book, regardless of whether you even have a child! But as far as doing Self-Reg with our kids goes, the truth is that babies tell us through their body language, virtually from the moment of birth, what they find soothing and what is agitating. The baby who tenses up when you stroke her a little too vigorously or deeply is "telling" you through her reaction to try a different kind of massage; when you slow it down or lighten your touch and her body melts into you, she might as well be saying, "Ahhhh."

Perhaps most important of all is this: There is never an age at which it's too late to start. Parents are bombarded every day with messages about the "importance of the early years"—the idea that brain trajectories are set by the age of six, if not younger. For some parents this has the unintended effect of dramatically intensifying their stress. "Oh my God," they think, "I missed out the chance to lay down a good foundation and now it's too late." I've heard this lament more than once! But the truth is, it is *never* too late to start Self-Reg with your child—or yourself. This applies to the entire life span, not simply to older children and teens.

9. Consider Whose Trajectory Needs to Change

I've seen so many children who were constantly yelled at, punished, identified as "that child," that I have to wonder: To what extent are we the ones who are ultimately responsible for the trajectories that we're trying to change? It's a chilling thought. Under the sway of an ancient view of self-control, we may have thought that we were doing the best we could to help a child by punishing or rewarding him. And when the child simply can't respond to this regimen, we start to perceive him as the one who is at fault: as not trying hard enough, as knowing full well that the path he was choosing was going to lead to trouble.

What I find even more disturbing is how the influential adults in a child's life—teachers, coaches, neighbors—will persuade a child's parents to start thinking this way: "Your child needs to try harder/ think before he acts/tell the truth!" These well-intentioned messages miss the mark—do nothing to address self-regulation—and only make parents more anxious. It is partly just to quell their own anxiety that they begin to repeat these damaging messages to their child, and maybe even start to believe it themselves.

The whole point of Self-Reg is, of course, to become aware of and explore these issues and develop strategies to help your child develop the core emotional, cognitive, social, and prosocial competencies needed to deal with the stressors that life throws at him. But the starting point for changing a child's trajectory begins with our perception of that child; for this has far more bearing on how he perceives himself than we might ever dream.

10. Take It Personally

Self-regulation is always personal. Self-regulation is made possible by, and proceeds from, a strong relationship—it's the core strength of the interbrain—and we need to honor our own personal needs to do Self-Reg. Just like Jonah, the teen who ate junk food as if on autopilot, you need to recognize your own signals that you're in a state of low energy coupled with high tension; that's the "meaning," as it were, of a recurrent worry or an intrusive thought or a particular craving. You need to figure out what your stressors are, especially the hidden ones, and what you can do to reduce them. And just like all the children and teens we've looked at in this book, you need to be aware of when you are becoming hypo- or hyperaroused, and most important of all, what it feels like to be calm, resting, and recovering from the countless stresses of your daily lives.

Parents frequently share stories of their *aha* moments when they realize that the Self-Reg steps that are helping their children can help adults in precisely the same way. One mother shared with me that she had struggled with her weight since puberty and had been a yo-yo dieter her entire adult life, forever beating herself up for her lack of willpower. In working with the Self-Reg principles with her young son, it dawned on her that her weight problem had very little to do with willpower; the real problem was that she had used food to self-soothe since childhood. It had become a kind of self-regulation.

There are several reasons why eating can in fact have a calming effect. Some are psychological (associations formed by previous experiences) and some are physiological (endorphins released by the experience of eating certain kinds of foods). However, eating makes a poor tool for self-regulation, first because its effect as a stress reliever is only temporary, and second, the physical side effects, such as obesity, are bad for you.

Using the Self-Reg steps, this mother was able to shift her attention from the struggle for self-control and focus instead on ways to reduce her overall stress level. When she looked for hidden stressors coinciding with her impulses to overeat on comfort foods, she quickly discovered a pattern. On a good day at work or a relaxing evening or weekend with her family, she felt no draw to those foods that triggered craving and overeating. But after an especially stressful day at work or at home she felt desperate to tune it all out and just sit and eat—cake, chips, leftovers, you name it—until she couldn't swallow another bite. She never felt better afterward, only guilty and ashamed.

With this new awareness, she said, she realized that although she couldn't change her boss's sometimes abrasive management style or certain aspects of her family's personalities, she felt calmer dealing with both when she added a walk or other positive experiences to her day. The craving simply fell away. So did the excess pounds. It wasn't determination to stick with a diet that did it or because she had a sudden surge of willpower, but because, when she became more self-aware and learned how to deal effectively with her stressors, the cravings and stress-eating behavior simply diminished on their own. The Self-Reg plus: Whether a walk, a calming breath, or even knitting, when she chose what to do based on what would help her relax and restore, she found herself *doing* something instead of *eating* something. By taking better care of herself, she discovered she had more energy and patience for her son.

A Parent's Self-Reg Guide to Self-Care, Sanity, and Survival

Develop Your Own Self-Awareness as a Parent

Notice the way you up-regulate and down-regulate through the day to adjust to demands and the rhythm of the day. Get in touch with how your mind and body feel when you're stressed and how that affects the way you talk to your child or react to her behavior. For instance, could you be hypersensitive because you're overtired, anxious, or concerned about something else? Or could a past experience with this behavior in someone else be making you worry more about where it may lead for your child? Look for your own sources of stress in each of the five domains and identify ways to reduce that energy drain.

Create the Conditions That Support Optimal Self-Regulation for You

Establish a healthy sleeping, eating, and exercise regimen not just for your child but also for yourself. This also includes creating a calm, peaceful environment at home. If you have a hard time doing this just because it's good for you, then do it for your child. Remember that you serve not only as a model but also as a partner in co-regulation and in teaching your child how to self-regulate. Your child needs you to take good care of yourself.

Forgive Yourself

Part of shifting from the blame-and-shame paradigm is that you stop punishing yourself and focus instead on kinder ground, not only for your child but for yourself too. Be compassionate. We all make mistakes as parents. Apologize to your child when you've erred or fallen short of your better self; your child is watching you for cues about how to handle the stresses of everyday life and what to do when you mess up.

Aim for Calmness

Don't get attached to parenting styles or labels. They oversimplify the challenge of real parenting and they underestimate your capacity to come fresh to whatever moment unfolds for you and your child. Instead, develop a calm and consistent response style.

Make Time to Play with Your Child and
Simply Enjoy Each Other

Let your child help ground you in what's really important. Seeing the world through your child's eyes can reawaken you to the wonder and beauty of moments you might otherwise rush past. This is inherently calming for you and for your child.

Several years ago I was asked to consult on a large regeneration project taking place in Ireland. The community in question was in acute distress as a result of years of political and social neglect. Violence, drugs, and vandalism were rife. Those who could got out; those who couldn't were forced to join or hide from one of the two rival gangs. Walking through the neighborhood the first day, past burned-out houses and a littered park, I remarked to my host that it reminded me all too vividly of walking through the streets of Gaza. But the leaders of this project had brought in some of Ireland's finest minds to revive the physical and social environment, and despite the challenges they faced, the overall mood was one of great optimism.

I did not share their mood. At my visit to the primary school I had seen a group of children who, quite frankly, all appeared to have been traumatized. As for the teachers I met, they were the most wonderful and compassionate people imaginable, but they didn't know what to do, and every one of them displayed all the signs of burnout, or what psychologists refer to as "compassion fatigue."

Late that afternoon I met the local parish priest for a cup of tea; let us call him Father Pat. I suppose I must have given voice to my feelings of despair, for Father Pat looked at me gently and, in his thick Irish brogue, remarked: "Och, but they're only children, Stuart. Surely with all your science you can figure out some way to help them?" I instantly realized that the answer to Father Pat's question was a resounding *yes*, that the need for this knowledge and these practices had never been more acute for children and their parents and teachers. At that very moment the large-scale initiative to use Self-Reg in schools was born in Canada, beginning with school systems in British Columbia and Ontario.

Worrying about our children is a *human*, not a class or cultural, phenomenon. No demographic has a corner on the market of parental concern—or love. And no population of children is exempt from the myriad stresses that children have to deal with today. Certainly some of these stressors come wrapped in very different packaging, from gang violence to the pressure of college admissions. But at a human level it is about doing right by children and helping them develop the capacity to manage themselves to meet all challenges and live up to their fullest potential.

ACKNOWLEDGMENTS

A book's acknowledgments are more than just an occasion to thank those who have strongly influenced an author's thinking; it is also an opportunity to identify the book's intellectual pedigree. My own approach belongs to the logical empiricist tradition beginning, as Friedrich Waismann once remarked, with John Stuart Mill and culminating with Ludwig Wittgenstein. The two modern empiricists who have most influenced *Help Your Child Deal With Stress – and Thrive* are Stanley Greenspan and Stephen Porges. It is no coincidence that they worked closely together at the start of their careers, as there is a deep synergy between Greenspan's developmental and Porges's physiological outlook. Five others whose contribution must be highlighted are Alan Fogel, Robert Thayer, Allan Schore, Ross Greene, and my remarkable teacher at Oxford Jerome Bruner: Each of them is an outstanding philosopher as much as a remarkable scientist. Every one of the authors cited in the notes has played a vital role, but especially important are Paul MacLean, Walter Cannon, Hans Selye, and the legion of DIR therapists and theorists around the world.

Help Your Child Deal With Stress – and Thrive would not have been possible without the support of Milt and Ethel Harris and, following

Milt's untimely death, his children David, Judith, and Naomi and his nephew John. I do not know how to express my gratitude to the full MEHRI team: most important of all, our research director, Devin Casenhiser, who was such a joy to work with; neuroscience director, Jim Stieben; therapists Amanda Binns, Eunice Lee, Fay McGill, Narmilee Dhayanandhan, and Nadia Noble; research manager, Olga Morderer; community officer Alicia Allison; senior scientists Sonia Mostrangelo, Lisa Bayrami, Ljiljana Radenovic, and Shereen Hassanein; executive assistants Giselle Tedesco and Ana Bojcun; and all of the graduate and undergraduate students who worked tirelessly on our research.

I need to mention separately Chris Robinson, who was MEHRI's occupational therapist and who went on to be the clinical director of the MEHRIT Centre. So many of the ideas contained in *Help Your Child Deal With Stress – and Thrive* evolved from our work together.

I cannot mention my debt to MEHRI without in the same breath mentioning my debt to my colleagues in the Faculties of Health and Philosophy at York University and, most of all, my deans Rhonda Lenton and Harvey Skinner, who time and again provided us with support and guidance when this was most urgently needed.

My research over the years has been generously supported by several granting agencies in addition to the Harris Steel Foundation: the Canada Council and SSHRC; the Unicorn Foundation; Cure Autism Now; Public Health Agency of Canada; Templeton Foundation; Stars Foundation; IDRC; FIRA; Ministry of Health Promotion in Ontario; CIHR; and Roots of Empathy.

Over the years I worked with a number of individuals whose friendship was as important to me as their help and advice: in particular, Rod Allen, Jeremy Burman, Roger Downer, Norah Fryer, John Hoffman, Barbara King, Mike McKay, Mary Helen Moes, and, most especially, my children's godfather and my personal touchstone, Michel Maila.

The team at the MEHRIT Centre is a never-ending source of inspiration: Linda Warren, Brenda Smith-Chant, Jill Fergus, Sophie Davidson, Stephen Retallick, and Meaghan Trewin. Again I have to mention someone separately: Susan Hopkins, our executive director, whose contribution to *Help Your Child Deal With Stress – and Thrive* goes far beyond what anyone would have thought humanly possible.

There are three people in particular who have made this book possible: my agent, Jill Kneerim; our editor, Ann Godoff; and most of all my cowriter Teresa Barker. There is not a single word in this book that she hasn't agonized over, and not a single idea that she hasn't scrutinized from every conceivable angle, and then some. Writing this book with Teresa has been the most exciting intellectual experience of my life.

Finally, I must thank my executive assistant, Jade Calver, who not only managed the extraordinary demands being made on her but also remained remarkably cheerful throughout.

So many others have inspired *Help Your Child Deal With Stress – and Thrive*: not just psychologists, psy-chiatrists, therapists, and philosophers but every child, youth, parent, teacher, administrator, civil servant, and government minister I have ever had the good fortune to work with. We have taken great pains to conceal the identities of the children and parents mentioned throughout the book, in many cases combining different profiles that presented similar issues. I am deeply grateful to these families for their permission to tell their stories in this highly disguised form.

My parents and sister are never far from my thoughts, and I have been blessed with two wonderfully supportive in-laws, Kenneth Rotenberg and Doris Sommer-Rotenberg. But my greatest debt of all is, as always, to my wife and children; I wrote this book because of them, for them, and in a very real sense with them.

From Teresa:

My gratitude to Stuart for asking me to partner with him on this book and for the vision that has driven the work—our collaboration has been a special privilege and joy; to our editor, Ann Godoff, for her intuitive brilliance and the enthusiasm and meticulous care she brought to the manuscript; to our Penguin editorial and design team; and to agents Jill Kneerim and Madeleine Morel. I also want to thank Sherry Laten, Michael Thompson, and Catherine Steiner-Adair for their insightful perspectives. As always, I am in debt to my loving family and friends for their generosity, wisdom, and inspiration in support of this work.

NOTES

For continuing *Help Your Child Deal With Stress – and Thrive* updates, to follow Dr. Stuart Shanker's blog, *The Self-Reg View*, or to access parenting, educator, and media resources, visit the MEHRIT Centre at http://www.self-reg.ca/.

Introduction

2 **Yet we react as if:** The scientific understanding of "temperament" has advanced dramatically in recent years, largely as the result of Mary Rothbart's research on the influence of physiology. See M. K. Rothbart, *Becoming Who We Are: Temperament and Personality in Development* (Guilford Press, 2011).

5 **This technique is the result:** R. F. Baumeister and K. D. Vohs, *Handbook of Self-Regulation: Research, Theory and Applications* (New York: Guilford Press, 2004).

5 **The term "self-regulation":** J. T. Burman, C. D. Green, and S. G. Shanker, "The Six Meanings of Self-Regulation," *Child Development* (2015, in press).

5 **And "stress," in its original sense:** W. B. Cannon, *The Way of an Investigator: A Scientist's Experiences in Medical Research* (W. W. Norton, 1945); M. Jackson, *The Age of Stress: Science and the Search for Stability* (Oxford University Press, 2013); H. Selye, *Stress Without Distress* (New York: Hodder & Stotten Ltd., 1977); E. M. Sternberg, *The Balance Within: The Science Connecting Health and Emotions* (Macmillan, 2001).

6 **It's not easy to know:** S. I. Greenspan and J. Salmon, *The Challenging Child: Understanding, Raising, and Enjoying the Five "Difficult" Types of Children* (Da Capo Press, 1996).

6 **Since Plato's time self-control:** S. Shanker and D. Casenhiser, "Reducing the Effort in Effortful Control," in T. Racine and K. Slaney, eds., *Conceptual Analysis and Psychology* (New York: Macmillan, 2013); Christopher Peterson and Martin Seligman, *Character Strengths and Virtues* (Oxford: Oxford University Press, 2004).

6 **Self-control is about:** W. Mischel, *Marshmallow Test* (Random House, 2014).

7 **Then we need to help:** See S. Lupien, *Well Stressed: Manage Stress Before It Turns Toxic* (John Wiley & Sons, 2012).

Chapter 1: The Power of Self-Reg

11 **Have more willpower, more self-control:** N. Ryan, *"Willpower: Rediscovering the Greatest Human Strength*, by Roy F. Baumeister and John Tierney (book review), *Journal of Positive Psychology* 7, no. 5 (2012): 446–48.

13 **One of the big modern breakthroughs:** J. LeDoux, *The Emotional Brain: The Mysterious Underpinnings of Emotional Life* (Simon & Schuster, 1998).

13 **In times past it was initially:** S. T. von Sömmerring, *Vom Baue des menschlichen Körpers*, vol. 1 (Varrentrapp und Wenner, 1791).

13 **The ancient and unchallenged idea:** The source for this classical view of "self-control" was Plato's reading of the *Iliad*; see S. Shanker, "Emotion Regulation Through the Ages" (2012), in *Moving Ourselves, Moving Others: Motion and Emotion in Intersubjectivity, Consciousness and Language*, vol. 6, ed. A. Foolen et al. (John Benjamins, 2012).

14 **The capacity of the prefrontal cortex:** Nora Volkow has done groundbreaking research on this "dampening" of the DLPFC; see, for example, Volkow and Ruben Baler, "Addiction: A Disease of Self-Control."

14 **In the 1960s Paul MacLean:** P. D. MacLean and V. A. Kral, *A Triune Concept of the Brain and Behaviour* (University of Toronto Press, 1973).

16 **The cold outside is a classic:** H. Selye, *Stress Without Distress* (Springer US, 1976), 137–46.

16 **These neurochemicals raise heart rate:** W. B. Cannon, *Bodily Changes in Pain, Hunger, Fear and Rage*, 2nd ed. (New York: D. Appleton, 1929).

17 **Some of the other metabolic functions:** Gabor Maté, *When the Body Says No: The Hidden Costs of Stress* (Vintage Canada, 2004).

18 **Fascinating discoveries are being made:** S. W. Porges, *The Polyvagal Theory: Neurophysiological Foundations of Emotions, Attachment, Communication, and Self-Regulation*, Norton Series on Interpersonal Neurobiology (W. W. Norton, 2011).

18 **The autonomic nervous system (ANS) regulates:** C. Lillas and J. Turnbull, *Infant/Child Mental Health, Early Intervention, and Relationship-Based Therapies: A Neurorelational Framework for Interdisciplinary Practice* (W. W. Norton, 2009).

19 **All day every day:** To speed up or ascend a hill you press on the gas (SNS activation—think *S* for "speed"); to slow down or come to a stop you press on the brake (PNS inhibition—think *P* for "pause"). In heavy traffic you're constantly pressing on the gas and the brake without too many starts or stops. So too in highly challenging situations: The brain shifts unconsciously and seamlessly between SNS and PNS. In fact, these two systems are operating with every single breath we take: The SNS raises our heart rate and blood pressure, expands our lungs, and suffuses them with oxygen; we pause ever so slightly at the height of the breath, and then the PNS sets in train the recovery process, lowering our heart rate and blood pressure as our lungs deflate and CO_2 is discharged.

19 **The recovery function begins:** B. S. McEwen and H. M. Schmeck, *The Hostage Brain* (New York: Rockefeller University Press, 1994).

20 **This hierarchy of stress responses:** S. Porges, *Polyvagal Theory* (New York: W. W. Norton, 2011), p. 283.

20 **In chronic hypo- or hyperarousal:** J. D. Ford and J. Wortmann, *Hijacked by Your Brain: How to Free Yourself When Stress Takes Over* (Sourcebooks, 2013); S. J. Blakemore and U. Frith, *The Learning Brain: Lessons for Education* (Blackwell, 2005). See also M. I. Posner and M. K. Rothbart, *Educating the Human Brain* (American Psychological Association, 2007).

21 **A chronic state of heightened arousal:** P. A. Levine and A. Frederick, *Waking the Tiger: Healing Trauma: The Innate Capacity to Transform Overwhelming Experiences* (Berkeley, CA: North Atlantic Books, 1997).

22 **The 2,500-year-old idea:** Shanker, "Emotion Regulation Through the Ages." Both of Marc Lewis's recent books, *Memoirs of an Addicted Brain* and *The Biology of Desire*, are a must read on this topic.

23 **But arousal isn't the enemy:** K. McGonigal, *The Upside of Stress: Why Stress Is Good for You, and How to Get Good at It* (Penguin, 2015).

24 **This is especially important:** M. S. William and S. Shellenberger, *How Does Your Engine Run?: A Leader's Guide to the Alert Program for Self-Regulation* (TherapyWorks, 1996).

26 **Children of all ages:** S. Shanker, *Calm, Alert, and Learning: Classroom Strategies for Self-Regulation* (Pearson, 2013).

27 **This starts close to home:** The idea of "reframing behavior" was inspired by Ludwig Wittgenstein's *Philosophical Investigations* (Oxford: Blackwell, 1958). Wittgenstein uses an image from Gestalt psychology to convey the "aspect-shift" required to see an intractable logical problem in a different light:

> A similar point applies here: Seen from one perspective, a child's behavior appears "problematic," something that needs to be "managed" or "suppressed." But seen from a different perspective, the child's behavior is recognized as a sign of an overloaded nervous system. L. Wittgenstein, *Philosophical Investigations* (1958).

29 **And those systems in your PFC:** *Reappraisal* is as much about realizing that something you initially thought was benign is actually a danger as it is about recognizing that what you initially thought was a danger is actually benign. Reappraisal is profoundly influenced by the messages coming in from the body. In chronic anxiety the PFC is bombarded by alarm signals, leading to a reappraisal system that is primed to see everything as a threat. The reason why this happens lies in the biology of the flight-or-fight system. When the hypothalamus and ventral striatum process signals associated with danger, they activate the sympathetic nervous system, which releases adrenaline and noradrenaline, causing a cascade of cardiovascular, respiratory, digestive, excretory, and endocrine changes that prepare us for protective action. The hippocampus then sets out to identify the danger by searching through its storehouse of previous experiences associated with those internal sensations, while the amygdala continues to sound the danger alarm. If the alarm does not shut off, the PFC starts searching for threats, and if it can't find any, then the sensations themselves become the threat; for if the alarm is ringing, there must be a fire.

29 **One way to interrupt:** J. Kabat-Zinn, *Mindfulness for Beginners: Reclaiming the Present Moment—and Your Life* (Sounds True, 2011).

30 **Humans aren't very good:** R. E. Thayer, *Calm Energy: How People Regulate Mood with Food and Exercise* (Oxford University Press, 2003).

Chapter 2: More Than Marshmallows: Self-Regulation Versus Self-Control

33 **In 1963 American psychologist:** W. Mischel, *The Marshmallow Test* (Random House, 2014).

34 **It's also a bit scary:** First reported in W. Mischel, Y. Shoda, and M. I. Rodriguez, "Delay of Gratification in Children," *Science* 244, no. 4907 (1989): 933–38. Terrie Moffitt and her colleagues then did a remarkable follow-up study on the different life trajectories of children who were able to delay gratification versus those who weren't. See T. E. Moffitt et al., "A Gradient of Childhood Self-Control Predicts Health, Wealth, and Public Safety," *Proceedings of the National Academy of Sciences* 108, no. 7 (2011): 2693–98.

34 **circulating on the Internet:** "Me Want It (but Me Wait)," *Sesame Street*, August 5, 2013, https://youtu.be/9PnbKL3wuH4.

34 **In fact, if you have the child:** Sherrod (1974) was one of the first to demonstrate this:

D. R. Sherrod, "Crowding, Perceived Control, and Behavioral After-effects," *Journal of Applied Social Psychology* 4 (1974): 171–86. See also A. Duckworth and M. Seligman, "Self-Discipline Outdoes IQ in Predicting Academic Performance of Adolescents," *Psychological Science* 16, no. 12 (2005): 939–94.

35 **This is a stress test:** This is one of my favorite depictions of the test: ppproductions1000, "Very Tempting Marshmallow Test," September 19, 2009, https://youtu .be/x3S0xS2hdi4.

35 **These processes all require:** R. E. Robert Thayer, *The Biopsychology of Mood and Arousal* (Oxford University Press, 1989).

35 **The recovery system loses:** Bruce S. McEwen and Elizabeth Norton Lasley, *The End of Stress as We Know It* (Joseph Henry Press, 2002).

35 **Self-regulation calms the emotional:** H. Benson, *The Relaxation Response* (New York: William Morrow, 1975), 278.

36 **Further, if you focus:** Jennifer Lansford, from the Center for Child and Family Policy at Duke, and a team she put together from around the world compared the attitudes and effects of physical discipline in six different countries, ranging from Thailand, which reported the lowest levels of corporal punishment, to Kenya, which had the highest. They found that the harsher the discipline, the more aggression and anxiety seen in the children and youth. J. E. Lansford, et al., "Ethnic Differences in the Link Between Physical Discipline and Later Adolescent Externalizing Behaviors," *Journal of Child Psychology and Psychiatry*, 45 (2004), 801–12.

36–37 **It leads us to assume:** M. R. Muraven and R. F. Baumeister, "Self-Regulation and Depletion of Limited Resources: Does Self-Control Resemble a Muscle?" *Psychological Bulletin* 126 (2000): 247–59; B. J. Schmeichel and R. F. Baumeister, "Self-Regulatory Strength," in *Handbook of Self-Regulation*, ed. R. F. Baumeister and K. D. Vohs (New York: Guilford Press, 2004), 84–98.

37 **The behaviorist view, as it is:** J. B. Watson, "Psychology as the Behaviorist Views It," *Psychological Review* 20, no. 2 (1913): 158.

37 **The epidemic levels of childhood obesity:** Scattered about my office are dozens of articles reporting on epidemics in obesity, diabetes, allergies, asthma, tooth decay, heart disease, gastrointestinal disorders, and sleep deprivation; autism, ADHD, developmental disorders, depression, self-harm, and eating disorders; violence, anger, oppositional defiance, bullying, narcissism, and selfishness; illiteracy, learning disorders, dyslexia, and truancy. An epidemic of physical inactivity and what goes hand in hand with this: video-game addiction. That's a lot of epidemics. And by no means is this a complete list. "Epidemic" has become the new buzzword. But the ubiquity of the term is more than just a way of grabbing readers' attention: It's a manifestation of a pervasive societal anxiety about the state of children and most certainly a cause of an "epidemic of stressed parents raising stressed kids" K. Race, "The Epidemic of Stressed Parents Raising Stressed Kids," *Huffington Post*, February 21, 2014, www.huffingtonpost.com/kristen-race-phd/ the-epidemic-of-stressed-parents-raising-stressed-kids_b_4790658.html.

38 **Or the test might be timed:** Over the years Roy Baumeister and his colleagues have performed a number of elegant experiments demonstrating the effects of "ego depletion." Baumeister and Tierney's *Willpower* is a wonderful introduction to this exciting and important field of research. R. F. Baumeister and J. Tierney, *Willpower: Rediscovering the Greatest Human Strength* (Penguin, 2011).

40 **I'm not even sure that the little guy:** S. W. Porges, *The Polyvagal Theory: Neurophysi-*

ological Foundations of Emotions, Attachment, Communication, and Self-Regulation, Norton Series on Interpersonal Neurobiology (W. W. Norton, 2011).

41 **Overwhelmed, the response system:** R. M. Sapolsky, *Why Zebras Don't Get Ulcers: The Acclaimed Guide to Stress, Stress-Related Diseases, and Coping* (Macmillan, 2004).

47 **The foundation of Self-Reg:** See D. Tantam, *Can the World Afford Autistic Spectrum Disorder? Nonverbal Communication, Asperger Syndrome and the Interbrain* (Jessica Kingsley, 2009).

Chapter 3: No Small Matter: Arousal Regulation and the Interbrain

50 **The great American biologist:** Stephen J. Gould, "Human Babies as Embryos," in *Ever Since Darwin* (New York: W. W. Norton, 1977), 72.

50 **But compared with the rest:** Gould, *Ever Since Darwin*. Gould was drawing on the work of the Dutch biologist Adolf Portmann, who first raised the idea. See H.M.N. McCain, J. F. Mustard, and S. Shanker, *Early Years Study* 2 (2007).

51 **Nature's ingenious solution:** K. Rosenberg and W. Trevathan, "Bipedalism and Human Birth: The Obstetrical Dilemma Revisited," *Evolutionary Anthropology: Issues, News, and Reviews* 4, no. 5 (1995): 161–68.

51 **Axons and dendrites—the roots:** P. R. Huttenlocher, *Neural Plasticity* (Harvard University Press, 2002); C. A. Nelson, K. M. Thomas, and M. De Haan, *Neuroscience of Cognitive Development: The Role of Experience and the Developing Brain* (John Wiley & Sons, 2012).

52 **A child's *stress reactivity:*** Martha Bronson, *Self-Regulation in Early Childhood* (New York: Guilford Press, 2001); S. J. Bradley, *Affect Regulation and the Development of Psychopathology* (New York: Guilford Press, 2003).

52 **The neural systems and connections:** J. F. Mustard, "Experience-Based Brain Development: Scientific Underpinnings of the Importance of Early Child Development in a Global World," *Paediatrics & Child Health* 11, no. 9 (2006): 571; J. Kagan and N. Herschkowitz, *A Young Mind in a Growing Brain* (Psychology Press, 2006).

52 **Talk about a shock:** D. Maurer and C. Maurer, *The World of the Newborn* (Basic Books, 1988); Tiffany Field, *The Amazing Infant* (Wiley-Blackwell, 2007).

54 ***Arousal* in the physiological context:** Porges's work with neonates, summarized in *The Polyvagal Theory*, was groundbreaking. See also H. J. Polan and M. A. Hofer, "Psychobiological Origins of Infant Attachment and Separation Responses," in *Handbook of Attachment: Theory, Research, and Clinical Application*, ed. J. Cassidy and P. R. Shaver (New York: Guildford Press, 1999), 162–80; J. Kagan, *Unstable Ideas: Temperament, Cognition and Self* (Boston: Harvard University Press, 1989); M. K. Rothbart, L. K. Ellis, and M. I. Posner, "Temperament and Self-Regulation," in *Handbook of Self-Regulation: Research, Theory, and Applications*, ed. R. F. Baumeister and K. D. Vohs (New York: Guilford Press, 2004), 357–70; M. Gunnar and K. Quevedo, "The Neurobiology of Stress and Development," *Annual Review of Psychology* 58 (2007).

57 **Over the course of the day:** C. Lillas and J. Turnbull, *Infant/Child Mental Health, Early Intervention, and Relationship-Based Therapies: A Neurorelational Framework for Interdisciplinary Practice* (W. W. Norton, 2009).

59 **The interbrain lays the deep neurological:** On the importance of "sensory integration," see A. C. Bundy, S. J. Lane, and E. A. Murray, *Sensory Integration: Theory and Practice* (Philadelphia: F. A. Davis Co., 2002); F. A. Davis, N. Kashman, and J. Mora,

The Sensory Connection: An OT and SLP Team Approach (Arlington, TX: Future Horizons, 2005).

60 **Much as a newborn instinctively seeks:** Laura Berk and Stuart Shanker, *Child Development* (Pearson, 2006); M. Numan and T. R. Insel, *The Neurobiology of Parental Behavior* (Springer, 2003).

60 **The challenge here is that:** S. I. Greenspan and N. Lewis, *Building Healthy Minds: The Six Experiences That Create Intelligence and Emotional Growth in Babies and Young Children* (Da Capo Press, 2000).

60 **By the same token:** S. I. Greenspan, *Secure Child: Helping Our Children Feel Safe and Confident in a Changing World* (Da Capo Press, 2009).

61 **The interbrain begins as:** Allan Schore has published many seminal papers on the topic, nicely summarized in the first chapter of A. N. Schore, *The Science of the Art of Psychotherapy*, Norton Series on Interpersonal Neurobiology (W. W. Norton, 2012). See also Ed Tronick, *The Neurobehavioral and Social-Emotional Development of Infants and Children* (W. W. Norton, 2007) and J. Freed and L. Parsons, *Right-Brained Children in a Left-Brained World: Unlocking the Potential of Your ADD Child* (Simon & Schuster, 1998).

62 *A baby's baseline arousal:* See A. N. Schore, *Affect Regulation and the Origin of the Self: The Neurobiology of Emotional Development* (Psychology Press, 1994).

64 **Melanie's sleeplessness proved to be:** In *Calm, Alert, and Learning* I present a number of techniques for reducing stress in the classroom that parents have also found very useful for the home environment; see especially chapter 1: S. Shanker, *Calm, Alert, and Learning: Classroom Strategies for Self-Regulation* (Pearson, 2012).

66 **The baby's positive reaction:** Schore reviews this large body of research in *Affect Regulation and the Origin of Self*.

66 **They try desperately to bring Mommy back:** E. Z. Tronick, "Emotions and Emotional Communication in Infants," *American Psychologist* 44 (1989): 112–19. There is a clip of the Still Face experiment on YouTube: https://youtu.be/apzXGEbZht0.

66 **The interbrain serves not just:** Dan Siegel has written several wonderful books about this. One of my favorites is *The Developing Mind* (New York: Guilford Press, 1999; second edition 2012).

69 **Our relationship with our child:** A. Fogel, *Developing Through Relationships* (University of Chicago Press, 1993); A. Sameroff, *The Transactional Model* (American Psychological Association, 2009).

Chapter 4: Under the Boab Tree: The Five-Domain Model for Self-Reg

73 **The Five Domains of Stress and Self-Regulation:** M. G. Baron and J. Grodon, *Stress and Coping in Autism* (Oxford University Press, 2006). This is an invaluable guide to understanding the different kinds of stressors all children deal with, not just those on the spectrum. The authors' "Stress Inventory" is particularly informative.

73 **Because self-regulation involves these multiple:** A. Fogel, B. J. King, and S. G. Shanker, eds., *Human Development in the Twenty-first Century: Visionary Ideas from Systems Scientists* (Cambridge University Press, 2007).

74 **Signs of stress in the biological domain:** P. Ogden, *Sensorimotor Psychotherapy: Interventions for Trauma and Attachment* (W. W. Norton, 2015).

Chapter 5: Eat, Play, Sleep: The Biological Domain

91 *misbehavior* **is fundamentally tied:** See S. Shanker and D. Casenhiser, *Reducing the Effort in Effortful Control: A Wittgensteinian Perspective on the Use of Conceptual Analysis in Psychology.* (Palgrave Macmillan, 2013).

93 **The reason for this lies:** See T. Lewis, F. Amini, and R. Lannon, *A General Theory of Love* (Vintage, 2007).

97 **A stressor, according to the classic:** W. B. Cannon, *The Wisdom of the Body* (W. W. Norton, 1932).

98 **"Sensitive caregiving" means recognizing:** See K. Lee Raby et al., "The Enduring Predictive Significance of Early Maternal Sensitivity: Social and Academic Competence Through Age 32 Years," *Child Development* 17 (December 2014), 695–708.

100 **The hypothalamus responds not just:** P. Meerlo et al., "Sleep Restriction Alters the Hypothalamic-Pituitary-Adrenal Response to Stress," *Journal of Endocrinology* 14 (2002), 397–402.

101 **There is also the matter:** M. Edlund, *The Power of Rest: Why Sleep Alone Is Not Enough: A 30-Day Plan to Reset Your Body* (HarperCollins, 2010).

102 **To some extent you can:** S. Shanker, *Calm, Alert, and Learning: Classroom Strategies for Self-Regulation* (Pearson, 2012).

103 **The more we practice:** A. Fogel, *The Psychophysiology of Self-awareness: Rediscovering the Lost Art of Body Sense* (W. W. Norton, 2009).

103 **master mindfulness techniques:** Our clinical director, Chris Robinson, was instrumental in the development of this method. See also S. K. Greenland, *The Mindful Child: How to Help Your Kid Manage Stress and Become Happier, Kinder, and More Compassionate* (Simon & Schuster, 2010).

104 **Self-awareness is central to your child's:** This point was central to the work of the great "somatic educators" of the last century, e.g., Jean Ayres, Moshe Feldenkrais, Elsa Gindler, Alexander Lowen, Wilhelm Reich, and Ida Rolf. In Self-Reg the very thing that we want the child or youth to become aware of (her low energy and high tension) is what is blocking such awareness. The somatic educators all developed powerful therapeutic techniques for breaking this logjam and thereby releasing what Lowen called the body's "bioenergy."

107 **It was essential that Rosie:** See Robin Alter, *Anxiety and the Gift of Imagination: A New Model for Helping Parents and Children Manage Anxiety* (Createspace, 2011); G. M. Biegel, *The Stress Reduction Workbook for Teens: Mindfulness Skills to Help You Deal with Stress* (New Harbinger, 2009); G. Hawn and W. Holden, *10 Mindful Minutes: Giving Our Children—and Ourselves—the Social and Emotional Skills to Reduce Stress and Anxiety for Healthier, Happy Lives* (Penguin, 2011); X. Vo. Dzung, *The Mindful Teen: Powerful Skills to Help You Handle Stress One Moment at a Time* (New Harbinger, 2015).

Chapter 6: Monster in the Attic: The Emotion Domain

110 **To be sure, it's important:** Over the past few decades developmental psychologists have been looking carefully at the role of emotional functioning on children's well-being. See, e.g., C. Izard, et al. (2001), "Emotional Knowledge as a Predictor of Social Behavior and Academic Competence in Children at Risk," *Psychological Science*, 12, 18–23; N. Eisenberg, et al. (2004), "The Relation of Effortful Control and Impulsivity

to Children's Resiliency and Adjustment," *Child Development*, 75, 25–46; S. Denham, P. Ji, and B. Hamre (2010), *Compendium of Preschool Through Elementary School Social-Emotional Learning and Associated Assessment Measures*; Social and Emotional Learning Research Group: University of Illinois at Chicago. Recent findings indicate that emotional intelligence is more important than IQ as far as academic attainment is concerned: P. Salovey and J. D. Mayer, (1990), "Emotional Intelligence," *Imagination, Cognition, and Personality*, 9, 185–211; D. Goleman, *Emotional Intelligence* (New York: Bantam Dell, 1995); J. Shonkoff and D. Phillips, *From Neurons to Neighborhoods: The Science of Early Childhood Development* (Washington, D.C.: National Academy Press, 2000); S. Denham, et al. (2009), "Assessing Social Emotional Development in Children from a Longitudinal Perspective," *Journal of Epidemiology and Community Health*, 63 (Suppl II), 37–52. For a review of this extremely important field of research, see Shanker, "Broader Measures of Success: Social/Emotional Learning," Toronto, *People for Education*, 2015.

111 **Philosophers have talked about:** Stuart Shanker, "A Dynamic Developmental Model of Emotions," *Philosophy, Psychiatry and Psychology* 11 (2004): 219–33.

111 **A child who is frightened:** Carrol Izard, *The Psychology of Emotions* (Springer, 1991); Jaak Panksepp, *Affective Neuroscience* (Oxford University Press, 1998); Marc Lewis and Jeanette Haviland-Jones, *Handbook of Emotions*, 3rd ed. (Guilford Press, 2010).

113 **But they can't control:** C. E. Izard, *The Psychology of Emotions* (Springer Science & Business Media, 1991).

114 **For one of the complications:** P. E. Griffiths, *What Emotions Really Are: The Problem of Psychological Categories* (Chicago: University of Chicago Press, 1997), 114.

114 **Important here is how these reflexes:** S. I. Greenspan and J. I. Downey, *Developmentally Based Psychotherapy* (Madison, CT: International Universities Press, 1997).

115 **A child whose parents delight:** Stanley Greenspan with Nancy Thorndike Greenspan, *First Feelings: Milestones in the Emotional Development of Your Infant and Child from Birth to Age 4* (Viking, 1985).

116 **"Emotion regulation" is standardly defined:** James J. Gross, *Handbook of Emotion Regulation*, 2nd ed. (Guilford Press, 2015).

117 **Her approach was like many:** There have been hundreds of studies evaluating the outcomes of programs designed to foster SEL. A full listing, with reviews, can be found at www.casel.org/guide. See also Shanker, "Broader Measures of Success: Social/Emotional Learning," Toronto, *People for Education*, 2015.

121 **As it turned out:** This point is central to the field of "bioenergetics" (see note "Self-awareness is central to your child's" in chapter 5 above). Bessel van der Kolk is a major contributor to this field. B. van der Kolk, *The Body Keeps the Score: Brain, Mind, and Body in the Healing of Trauma* (Penguin, 2014).

125 **Without these formative experiences:** This argument is developed in greater detail in S. I. Greenspan and S. Shanker, *The First Idea: How Symbols, Language, and Intelligence Evolve, from Primates to Humans* (Perseus Books, 2004).

127 **Does a child's anger alone:** T. Ross, M. I. Fontao, and R. Schneider, "Aggressive Behavior in Male Offenders: Preliminary Analyses of Self-Regulatory Functions in a Sample of Criminals," *Psychological Reports* 100, no. 3, part 2 (2007): 1171–85; A. Raine, *The Anatomy of Violence: The Biological Roots of Crime* (Vintage, 2013); R. E. Tremblay, W. W. Hartup, and J. Archer, eds., *Developmental Origins of Aggression* (Guilford Press, 2005). But for a riveting counterpoint, see J. Fallon, *The Psychopath Inside: A Neuroscientist's Personal Journey into the Dark Side of the Brain* (Penguin, 2013).

128 **That is a core part:** J. Panksepp, *Affective Neuroscience* (New York: Oxford University Press, 1998).

Chapter 7: Calm, Alert, and Learning: The Cognitive Domain

133 **But our research focus:** We have been highly influenced in our clinical work with children with ADHD by S. I. Greenspan and J. Greenspan, *Overcoming ADHD: Helping Your Child Become Calm, Engaged, and Focused—Without a Pill* (Da Capo Press, 2009); E.M.M. Hallowell and J. J. Ratey, *Driven to Distraction: Recognizing and Coping with Attention Deficit Disorder from Childhood Through Adulthood* (Anchor, 2011); and M. L. Kutscher, *ADHD: Living Without Brakes* (Jessica Kingsley, 2009).

134 **What can I do to strengthen:** I have been profoundly influenced here by S. I. Greenspan and N. T. Greenspan, *The Learning Tree: Overcoming Learning Disabilities from the Ground Up* (Da Capo Press, 2010).

135 **EF coaching works on things:** There are several excellent guides; I have found P. Dawson and R. Guare, *Executive Skills in Children and Adolescents: A Practical Guide to Assessment and Intervention* (Guilford Press, 2010) particularly helpful. For a more theoretical understanding, see R. A. Barkley, *Executive Functions: What They Are, How They Work, and Why They Evolved* (Guilford Press, 2012). E. Galinsky, *Mind in the Making: The Seven Essential Life Skills Every Child Needs* (HarperStudio, 2010) is an outstanding resource.

136 **There are a number of reasons:** J. T. Nigg, *What Causes ADHD? Understanding What Goes Wrong and Why* (Guilford Press, 2006).

137 **He couldn't be bothered:** Daniel Pink, *Drive: The Surprising Truth About What Motivates Us* (New York: Penguin, 2009), 138 and 240.

138 **"blooming, buzzing confusion":** William James, *Principles of Psychology* (Cambridge, MA: Harvard University Press, 1981), 462. Originally published in 1890.

139 **Patterns make the world:** Stuart Shanker, *Wittgenstein's Remarks on the Foundations of AI* (London: Routledge, 1998). Jerome Bruner has been one of the big influences on my thinking, especially in regard to this topic. See J. Bruner, *Child's Talk* (Oxford: Oxford University Press, 1983); J. Bruner, "Child's Talk: Learning to Use Language," *Child Language Teaching and Therapy* 1, no. 1 (1985): 111–14.

143 **A colleague once told me:** The colleague in question was Chris Robinson. So much of this chapter is the result of going back and forth with her as we worked on individual cases.

144 **Ordinarily we are so used:** One of the better books I've read on self-regulation, even though the term is never mentioned, is Chris Hadfield's *An Astronaut's Guide to Life on Earth* (Pan Macmillan, 2013).

144 **Part of the answer lies:** Richard Davidson has written several critical books in this area: See Richard Davidson and Daniel Goleman, *Training the Brain* (Amazon Digital Services, 2012); Richard Davidson and Sharon Begley, *The Emotional Life of Your Brain* (Hachette UK, 2012); Jon Kabat-Zinn and Richard Davidson, eds. *The Mind's Own Physician: A Scientific Dialogue with the Dalai Lama on the Healing Power of Meditation* (New Harbinger, 2012).

145 **Attention is a full-body phenomenon:** S. W. Porges, *The Polyvagal Theory: Neurophysiological Foundations of Emotions, Attachment, Communication, and Self-Regulation*, Norton Series on Interpersonal Neurobiology (W. W. Norton, 2011).

146 **"the mental act that energizes,":** See Huitt, W. (2011), "Motivation to Learn: An Overview," *Educational Psychology Interactive* (Valdosta, GA: Valdosta State University).

148 **But every child has to learn:** S. Shanker, *Calm, Alert, and Learning: Classroom Strategies for Self-Regulation* (Pearson, 2013).

150 **This is not simply a matter:** B. J. Zimmerman and D. H. Schunk, eds., *Self-Regulated Learning and Academic Achievement: Theoretical Perspectives* (Routledge, 2001).

150 **It has also been discovered:** Terje Sagvolden reported that children with ADHD often have an abnormal sense of time. Scientists at the Gilden Lab of the University of Texas at Austin have been able to show that many children with ADHD operate on a faster time scale than typically developing children. T. Sagvolden et al., "A Dynamic Developmental Theory of Attention-Deficit/Hyperactivity Disorder (ADHD) Predominantly Hyperactive/Impulsive and Combined Subtypes," *Behavioral and Brain Sciences* 28, no. 3 (2005): 397–418.

153 **The most important element:** See S. I. Greenspan, *Secure Child: Helping Our Children Feel Safe and Confident in a Changing World* (Da Capo Press, 2009); and, of course, J. Bowlby, *A Secure Base: Clinical Applications of Attachment Theory*, vol. 393 (Taylor & Francis, 2005).

153 **I am a big believer:** R. Louv, *Last Child in the Woods: Saving Our Children from Nature-Deficit Disorder* (Algonquin Books, 2008); R. Louv, *The Nature Principle: Reconnecting with Life in a Virtual Age* (Algonquin Books, 2012). The question of why exposure to nature should have such a calming effect on the brain takes us deep into the theory of "biophilia." See E. O. Wilson, *Consilience: The Unity of Knowledge*, vol. 31 (Vintage, 1999). For an important overview of the neuroscience that's been done in this area, see E. M. Sternberg, *Healing Spaces: The Science of Place and Well-being* (Harvard University Press, 2009).

156 **Our intention had never been:** But see S. Olfman and B. D. Robbins, eds., *Drugging Our Children: How Profiteers Are Pushing Antipsychotics on Our Youngest, and What We Can Do to Stop It* (ABC-CLIO, 2012).

157 **What exactly were we trying:** See the wonderful TEDx talk by Stephen Tonti (April 10, 2013), "ADHD as a Difference in Cognition, Not a Disorder," https://youtu.be/uU6o2_UFSEY; and Jim Jacobson's blog, *Living Amongst Humans*, at www.amongsthumans.com.

Chapter 8: A New Lens for Looking at Social Development: The Social Domain

162 **The answer lies in what:** S. W. Porges, *The Polyvagal Theory: Neurophysiological Foundations of Emotions, Attachment, Communication, and Self-Regulation*, Norton Series on Interpersonal Neurobiology (W. W. Norton, 2011).

164 **This remarkable micromanaged dance:** A. Fogel, *Developing Through Relationships* (University of Chicago Press, 1993).

164 **It is, in fact, the foundation:** Stuart Shanker and Jim Stieben, "The Roots of Mind-blindness," in *Against Theory of Mind*, ed. Ivan Leudar (London: Palgrave Macmillan, 2009).

165 **One of Tronick's research assistants:** E. Tronick, "Why Is Connection with Others So Critical?" (2004), in *Emotional Development*, ed. J. Nadel and D. Muir (Oxford University Press, 2004). The "research assistant" was Lisa Bohne.

166 **What we are looking at here:** A. N. Schore, *Affect Regulation and the Origin of the Self: The Neurobiology of Emotional Development* (Psychology Press, 1994).

166 **Perhaps the most fascinating thing:** S. Savage-Rumbaugh, S. G. Shanker, and T. J. Taylor, *Apes, Language, and the Human Mind* (Oxford University Press, 1998).

168 **These patterns can be hard to break:** M. D. Lewis, "Bridging Emotion Theory and Neurobiology Through Dynamic Systems Modeling," *Behavioral and Brain Sciences* 28, no. 2 (2005): 169–94.

170 **The brain has shifted:** J. D. Ford and J. Wortmann, *Hijacked by Your Brain: How to Free Yourself When Stress Takes Over* (Sourcebooks, 2013).

173 **If for whatever reason:** D. M. Casenhiser, S. G. Shanker, and J. Stieben, "Learning Through Interaction in Children with Autism: Preliminary Data from Asocial-Communication-Based Intervention," *Autism* 17, no. 2 (2013): 220–41.

174 **This is the world that Temple Grandin:** T. Grandin, *Thinking in Pictures: My Life with Autism*, expanded ed. (New York: Vintage, 2006).

Chapter 9: The Better Self: Empathy and the Prosocial Domain

186 **Every single child is born:** See the quite remarkable research by Jason Cowell and Jean Decety, "Precursors to Morality in Development as a Complex Interplay Between Neural, Socioenvironmental, and Behavioral Facets," *Proceedings of the National Academy of Science*, University of Chicago, May 2015.

188 **In other words, rather than:** N. Eisenberg and P. H. Mussen, *The Roots of Prosocial Behavior in Children* (Cambridge University Press, 1989).

189 **The idea that a child has to learn:** T. Hobbes, *Leviathan* (New York: Oxford University Press, 1651; 2009, XIII.9), 581–735; for a modern version see W. Golding, *Lord of the Flies* (New York: Penguin, 1954; 1983).

189 **The crux of Self-Reg is that:** In 2005 Jorge Moll discovered that the act of giving activates the same part of the brain that releases affiliative neurotransmitters in bonding: the phenomenon now referred to as "helper's high." See J. Moll et al., "The Neural Basis of Human Moral Cognition," *Nature Reviews Neuroscience* 6, no. 10 (2005): 799–809.

189 **The work of evolutionary biologists:** B. J. King, *The Dynamic Dance: Nonvocal Communication in African Great Apes* (Harvard University Press, 2009); F. De Waal, *The Age of Empathy: Nature's Lessons for a Kinder Society* (Broadway Books, 2010); M. Bekoff and J. Goodall, *The Emotional Lives of Animals: A Leading Scientist Explores Animal Joy, Sorrow, and Empathy—and Why They Matter* (New World Library, 2008).

190 **Prosocial development rests first:** Stanley Greenspan and Stuart Shanker, *Toward a Psychology of Global Interdependency: A Framework for International Collaboration* (Washington, DC: ICDL Press, 2002).

192 **A large body of scientific literature:** Arthur Brooks found that givers are 42 percent more likely to describe themselves as being "very happy" and 25 percent more likely to describe themselves as being "in excellent health." See A. Brooks, *Who Really Cares* (New York: Basic Books, 2006); Canadian Institute for Health Information, *The Role of Social Support in Reducing Psychological Distress* (Canadian Institute for Health Information, 2012).

192 **What is particularly noteworthy:** See Esther Sternberg, *The Balance Within* (New York: Times Books, 2001).

193 *Being exposed to someone else's stress:* See J. T. Cacioppo and J. Decety, "Social Neuroscience: Challenges and Opportunities in the Study of Complex Behavior," *Annals of the New York Academy of Sciences* 1224, no. 1 (2011): 162–73. Decety's work on the neuroscience of empathy has been groundbreaking; see, e.g., J. Decety and C. D. Batson,

"Social Neuroscience Approaches to Interpersonal Sensitivity" (2007), in *Suffering and Bioethics*, ed. R. M. Green and N. J. Palpant (New York: Oxford University Press, 2014), 89–105.

197 **A large part of the problem:** D. Goleman, *Social Intelligence* (Random House, 2007).

199 **The one thing I felt certain about:** R. W. Wrangham and D. Peterson, *Demonic Males: Apes and the Origins of Human Violence* (Houghton Mifflin Harcourt, 1997). This book reinforced the Hobbesian view of human nature. But the work of Frans de Waal (cited above) has led us to recognize that early humans were more akin to bonobos than to chimpanzees: a species based on the cultivation of empathy. One of my favorite books on the topic of children's natural empathetic instinct is Mary Gordon, *Roots of Empathy: Changing the World Child by Child* (Workman, 2009).

200 **It means recognizing:** See Stanley Greenspan and Stuart Shanker, *Toward a Psychology of Global Interdependency: A Framework for International Collaboration* (Washington, D.C.: ICDL Press, 2002).

205 **But intuitively we all know:** This knowledge is "intuitive" because, as one of the greatest of all my professors, Northrop Frye, explained, our thinking is grounded in the Bible, in this particular case Psalm 15. David starts off by asking: "Lord, who may dwell in your tent?" He then rather brazenly proceeds to answer this question himself: "Only those," he argues, "who are blameless and righteous"; "who only speak the truth, and speak it from the heart"; "who never harm another, neither in words nor actions"; "who keep their word, regardless of how hard this might be"; "who hate those who are evil and embrace those who are noble." "Whoever does these things," David concludes, "will never be shaken." His point in the first part of this verse is that it's just not saying these things that matters but living this way. And his point in the second part is that the reason to do these things is not simply to gain entrance to the kingdom of heaven; if you live this way, the benefits are here and now, in this life, for only in this way will you be able to enjoy moments of true peace and calmness.

Chapter 10: The Power and Perils of Adolescence

210 **As I'll explain in this chapter:** G. E. Weisfeld, *Evolutionary Principles of Human Adolescence* (Basic Books, 1999).

213 **Kids often don't know:** Yet another "epidemic" that we are seeing today is what the National Institute on Drug Abuse calls the "Rx Generation." An unbelievable number of teens are using pain relievers or cough and cold medications to suppress what are in fact symptoms of anxiety. Over time this exacerbates the anxiety and often leads to more serious forms of prescription drug abuse.

213 **And "depression," in the words of Philip W. Gold:** See P. W. Gold, "The Organization of the Stress System and Its Dysregulation in Depressive Illness." *Molecular Psychiatry.* 2015; 20: 32–47.

213 **It's as if what the German Romantics:** Dan Siegel's *Brainstorm* is not just extremely insightful on this topic but also a great help to parents and teens. D. J. Siegel, *Brainstorm: The Power and Purpose of the Teenage Brain* (Hachette UK, 2014).

214 **A "mismatch," as Peter Gluckman:** P. Gluckman and M. Hanson, *Mismatch: Why Our World No Longer Fits Our Bodies* (Oxford University Press, 2006).

214 **In other words, a major:** See anything and everything by Jay Giedd, starting with "The Teen Brain: Primed to Learn, Primed to Take Risks," *Cerebrum*, February 26,

2009; see also L. Steinberg, *Age of Opportunity: Lessons from the New Science of Adolescence* (Houghton Mifflin Harcourt, 2014).

215 **This is not the only:** L. Steinberg, "A Dual Systems Model of Adolescent Risk-Taking," *Developmental Psychobiology* 52, no. 3 (2010): 216–24.

216 **nature's way of forcing your child:** See Jay Giedd's *Frontline* piece, "Inside the Teenage Brain," January 31, 2002.

218 **There is heightened sensitivity:** Steinberg, "Dual Systems Model of Adolescent Risk-Taking."

219 **What sorts of things can your teen do:** Walter Hess introduced the terms "ergotropic" and "tropotrophic," based on his research on the effects of stimulating different parts of the hypothalamus, to distinguish between the energy that an organism expends when exposed to a threat (ergotropic) and the mechanisms that promote recovery and the restoration of energy (tropotrophic).

220 **More than a hundred years ago:** Stuart Shanker, "Descartes' Legacy: The Mechanist/Vitalist Debates," in *Philosophy of Science, Logic, and Mathematics in the 20th Century* (London: Routledge, 1996).

223 **The government has become deeply alarmed:** Y. Zhao, *Who's Afraid of the Big Bad Dragon: Why China Has the Best (and Worst) Education System in the World* (John Wiley & Sons, 2014).

224 **The shape of our teeth:** Daniel Lieberman, *The Story of the Human Body: Evolution, Health, and Disease* (Penguin, 2014).

225 **Of all the mismatches:** Ibid. See also J. J. Ratey and E. Hagerman, *Spark: The Revolutionary New Science of Exercise and the Brain* (Little Brown, 2008).

227 **The challenge for parents:** J. Abbott, *Overschooled but Undereducated: How the Crisis in Education Is Jeopardizing Our Adolescents* (A&C Black, 2010). See also R. Epstein, *The Case Against Adolescence: Rediscovering the Adult in Every Teen* (Quill Driver Books, 2007).

Chapter 11: More: Desire, Dopamine, and the Surprising Biology of Boredom (the Reward System)

236 **Studies have shown how overstimulation:** This has been demonstrated by one of my colleagues at York, John Eastwood. See Eastwood et al., "The Unengaged Mind: Defining Boredom in Terms of Attention," *Perspectives on Psychological Science* 7, no. 5 (2012): 482–95; Kimberley B. Mercer-Lynn, Rachel J. Bar, and John D. Eastwood, "Causes of Boredom: The Person, the Situation, or Both?" *Personality and Individual Differences* 56 (2014): 122–26.

237 **That's a major finding:** There has been so much research over the past decade on the neurobiology of the reward system, wonderfully summarized in Marc Lewis, *The Biology of Desire: Why Addiction Is Not a Disease* (Penguin Random House Canada, 2015). See also G. Wilson, *Your Brain on Porn: Internet Pornography and the Emerging Science of Addiction* (Commonwealth, 2014).

237 **And then dopamine—the source:** Matthias Koepp et al., "Evidence for Striatal Dopamine Release During a Video Game," *Nature* 393 (1998), 266–68.

238 **Dopamine is released when:** M. Lewis, *Memoirs of an Addicted Brain: A Neuroscientist Examines His Former Life on Drugs* (Doubleday Canada, 2013).

239 **Violence-themed role-playing:** D. Grossman, *On Killing: The Psychological Cost of Learning to Kill in War and Society* (Little, Brown, 2009).

239 **These films are designed:** Scott Brown, "How Movies Activate Your Neural G-Spot," *Wired*, January 25, 2010.

239 **"willing suspension of disbelief":** Samuel T. Coleridge, *Biographia Literaria*, chapter XIV (West Sussex, UK: Littlehampton Book Services, 1817 and 1975).

239 **Junk food falls into the same:** D. A. Kessler, *The End of Overeating: Taking Control of the Insatiable American Appetite* (Rodale, 2010).

242 **What's more, studies show:** Clinicians refer to this state as "allostatic overload." As we saw in chapter 1, the autonomic nervous system (ANS) responds to stress with metabolic processes that consume energy and then sets in motion compensating processes that promote recovery and growth. The demands on this homeostatic system is called allostatic load. Allostatic overload occurs when the recovery mechanisms are overstretched and become compromised.

245 **We are all, children and adults:** R. E. Thayer, *The Origin of Everyday Moods: Managing Energy, Tension, and Stress* (Oxford University Press, 1997).

246 **Time spent in nature:** Marc Berman et al., "Interacting with Nature Improves Cognition and Affect for Individuals with Depression," *Journal of Affective Disorders* 140, no. 3 (2012): 300–305.

247 **An estimated 50 percent of children:** Based on the UNICEF study "An Urban World" published March 7, 2012 (see www.urbanizationproject.org); and the 2010 U.S. census data released March 26, 2012 (see www.census.gov).

247 **A flurry of scientific papers:** The concern that city living might be a significant factor in the rise of mental illness dates back to a study done in Camberwell, UK, between 1965 and 1984. The number of people in the borough diagnosed with schizophrenia doubled during that period while there was virtually no rise in rural areas. We know that stress is a critical factor in the expression of schizophrenia, so the study naturally led to the worry that, as one of the lead authors Jane Boydell put it, "cities may be making us sick." Of course, it might simply be that affected individuals living in cities are more likely to receive a diagnosis than their rural counterparts. Or maybe there was a "migration" effect operating here: That is, people with psychological disorders move to the city in order to secure better services. Or maybe the Camberwell study reveals something about the stress involved in uprooting yourself: e.g., leaving a strong social support network for the isolation of a big city. Or perhaps what was missing was walking in the woods or going down to the creek for a spot of fishing. Maybe the big culprit here was the increase in domestic and child abuse that seems to go hand in hand with urbanization. Or maybe there was just something particularly stressful about living in Camberwell. Noel Kennedy et al., "Gender Differences in Incidence and Age at Onset of Mania and Bipolar Disorder Over a 35-Year Period in Camberwell, England," *American Journal of Psychiatry*, 162 (2005): 257–62.

248 **It was a paper that Andreas:** Florian Lederbogen et al., "City Living and Urban Upbringing Affect Neural Social Stress Processing in Humans," *Nature* 474, no. 7352 (2011): 498–501.

248 **The work of Gary Evans:** G. W. Evans, J. Brooks-Gunn, and P. K. Klebanov, "Stressing Out the Poor," *Pathways* (2011), Community Investments 23(2): 22–27.

Chapter 12: Parents Under Pressure: Where Do We Go from Here?

250 **Parents are under extraordinary pressure:** Of the many recent books addressing this issue, I have found especially helpful *Parenting Through the Storm* by Ann Douglas (HarperCollins, 2015); *The Parents We Mean to Be* by R. Weissbourd (Houghton

Mifflin Harcourt, 2009); and the deeply inspiring *Child Honouring: How to Turn This World Around* by Sharna Olfman and Raffi Cavoukian (APG Books, 2015).

253 **This idea is based on work:** D. Baumrind, "Effects of Authoritative Parental Control on Child Behavior," *Child Development* 37, no. 4 (1966): 887–907; D. Baumrind, "Childcare Practices Anteceding Three Patterns of Preschool Behavior," *Genetic Psychology Monographs* 75, no. 1 (1967): 43–88.

253 **Ever since, scientists have tended:** E. E. Maccoby and J. A. Martin, "Socialization in the Context of the Family: Parent-Child Interaction," in *Handbook of Child Psychology*, vol. 4, *Socialization, Personality, and Social Development*, 4th ed., ed. P. H. Mussen and E. M. Hetherington (New York: Wiley, 1983).

BIBLIOGRAPHY

Abbott, J. *Overschooled but Undereducated: How the Crisis in Education Is Jeopardizing Our Adolescents.* London: A&C Black, 2010.

Alter, R. *Anxiety and the Gift of Imagination: A New Model for Helping Parents and Children Manage Anxiety.* Createspace, 2011.

Barkley, R. A. *Executive Functions: What They Are, How They Work, and Why They Evolved.* New York: Guilford Press, 2012.

Baron, M. G., and J. Grodon. *Stress and Coping in Autism.* Oxford: Oxford University Press, 2006.

Baumeister, R. F., and K. D. Vohs. *Handbook of Self-Regulation: Research, Theory and Applications.* New York: Guilford Press, 2004.

———, and J. Tierney. *Willpower: Rediscovering the Greatest Human Strength.* Penguin, 2011.

Baumrind, D. "Childcare Practices Anteceding Three Patterns of Preschool Behavior," *Genetic Psychology Monographs* 75, no. 1 (1967).

———. "Effects of Authoritative Parental Control on Child Behavior." *Child Development* 37, no. 4 (1966): 887–907.

Bekoff, M., and J. Goodall. *The Emotional Lives of Animals: A Leading Scientist Explores Animal Joy, Sorrow, and Empathy—and Why They Matter.* Novato, CA: New World Library, 2008.

Benson, H. *The Relaxation Response.* New York: William Morrow, 1975.

Berk, L., and Stuart Shanker. *Child Development.* New York: Pearson, 2006.

Berman, M., et al. "Interacting with Nature Improves Cognition and Affect for Individuals with Depression." *Journal of Affective Disorders* 140, no. 3 (2012): 300–305.

Biegel, G. M. *The Stress Reduction Workbook for Teens: Mindfulness Skills to Help You Deal with Stress.* Oakland, CA: New Harbinger, 2009.

Blakemore, S. J., and U. Frith. *The Learning Brain: Lessons for Education.* Oxford: Blackwell, 2005.

Bowlby, J. A. *Secure Base: Clinical Applications of Attachment Theory.* London: Taylor & Francis, 2005.

Bradley, S. J. *Affect Regulation and the Development of Psychopathology.* New York: Guilford Press, 2003.

Bronson, M. *Self-Regulation in Early Childhood.* New York: Guilford Press, 2001.

Brooks, A. *Who Really Cares.* New York: Basic Books, 2006.

Brown, S. "How Movies Activate Your Neural G-Spot." *Wired,* January 25, 2010.

Bruner, J. *Child's Talk.* Oxford: Oxford University Press, 1983.

———. "Child's Talk: Learning to Use Language." *Child Language Teaching and Therapy* 1, no. 1 (1985): 111–14.

Bundy, A. C., S. J. Lane, and E. A. Murray. *Sensory Integration: Theory and Practice.* Philadelphia: F. A. Davis, 2002.

Burman, J. T, C. D. Green, and S. G. Shanker. "The Six Meanings of Self-Regulation." *Child Development* (2015, in press).

Cacioppo, J. T., and J. Decety. "Social Neuroscience: Challenges and Opportunities in the Study of Complex Behavior." *Annals of the New York Academy of Sciences* 1224, no. 1 (2011): 162–73.

Canadian Institute for Health Information. *The Role of Social Support in Reducing Psychological Distress.* Ottawa, Canada: Canadian Institute for Health Information, 2012.

Cannon, W. B. *The Wisdom of the Body.* New York: W. W. Norton, 1932.

———. *Bodily Changes in Pain, Hunger, Fear and Rage,* 2nd ed. New York: D. Appleton, 1929.

———. *The Way of an Investigator: A Scientist's Experiences in Medical Research.* New York: W. W. Norton, 1945.

Casenhiser, D. M., S. G. Shanker, and J. Stieben. "Learning Through Interaction in Children with Autism: Preliminary Data from Asocial-Communication-Based Intervention." *Autism* 17, no. 2 (2013): 220–41.

Coleridge, Samuel T. *Biographia Literaria,* chapter XIV. West Sussex, England: Littlehampton Book Services, 1817; 1975.

Cowell, J., and Jean Decety. "Precursors to Morality in Development as a Complex Interplay Between Neural, Socioenvironmental, and Behavioral Facets." *Proceedings of the National Academy of Science,* University of Chicago, May 2015.

Davidson, R., and Sharon Begley. *The Emotional Life of Your Brain.* London: Hachette UK, 2012.

Davis, F. A., N. Kashman, and J. Mora. *The Sensory Connection: An OT and SLP Team Approach.* Arlington, TX: Future Horizons, 2005.

Dawson, P., and R. Guare. *Executive Skills in Children and Adolescents: A Practical Guide to Assessment and Intervention.* New York: Guilford Press, 2010.

Decety, J., and C. D. Batson. "Social Neuroscience Approaches to Interpersonal Sensitivity." *Social Neuroscience* 2 (3–4)(2007): 151–57.

Denham, S., P. Ji, and B. Hamre. *Compendium of Preschool Through Elementary School Social-Emotional Learning and Associated Assessment Measures.* Chicago: Social and Emotional Learning Research Group, University of Illinois, 2010.

———, et al. (2009). "Assessing Social Emotional Development in Children from a Longitudinal Perspective." *Journal of Epidemiology and Community Health* 63(Suppl II), 37–52.

De Waal, F. *The Age of Empathy: Nature's Lessons for a Kinder Society.* New York: Broadway Books, 2010.

Douglas, A. *Parenting Through the Storm.* New York: HarperCollins, 2015.

Duckworth, A., and M. Seligman. "Self-Discipline Outdoes IQ in Predicting Academic Performance of Adolescents." *Psychological Science* 16, no. 12 (2005): 939–94.

Dzung, X. *The Mindful Teen: Powerful Skills to Help You Handle Stress One Moment at a Time.* Oakland, CA: New Harbinger, 2015.

Eastwood, John, et al. "The Unengaged Mind: Defining Boredom in Terms of Attention." *Perspectives on Psychological Science* 7, no. 5 (2012): 482–95.

Edlund, M. *The Power of Rest: Why Sleep Alone Is Not Enough: A 30-Day Plan to Reset Your Body*. New York: HarperCollins, 2010.

Eisenberg, N., and P. H. Mussen. *The Roots of Prosocial Behavior in Children*. Cambridge, UK: Cambridge University Press, 1989.

———, et al. "The Relation of Effortful Control and Impulsivity to Children's Resiliency and Adjustment." *Child Development* 75 (2004): 25–46.

Epstein, R. *The Case Against Adolescence: Rediscovering the Adult in Every Teen*. Fresno, CA: Quill Driver Books, 2007.

Evans, G. W., J. Brooks-Gunn, and P. K. Klebanov. "Stressing Out the Poor." *Pathways* (2011), Community Investments 23(2):22–27.

Fallon, J. *The Psychopath Inside: A Neuroscientist's Personal Journey into the Dark Side of the Brain*. New York: Penguin, 2013.

Field, Tiffany. *The Amazing Infant*. Hoboken, NJ: Wiley-Blackwell, 2007.

Fogel, A. *Developing Through Relationships*. Chicago: University of Chicago Press, 1993.

———. *The Psychophysiology of Self-awareness: Rediscovering the Lost Art of Body Sense*. New York: W. W. Norton, 2009.

———, B. J. King, and S. G. Shanker, eds. *Human Development in the Twenty-first Century: Visionary Ideas from Systems Scientists*. Cambridge, UK: Cambridge University Press, 2007.

Ford, J. D., and J. Wortmann. *Hijacked by Your Brain: How to Free Yourself When Stress Takes Over*. Naperville, IL: Sourcebooks, 2013.

Freed, J., and L. Parsons. *Right-Brained Children in a Left-Brained World: Unlocking the Potential of Your ADD Child*. New York: Simon & Schuster, 1998.

Galinsky. E. *Mind in the Making: The Seven Essential Life Skills Every Child Needs*. New York: HarperStudio, 2010.

Giedd, J. "The Teen Brain: Primed to Learn, Primed to Take Risks." *Cerebrum*, February 26, 2009.

———. "Inside the Teenage Brain." *Frontline*, January 31, 2002.

Gluckman, P., and M. Hanson. *Mismatch: Why Our World No Longer Fits Our Bodies*. Oxford: Oxford University Press, 2006.

Goleman, D. *Emotional Intelligence*. New York: Bantam Dell, 1995.

———. *Social Intelligence*. New York: Random House, 2007.

Gordon, M. *Roots of Empathy: Changing the World Child by Child*. New York: Workman, 2009.

Gould, Stephen J. "Human Babies as Embryos," in *Ever Since Darwin*, New York: W. W. Norton, 1977.

Grandin, Temple. *Thinking in Pictures: My Life with Autism*, expanded ed. New York: Vintage, 2006.

Greene, R. W. *The Explosive Child*. New York: Harper Paperbacks, 2001.

Greenland, S. K. *The Mindful Child: How to Help Your Kid Manage Stress and Become Happier, Kinder, and More Compassionate*. New York: Simon & Schuster, 2010.

Greenspan, S. I. *Secure Child: Helping Our Children Feel Safe and Confident in a Changing World*. Boston: Da Capo Press, 2009.

———, and Stuart Shanker. *Toward a Psychology of Global Interdependency: A Framework for International Collaboration*. Washington, DC: ICDL Press, 2002.

———, with N. T. Greenspan. *First Feelings: Milestones in the Emotional Development of Your Infant and Child from Birth to Age 4*. New York: Viking, 1985.

———, and N. T. Greenspan. *The Learning Tree: Overcoming Learning Disabilities from the Ground Up*. Boston: Da Capo Press, 2010.

————, and J. Greenspan. *Overcoming ADHD: Helping Your Child Become Calm, Engaged, and Focused—Without a Pill.* Boston: Da Capo Press, 2009.

————, and S. Shanker. *The First Idea: How Symbols, Language, and Intelligence Evolve, from Primates to Humans.* New York: Perseus Books, 2004.

————, and N. Lewis. *Building Healthy Minds: The Six Experiences That Create Intelligence and Emotional Growth in Babies and Young Children.* Boston: Da Capo Press, 2000.

————, and J. I. Downey. *Developmentally Based Psychotherapy.* Madison, CT: International Universities Press, 1997.

————, and J. Salmon. *The Challenging Child: Understanding, Raising, and Enjoying the Five "Difficult" Types of Children.* Boston: Da Capo Press, 1996.

Griffiths, P. E. *What Emotions Really Are: The Problem of Psychological Categories.* Chicago: University of Chicago Press, 1997.

Gross, J. *Handbook of Emotion Regulation,* 2nd ed. New York: Guilford Press, 2015.

Grossman, D. *On Killing: The Psychological Cost of Learning to Kill in War and Society.* New York: Little, Brown, 2009.

Gunnar, M., and K. Quevedo. "The Neurobiology of Stress and Development." *Annual Review of Psychology* 58 (2007).

Hadfield, C. *An Astronaut's Guide to Life on Earth.* London: Pan Macmillan, 2013.

Hallowell, E.M.M., and J. J. Ratey. *Driven to Distraction: Recognizing and Coping with Attention Deficit Disorder from Childhood Through Adulthood.* New York: Anchor, 2011.

Hawn, G., and W. Holden. *10 Mindful Minutes: Giving Our Children—and Ourselves—the Social and Emotional Skills to Reduce Stress and Anxiety for Healthier, Happy Lives.* New York: Penguin, 2011.

Hobbes, T. *Leviathan.* New York, Oxford University Press, 1651; 2009, XIII.9, 581–735; for a modern version, see William Golding. *Lord of the Flies.* New York: Penguin, 1954; 1983.

Huitt, W. "Motivation to Learn: An Overview." *Educational Psychology Interactive.* Valdosta, GA: Valdosta State University, 2011.

Huttenlocher, P. R. *Neural Plasticity.* Cambridge, MA: Harvard University Press, 2002.

Izard, C. *The Psychology of Emotions.* London: Springer, 1991.

————, et al. "Emotional Knowledge as a Predictor of Social Behavior and Academic Competence in Children at Risk." *Psychological Science* 12 (2001): 18–23.

Jackson, M. *The Age of Stress: Science and the Search for Stability.* Oxford: Oxford University Press, 2013.

James, W. *Principles of Psychology.* Cambridge, MA: Harvard University Press, 1981, p. 462. Originally published in 1890.

Kabat-Zinn, J. *Mindfulness for Beginners: Reclaiming the Present Moment—and Your Life.* Louisville, CO: Sounds True, 2011.

————, and Richard Davidson, eds. *The Mind's Own Physician: A Scientific Dialogue with the Dalai Lama on the Healing Power of Meditation.* Oakland, CA: New Harbinger, 2012.

Kagan, J. *Unstable Ideas: Temperament, Cognition and Self.* Cambridge, MA: Harvard University Press, 1989.

————, and N. Herschkowitz. *A Young Mind in a Growing Brain.* East Sussex, England: Psychology Press, 2006.

Kennedy, N., et al. "Gender Differences in Incidence and Age at Onset of Mania and Bipolar Disorder Over a 35-Year Period in Camberwell, England." *American Journal of Psychiatry,* vol. 162 (2005): 257–62.

Kessler, D. A. *The End of Overeating: Taking Control of the Insatiable American Appetite.* Emmaus, PA: Rodale, 2010.

King, B. J. *The Dynamic Dance: Nonvocal Communication in African Great Apes*. Cambridge, MA: Harvard University Press, 2009.

Koepp, Matthias, et al. "Evidence for Striatal Dopamine Release During a Video Game." *Nature* 393 (1998): 266–68.

Kutscher, M. L. *ADHD: Living Without Brakes*. London: Jessica Kingsley, 2009.

Lansford, J. E., et al. "Ethnic Differences in the Link Between Physical Discipline and Later Adolescent Externalizing Behaviors." *Journal of Child Psychology and Psychiatry* 45 (2004): 801–12.

Lederbogen, A. F., et al. "City Living and Urban Upbringing Affect Neural Social Stress Processing in Humans." *Nature* 474, no. 7352 (2011): 498–501.

LeDoux, J. *The Emotional Brain: The Mysterious Underpinnings of Emotional Life*. New York: Simon & Schuster, 1998.

Levine, P.A., and A. Frederick. *Waking the Tiger: Healing Trauma: The Innate Capacity to Transform Overwhelming Experiences*. Berkeley, CA: North Atlantic Books, 1997.

Lewis, M. *The Biology of Desire: Why Addiction Is Not a Disease*. Toronto: Penguin Random House Canada, 2015.

———. *Memoirs of an Addicted Brain: A Neuroscientist Examines His Former Life on Drugs*. Toronto: Doubleday Canada, 2013.

———, and Jeanette Haviland-Jones. *Handbook of Emotions*, 3rd ed. New York: Guilford Press, 2010.

———, "Bridging Emotion Theory and Neurobiology Through Dynamic Systems Modeling." *Behavioral and Brain Sciences* 28, no. 2 (2005): 169–94.

Lewis, T., F. Amini, and R. Lannon. *A General Theory of Love*. New York: Vintage, 2007.

Lieberman, D. *The Story of the Human Body: Evolution, Health, and Disease*. New York: Penguin, 2014.

Lillas, Connie, and Janiece Turnbull. *Infant/Child Mental Health, Early Intervention, and Relationship-Based Therapies: A Neurorelational Framework for Interdisciplinary Practice*. New York: W. W. Norton, 2009.

Louv, R. *Last Child in the Woods: Saving Our Children from Nature-Deficit Disorder*. New York: Algonquin Books, 2008.

———. *The Nature Principle: Reconnecting with Life in a Virtual Age*. New York: Algonquin Books, 2012.

Lupien, S. *Well Stressed: Manage Stress Before It Turns Toxic*. New York: John Wiley & Sons, 2012.

McCain, H.N.M., J. F. Mustard, and S. Shanker. *Early Years Study 2*. Toronto: Council for Early Child Development, 2007.

Maccoby, E. E., and J. A. Martin. "Socialization in the Context of the Family: Parent-Child Interaction," in *Handbook of Child Psychology*, vol. 4: *Socialization, Personality, and Social Development*, 4th ed., P. H. Mussen and E. M. Hetherington, eds. New York: John Wiley & Sons, 1983.

McEwen, B. S., and Elizabeth Norton Lasley. *The End of Stress as We Know It*. Washington, D.C.: Joseph Henry Press, 2002.

McGonigal, K. *The Upside of Stress: Why Stress Is Good for You, and How to Get Good at It*. New York: Penguin, 2015.

MacLean, P. D., and V. A. Kral. *A Triune Concept of the Brain and Behaviour*. Toronto: University of Toronto Press, 1973.

Maté, G. *When the Body Says No: The Hidden Costs of Stress*. Toronto: Vintage Canada, 2004.

Maurer, D., and C. Maurer. *The World of the Newborn*. New York: Basic Books, 1988.

————, and H. M. Schmeck. *The Hostage Brain*. New York: Rockefeller University Press, 1994.

Meerlo, P., et al. "Sleep Restriction Alters the Hypothalamic-Pituitary-Adrenal Response to Stress." *Journal of Endocrinology*, vol. 14 (2002): 397–402.

Mercer-Lynn, K., Rachel J. Bar, and John D. Eastwood. "Causes of Boredom: The Person, the Situation, or Both?" *Personality and Individual Differences* 56 (2014): 122–26.

"Me Want It (but Me Wait)." *Sesame Street*, August 5, 2013, https://youtu.be/9PnbKL3wuH4.

Mischel, W. *Marshmallow Test*. New York: Random House, 2014.

————, Y. Shoda, and M. I. Rodriguez. "Delay of Gratification in Children." *Science* 244, no. 4907 (1989): 933–38.

Moffitt, T. E., et al. "A Gradient of Childhood Self-Control Predicts Health, Wealth, and Public Safety." *Proceedings of the National Academy of Sciences* 108, no. 7 (2011): 2693–98.

Moll, J., et al. "The Neural Basis of Human Moral Cognition." *Nature Reviews Neuroscience* 6, no. 10 (2005): 799–809.

Muraven, M.R., and R. F. Baumeister. "Self-Regulation and Depletion of Limited Resources: Does Self-Control Resemble a Muscle?" *Psychological Bulletin* 126 (2000): 247–59.

Mustard, J. F. "Experience-Based Brain Development: Scientific Underpinnings of the Importance of Early Child Development in a Global World." *Paediatrics & Child Health* 11, no. 9 (2006): 571.

Nelson, C. A., K. M. Thomas, and M. De Haan. *Neuroscience of Cognitive Development: The Role of Experience and the Developing Brain*. New York: John Wiley & Sons, 2012.

Nigg, J. T. *What Causes ADHD? Understanding What Goes Wrong and Why*. New York: Guilford Press, 2006.

Numan, M., and T. R. Insel. *The Neurobiology of Parental Behavior*. London: Springer, 2003.

Ogden, P. *Sensorimotor Psychotherapy: Interventions for Trauma and Attachment*. New York: W. W. Norton, 2015.

Olfman, S., and B. D. Robbins, eds. *Drugging Our Children: How Profiteers Are Pushing Antipsychotics on Our Youngest, and What We Can Do to Stop It*. Santa Barbara, CA: ABC-CLIO, 2012.

Panksepp, J. *Affective Neuroscience*. New York: Oxford University Press, 1998.

Peterson, Christopher, and Martin Seligman. *Character Strengths and Virtues*. New York: Oxford University Press, 2004.

Pink, D. *Drive: The Surprising Truth About What Motivates Us*. New York: Penguin, 2009, 138 and 240.

Polan, H. J., and M. A. Hofer. "Psychobiological Origins of Infant Attachment and Separation Responses," in *Handbook of Attachment: Theory, Research, and Clinical Application*, J. Cassidy and P. R. Shaver, eds. New York: Guilford Press, 1999, 162–80.

Porges, S. W. *The Polyvagal Theory: Neurophysiological Foundations of Emotions, Attachment, Communication, and Self-Regulation*, Norton Series on Interpersonal Neurobiology. New York: W. W. Norton, 2011, 283.

Posner, M. I., and M. K. Rothbart. *Educating the Human Brain*. Washington, D.C.: American Psychological Association, 2007.

Ppproductions1000, "Very Tempting Marshmallow Test," September 19, 2009, https://youtu.be/x3S0xS2hdi4.

Raby, K., et al. "The Enduring Predictive Significance of Early Maternal Sensitivity:

Social and Academic Competence Through Age 32 Years." *Child Development* 17 (December 2014): 695–708.

Race, K. "The Epidemic of Stressed Parents Raising Stressed Kids." *Huffington Post*, February 21, 2014, www.huffingtonpost.com/kristen-race-phd/the-epidemic-of-stressed-parents-raising-stressed-kids_b_4790658.html.

Raine, A. *The Anatomy of Violence: The Biological Roots of Crime.* New York: Vintage, 2013.

Ratey, J. J., and E. Hagerman. *Spark: The Revolutionary New Science of Exercise and the Brain.* New York: Little Brown, 2008.

Richard, D., and Daniel Goleman. *Training the Brain.* Amazon Digital Services, 2012.

Rosenberg, K., and W. Trevathan. "Bipedalism and Human Birth: The Obstetrical Dilemma Revisited." *Evolutionary Anthropology: Issues, News, and Reviews* 4, no. 5 (1995): 161–68.

Ross, T., M. I. Fontao, and R. Schneider. "Aggressive Behavior in Male Offenders: Preliminary Analyses of Self-Regulatory Functions in a Sample of Criminals." *Psychological Reports* 100, no. 3, part 2 (2007): 1171–85.

Rothbart, M. K. *Becoming Who We Are: Temperament and Personality in Development.* New York: Guilford Press, 2011.

———, L. K. Ellis, and M. I. Posner. "Temperament and Self-Regulation," in *Handbook of Self-Regulation: Research, Theory, and Applications.* R. F. Baumeister and K. D. Vohs, eds. New York: Guilford Press, 2004, 357–70.

Ryan, N. "Willpower: Rediscovering the Greatest Human Strength, by Roy F. Baumeister and John Tierney" (book review). *Journal of Positive Psychology* 7, no. 5 (2012): 446–48.

Sagvolden, T., et al. "A Dynamic Developmental Theory of Attention-Deficit/Hyperactivity Disorder (ADHD) Predominantly Hyperactive/Impulsive and Combined Subtypes." *Behavioral and Brain Sciences* 28, no. 3 (2005): 397–418.

Salovey, P., and J. D. Mayer. "Emotional Intelligence." *Imagination, Cognition, and Personality"* 9 (1990): 185–211.

Sameroff, A. *The Transactional Model.* Washington, D.C.: American Psychological Association, 2009.

Sapolsky, R. M. *Why Zebras Don't Get Ulcers: The Acclaimed Guide to Stress, Stress-Related Diseases, and Coping.* New York: Macmillan, 2004.

Savage-Rumbaugh, S., S. G. Shanker, and T. J. Taylor. *Apes, Language, and the Human Mind.* New York: Oxford University Press, 1998.

Schmeichel, B. J., and R. F. Baumeister. "Self-Regulatory Strength," in *Handbook of Self-Regulation.* R. F. Baumeister and K. D. Vohs, eds. New York: Guilford Press, 2004, 84–98.

Schore, A. N. *Affect Regulation and the Origin of the Self: The Neurobiology of Emotional Development.* East Sussex, England: Psychology Press, 1994.

———. *The Science of the Art of Psychotherapy*, Norton Series on Interpersonal Neurobiology. New York: W. W. Norton, 2012.

Selye, H. *Stress Without Distress.* New York: Springer US, 1976, 137–46.

Shanker, S. *Calm, Alert, and Learning: Classroom Strategies for Self-Regulation.* London: Pearson, 2013.

———. *Wittgenstein's Remarks on the Foundations of AI.* London: Routledge, 1998.

———, and D. Casenhiser. *Reducing the Effort in Effortful Control: A Wittgensteinian Perspective on the Use of Conceptual Analysis in Psychology.* London: Palgrave Macmillan, 2013.

———. "A Dynamic Developmental Model of Emotions." *Philosophy, Psychiatry and Psychology* 11 (2004): 219–33.

———. Broader Measures of Success: Social/Emotional Learning [report]. Toronto: People for Education, 2015.

———. "Descartes' Legacy: The Mechanist/Vitalist Debates," in *Philosophy of Science, Logic, and Mathematics in the 20th Century*. London: Routledge, 1996.

———. "Emotion Regulation Through the Ages" (2012), in *Moving Ourselves, Moving Others: Motion and Emotion in Intersubjectivity, Consciousness and Language*, vol. 6, A. Foolen et al., eds. Amsterdam, The Netherlands: John Benjamins, 2012.

——— and D. Casenhiser. "Reducing the Effort in Effortful Control," in *Conceptual Analysis and Psychology*, T. Racine and K. Slaney, eds. New York, Macmillan, 2013.

———, and Jim Stieben. "The Roots of Mindblindness," in *Against Theory of Mind*. Ivan Leudar, ed. London: Palgrave Macmillan, 2009.

Sherrod, D. R. "Crowding, Perceived Control, and Behavioral After-effects." *Journal of Applied Social Psychology* 4 (1974): 171–86.

Shonkoff, J., and D. Phillips. *From Neurons to Neighborhoods: The Science of Early Childhood Development*. Washington, D.C.: National Academy Press, 2000.

Siegel, D. *Brainstorm: The Power and Purpose of the Teenage Brain*. London: Hachette UK, 2014.

———. *The Developing Mind*. New York, Guilford Press, 1999; second edition 2012.

Steinberg, L. *Age of Opportunity: Lessons from the New Science of Adolescence*. Boston: Houghton Mifflin Harcourt, 2014.

———. "A Dual Systems Model of Adolescent Risk-Taking." *Developmental Psychobiology* 52, no. 3 (2010): 216–24.

Steiner-Adair, C. *The Big Disconnect: Protecting Childhood and Family Relationships in the Digital Age*. New York: HarperCollins, 2013.

Sternberg, E. *The Balance Within: The Science Connecting Health and Emotions*. New York: Times Books, 2001.

———. *Healing Spaces: The Science of Place and Well-being*. Cambridge, MA: Harvard University Press, 2009.

Tantam, D. *Can the World Afford Autistic Spectrum Disorder? Nonverbal Communication, Asperger Syndrome and the Interbrain*. London: Jessica Kingsley, 2009.

Thayer, R. E. *The Biopsychology of Mood and Arousal*. New York: Oxford University Press, 1989.

———. *The Origin of Everyday Moods: Managing Energy, Tension, and Stress*. New York: Oxford University Press, 1997.

———. *Calm Energy: How People Regulate Mood with Food and Exercise*. New York: Oxford University Press, 2003.

Thompson, M. G. *Raising Cain: Protecting the Emotional Life of Boys*. New York: Ballantine, 1999.

———. *It's a Boy! Understanding Your Son's Development from Birth to Eighteen*. New York: Ballantine, 2008.

Tremblay, R. E., W. W. Hartup, and J. Archer, eds. *Developmental Origins of Aggression*. New York: Guilford Press, 2005.

Tronick, E. Z. *The Neurobehavioral and Social-Emotional Development of Infants and Children*. New York: W. W. Norton, 2007.

———. "Why Is Connection with Others So Critical?," in *Emotional Development*. J. Nadel and D. Muir, eds. Oxford: Oxford University Press, 2004.

———. "Emotions and Emotional Communication in Infants," *American Psychologist* 44 (1989): 112–19.

Van der Kolk, B. *The Body Keeps the Score: Brain, Mind, and Body in the Healing of Trauma*. New York: Penguin, 2014.

Volkow, Nora, and Ruben Baler. "Addiction: A Disease of Self-Control." *Neurosciences and the Human Person: New Perspectives on Human Activities. Scripta Varia 121*. Vatican City: Pontifical Academy of Sciences, 2013.

Von Sömmerring, S. T. *Vom Baue des menschlichen Körpers*, vol. 1 Frankfurt, Germany: Varrentrapp und Wenner, 1791.

Watson, J. B. "Psychology as the Behaviorist Views It." *Psychological Review* 20, no. 2 (1913): 158.

Weisfeld, G. E. *Evolutionary Principles of Human Adolescence*. New York: Basic Books, 1999.

Weissbourd, R. *The Parents We Mean to Be*. Boston: Houghton Mifflin Harcourt, 2009.

William, M. S., and S. Shellenberger. *How Does Your Engine Run?: A Leader's Guide to the Alert Program for Self-Regulation*. Albuquerque, NM: TherapyWorks, 1996.

Wilson, E. O. *Consilience: The Unity of Knowledge*. New York: Vintage, 1999.

Wilson, G. *Your Brain on Porn: Internet Pornography and the Emerging Science of Addiction*. New Delhi, India: Commonwealth, 2014.

Wittgenstein, L. *Philosophical Investigations*. Oxford: Blackwell, 1958.

Wrangham, R. W., and D. Peterson. *Demonic Males: Apes and the Origins of Human Violence*. Boston: Houghton Mifflin Harcourt, 1997.

Zhao, Y. *Who's Afraid of the Big Bad Dragon: Why China Has the Best (and Worst) Education System in the World*. New York: John Wiley & Sons, 2014.

Zimmerman, B. J., and D. H. Schunk, eds. *Self-Regulated Learning and Academic Achievement: Theoretical Perspectives*. London: Routledge, 2001.

INDEX

You may also enjoy reading these books,

also published by Yellow Kite:

yellow
kite

books to help you live a good life

Join the conversation and tell
us how you live a #goodlife

 @yellowkitebooks

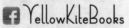 YellowKiteBooks

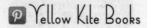 Yellow Kite Books

 YellowKiteBooks